Google

How Google Works

Eric Schmidt and Jonathan Rosenberg

with Alan Eagle

JOHN MURRAY

First published in Great Britain in 2014 by John Murray (Publishers)
An Hachette UK Company

1

© Google, Inc. 2014

All illustrations © Nishant Choksi 2014

A CIP catalogue record for this title is available
from the British Library

Hardback ISBN 978-1-444-79246-1
Trade Paperback ISBN 978-1-444-79247-8
Ebook ISBN 978-1-444-79248-5

Printed and bound in Great Britain by Clays Ltd, St Ives plc

John Murray policy is to use papers that are natural,
renewable and recyclable products and made from wood
grown in sustainable forests. The logging and manufacturing
processes are expected to conform to the environmental
regulations of the country of origin.

John Murray (Publishers)
338 Euston Road
London NW1 3BH

www.johnmurray.co.uk

To our favorite smart creatives, Wendy and Beryl.

Contents

Foreword

by Larry Page
Google Cofounder and CEO

When I was younger and first started thinking about my future, I decided to either become a professor or start a company. I felt that either option would give me a lot of autonomy—the freedom to think from first principles and real-world physics rather than having to accept the prevailing "wisdom."

As Eric and Jonathan explain in *How Google Works*, we've tried to apply this autonomy of thought to almost everything we do at Google. It's been the driving force behind our greatest successes and some impressive failures. In fact, starting from first principles was what got Google going. One night I had a dream (literally) and woke up thinking...what if you could download the whole Web and just keep the links? So I grabbed a pen and scribbled down the details to figure out whether it was really possible. The idea of building a search engine wasn't even on my radar at the time. It was only later that Sergey and I realized ranking web pages by their links could generate much better search results. Gmail started out as a pipe dream too. And when Andy Rubin started Android a decade ago, most people thought aligning the mobile industry around an open-source operating system was nuts.

Over time I've learned, surprisingly, that it's tremendously hard to get teams to be super ambitious. It turns out most people haven't been educated in this kind of moonshot thinking. They tend to assume that things are impossible, rather than starting from real-world physics and figuring out what's actually possible. It's why we've put so much energy into hiring independent thinkers at Google, and setting big goals. Because if you hire the right people and have big enough dreams, you'll usually get there. And even if you fail, you'll probably learn something important.

It's also true that many companies get comfortable doing what they have always done, with a few incremental changes. This kind of incrementalism leads to irrelevance over time, especially in technology, because change tends to be revolutionary not evolutionary. So you need to force yourself to place big bets on the future. It's why we invest in areas that may seem wildly speculative, such as self-driving cars or a balloon-powered Internet. While it's hard to imagine now, when we started Google Maps, people thought that our goal of mapping the entire world, including photographing every street, would prove impossible. So if the past is any indicator of our future, today's big bets won't seem so wild in a few years' time.

These are some of the principles that I think are important, and there are more in the pages that follow. Hopefully you can take these ideas and do some impossible things of your own!

How Google Works

Introduction—Lessons Learned from the Front Row

In July 2003, Eric Schmidt had been the CEO of Google Inc. for two years when he received an email from one of the company's board members and investors, Mike Moritz, a partner at Sequoia Capital. It included a suggestion:

> you may want to think about picking a three hour slot
> in mid-august when the management presents to the
> board our campaign to compete with finland. (i do not
> think we should wait until the september meeting.
> this is far too important a topic and we've all
> learned that the best way to discover how short a
> year happens to be is to compete with finland.)

To the uninformed, this note might have been confusing. Why would Google, a several-hundred-employee, five-year-old Internet start-up based in Mountain View, California, be competing with Finland, a country of five million people that was over five thousand miles away and generally considered to be a friendly, peaceful place?

The Finland email arrived just when Eric felt like he was finally settling into Google. He had come from Novell, where he had been the CEO, and had also worked at Sun Microsystems and Bell Labs. After growing up in northern Virginia, he graduated from Princeton with a degree in electrical engineering and received a master's degree and PhD in computer science from the University of California, Berkeley, so not only was he no stranger to working with engineers and computer scientists, he *was* one. Still, when he got to Google he stepped into a place very different from anywhere else he had been.

His "I have a feeling we're not in Kansas anymore" revelation started on his first day. When he arrived at the office that had been assigned to him, which was already quite modest by big-shot CEO standards, he found that it was occupied by several software engineers. Rather than kicking them out, he decamped to the next office over, which was more of a closet with a window than an actual office.

Then, a few weeks later, it got worse. One morning, as he walked down the hall to his ~~closet~~ office, he noticed that his assistant, Pam Shore, had a troubled look on her face.[1] He soon found out why: He had a new officemate. It was one of the search engineers, Amit Patel, who explained to Eric that *his* office had five inhabitants, with another on the way, and that his solution of sawing one of the desks in half to make more space hadn't worked. In comparison to his current space, Eric's spot seemed quite roomy, so Amit moved in. (The facilities crew had refused to move Amit's stuff into Eric's office, so he had done it himself.) Amit and Eric ended up sharing the office for several months. Clearly, this was not a measure-your-importance-in-square-feet kind of place.

Beyond the unusual facilities arrangements, the rest of Eric's transition into the company was fairly smooth. His relationship with the two founders, Larry Page and Sergey Brin, was strengthening every day. The company's advertising platform, AdWords, was starting to generate significant amounts of revenue (when the company filed for its initial public offering in 2004, the financial statements astonished most observers... in a good way), and even though "Google" as a verb

---

1. For Pam, anything other than a warm smile counts as "troubled."

wouldn't be added to the *Oxford English Dictionary* for another three years,[2] for millions of users Google search was already an important part of everyday life. The company was growing too, adding dozens of employees every month, including a new head of products, Jonathan Rosenberg, who came on board in February of 2002. Jonathan, like Eric, was the son of an economics professor. He joined Google after stints at Excite@Home and Apple, to build up the company's product management team and round out Eric's staff.

As Mike's email pointed out, though, there was a major competitor on the horizon, and it wasn't really our Nordic friends across the Atlantic. Finland was our internal code name for Microsoft,[3] at the time the most important tech company on the planet.[4] Eric knew that a huge chunk of Google's traffic came from people using Microsoft's Internet Explorer browser. Like everyone at Google, he believed that the Internet was the technology platform of the future and that search was one of its most useful applications. Therefore, it was only a matter of time before our friends from Redmond would take a real interest in what we were doing. And when Microsoft took a real interest in things start-ups were doing, things had a way of getting really interesting.[5]

The future of the company was at stake, and what to do was far from obvious. Moritz's note was a call to action. He asked Eric to rally the team and create a plan that would establish clear deliverables across

---

2. The *Oxford English Dictionary* added "Google" on June 15, 2006. Other new words added in this update included "geocaching," "mash-up," "self-storage," and "texting." See Candace Lombardi, "Google Joins Xerox as a Verb" (*CNET News*, July 6, 2006).

3. In fact, "Finland" is a code name for the code name we actually used. If we used the actual code name in this book, it wouldn't be much of a code name, would it?

4. To get an idea of the awe in which Microsoft was held in those days, just look at the titles of some of the books about the company: *Microsoft Secrets: How the World's Most Powerful Software Company Creates Technology, Shapes Markets, and Manages People* (1995), *Overdrive: Bill Gates and the Race to Control Cyberspace* (1997), and *How the Web Was Won: How Bill Gates and His Internet Idealists Transformed the Microsoft Empire* (2000).

5. In the 1980s and '90s, it was virtually impossible for Silicon Valley technology entrepreneurs to get funding for their companies without first articulating to their investors their Microsoft strategy. If you didn't have a clear plan, you wouldn't get a check.

the company: product, sales, marketing, finance, and corporate development. Every aspect of how Google operated was on the table, and there was even talk about transitioning the company from its quirky start-up structure to a more traditional one organized around business units, to make it easier to develop new revenue streams (another thing the new plan was supposed to address). Most important, the plan needed to establish milestones and a roadmap of which products would ship, and when. In short, Moritz wanted what any sensible, normal board member would want: a comprehensive business plan.

He closed the note with a flourish:

```
so why not pick an evening in mid august to mark the
completion of the plans for the mightiest campaign
any of us will ever be in.
```

Since products would be the crux of this plan, Eric gave the project to Jonathan. His instructions: "I would like to review this in two weeks."

There was a problem, though, besides the fact that a huge company was coming to compete with us. Moritz was right: To take on the biggest gorilla in the jungle, we needed a plan. But he was also wrong, and to understand why he was wrong, and why he was inadvertently putting the two of us in a rock-and-hard-place sort of situation, it helps to first understand just what kind of company Google was.

"Just go talk to the engineers"

When Sergey and Larry founded Google in 1998, they had no formal business training or experience. They considered this an advantage, not a liability. As the company grew out of its first home in a Stanford dorm room, to Susan Wojcicki's garage[6] in Menlo Park, to offices in

---

6. Susan went on to become an employee and eventually the leader of all ad products and then YouTube, but her first Google title was landlord.

Palo Alto and then Mountain View, the founders ran it on a few simple principles, first and foremost of which was to focus on the user. They believed that if they created great services, they could figure out the money stuff later. If all they did was create the world's best search engine, they would be very successful.[7]

Their plan for creating that great search engine, and all the other great services, was equally simple: Hire as many talented software engineers as possible, and give them freedom. This approach suited a company born in a university lab, since in academia the most valuable asset is intellect (also, for some American universities, the ability to throw a football fifty yards). But while most companies say that their employees are everything, Larry and Sergey actually ran the company that way. This behavior wasn't corporate messaging, and it wasn't altruism. They felt that attracting and leading the very best engineers was the *only* way for Google to thrive and achieve its lofty ambitions. And they really meant engineers: The founders stopped Eric's first attempt to hire the estimable Sheryl Sandberg, now Facebook's COO, because she wasn't an engineer. (Sheryl went on to spend over six very successful years at Google.) As the company grew, the founders relented in this single-mindedness, but only a little bit. To this day the rule of thumb is that at least half of Google employees (aka Googlers) should be engineers.

The management tactics the founders used to run the company were equally simplistic. Like the professors in their Stanford computer science lab, who did not dictate what their thesis projects should be but rather provided direction and suggestions, Larry and Sergey offered their employees plenty of freedom and used communication as a tool to keep everyone moving in the same general direction. They had a very strong belief in the profound importance of the Internet and the power

---

7. Although as business neophytes Sergey and Larry didn't realize this, their "focus on the user" mantra was consistent with Peter Drucker's idea of the purpose of business: "There is only one valid definition of a business purpose: to create a customer.... The customer is the foundation of a business and keeps it in existence." From *The Practice of Management*, (HarperBusiness, 1993 edition), page 37.

of search, and they communicated these points via informal meetings with the small engineering teams that populated the Google offices, and through company-wide "TGIF" meetings held every Friday afternoon, where any topic was fair game for discussion.

When it came to process, the founders ran things with a light touch. For years, Google's primary tool for managing the company's resources was a spreadsheet with a ranked list of the company's top 100 projects, which was available for anyone to see and debated in semi-quarterly meetings. These meetings were part status update, part resource allocation, and part brainstorming. The system was not very scientific: Most projects were prioritized on a scale of 1 to 5, but there was also room on the list for projects categorized as "new / far out" and "skunkworks." (Today we can't recall the distinction between the two, but at the time it all made perfect sense... sort of.) There was no concept of or recognized need for longer-range planning than this; if something more important came up, the engineers would figure it out and adjust the list.

This emphasis on engineering continued even as the company expanded the management team. The founders didn't hire Eric for his business acumen as much as for his track record as a technologist (Eric was a Unix expert and helped create Java—the software language, not the beverage or the island) and geek cred as an alum of Bell Labs. They hired Jonathan in spite of his economics and MBA degrees, because he was a proven product advocate and innovator from his days at Apple and Excite@Home. That we were business guys wasn't exactly a liability, but it wasn't a benefit either, at least not in Sergey's and Larry's minds.

Jonathan got a stark example of the founders' aversion to traditional business processes not long after he started at the company. As a seasoned executive in product management, he had plenty of experience in what's known as the "gate-based" approach to building products, which in most companies entails a series of well-defined phases and milestones, governed by various executive reviews, that escalate slowly up the corporate food chain. This approach is designed to conserve resources and funnel information up from far-flung silos to a small set of decision-makers. Jonathan assumed that he was meant to bring precisely this type of discipline to Google, and he was supremely confident that he was just the guy to do it.

A few months later, Jonathan presented Larry with a product plan that was a manifestation of the gate-based approach at its finest. There were milestones and approvals, priorities, and a two-year plan of what products Google would release and when. It was a masterpiece of textbook thinking. All that remained was for him to receive a rousing round of applause and a pat on the back. Sadly, this was not to be: Larry hated it. "Have you ever seen a scheduled plan that the team beat?" he asked. Um, no. "Have your teams ever delivered better products than what was in the plan?" No again. "Then what's the point of the plan? It's holding us back. There must be a better way. Just go talk to the engineers."

As Larry spoke, it dawned on Jonathan that the engineers he was talking about weren't engineers in the traditional definition of the role. Yes, they were brilliant coders and system designers, but along with their deep technical expertise many of them were also quite business savvy and possessed a healthy streak of creativity. Coming from an academic background, Larry and Sergey had given these employees unusual freedom and power. Managing them by traditional planning structures wouldn't work; it might guide them but it would also hem them in. "Why would you want to do that?" Larry asked Jonathan. "That would be stupid."

So when Mike Moritz and the board asked us to create a traditional, MBA-style business plan, we didn't want to be stupid. We knew that the Google patient would reject a formal, regimented plan as if it were an alien organ transplanted into its body, which in many respects it would be. As experienced business executives, we had joined Google with the idea of bringing "adult supervision" to a chaotic place. But by the summer of 2003 we had been at the company long enough to realize that it was run differently than most any other place, with employees who were uniquely empowered, and operating in a new, rapidly evolving industry. We understood the dynamics of our new industry enough to get that the way to fend off Microsoft was continuous product excellence, yet we also understood that the best way to achieve that excellence was not via a prescribed business plan, but rather by hiring the very best engineers we could and then getting out of the way. We understood that our founders intuitively grasped how to lead in this new era, but they—by their own admission—didn't know how to build a company to the scale where it could achieve their ambitious vision. They were great leaders of computer scientists, but we needed more than computer scientists to create a great company.

We also understood that the rules to guide us in this endeavor did not even exist yet, and they certainly couldn't be found in the type of traditional business plan that Mike Moritz wanted.

So we found ourselves, at this critical moment in the company's history, stuck in the middle. We could do what Moritz wanted and write a traditional business plan. That would keep our board happy, but it would not motivate or inspire our employees, it would not help attract the new talent the company so desperately needed, and it wouldn't address the strategic dynamics of this brand-new industry. Most important, the company's founders would kill it before it ever saw the light of day. And maybe fire the two of us while they were at it.

The Finland plan

The plan that we ultimately presented to the board bore a close enough resemblance to a traditional business plan that the members departed the meeting satisfied that, yes, we have a business plan! Looking back now on that document, we are surprised in how many ways it was spot on. It was all about how Google would focus on its users and build excellent platforms and products. It said that Google would always offer higher-quality services and make those services easily accessible.

It proposed that our foundation be built on users, and that more users would draw more advertisers. There were a few tactical points covering how we would fend off competitive threats, but basically the way to challenge Microsoft, we said, was to create great products.

Which was, as it turned out, exactly the right thing to do.

Microsoft did aggressively challenge us, reportedly spending nearly $11 billion[8] in an attempt to knock Google off its perch as a key player in the Internet search and advertising business. Microsoft programs like MSN Search, Windows Live, and Bing, and acquisitions like aQuantive, failed to achieve true prominence, not because they were poorly executed but because Google was so well prepared for them. We worked incessantly to make search better. We added images, books, YouTube, shopping data, and any other corpus of information we could find. We created our own set of applications, such as Gmail and Docs, and made them all web-based. We improved our infrastructure by leaps and bounds, so that we could more quickly crawl an index of online data and content that was growing exponentially.[9] We made search faster and available in more languages, and improved our user interface to make it easier to use. We added maps and better local results. We worked with partners to ensure that it was always easy for users to access us. We even expanded into some areas where Microsoft excelled, such as browsers, launching Google Chrome and making it the fastest and most secure browser in the industry from day one. And we monetized all of this with highly efficient and effective ad systems.

Eric used to warn his team that "Microsoft will come at us, wave after wave." They did, and still do, nevertheless the business plan that Moritz pushed us to develop worked beyond our wildest dreams. Today Google is a $50-billion company with over forty-five thousand

---

8. Jay Yarow, "Steve Ballmer's Huge Reorg of Microsoft Could Bury One of the Company's Biggest Embarrassments" (*Business Insider*, July 9, 2013).

9. This was remarkably challenging. Imagine repeatedly climbing a mountain that is rapidly growing in size, and every time you climb it you need to get to the top faster than your previous trip. That's what it was like, except the mountain was made out of data, not dirt and rocks.

employees in over forty countries. We have diversified from Internet search and search advertising into video and other forms of digital marketing, successfully transitioned from a PC-centric world to a mobile-centric one, produced a successful suite of hardware devices, and pushed the technology edge with new projects that promise, for example, to bring Internet access to everyone and create cars that drive themselves.

One of the biggest reasons for our success, though, is that the plan we delivered to the board that day in 2003 wasn't much of a plan at all. There were no financial projections or discussions of revenue streams. There was no market research on what users, advertisers, or partners wanted or how they fit into nicely defined market segments. There was no concept of market research or discussion of which advertisers we would target first. There was no channel strategy or discussion of how we would sell our ad products. There was no concept of an org chart, with sales doing this, product doing that, and engineering doing some other that. There was no product roadmap detailing what we would build and when. There was no budget. There were no targets or milestones that the board and company leaders could use to monitor our progress.

There were also no tactics on how we would build the company or, more specifically, how we would stay loyal to Larry and Sergey's "just go talk to the engineers" ethos while building an enterprise that could take on the world's most powerful technology company and achieve our audacious global ambition of transforming lives by the billions. We left that out for the simple reason that we didn't know how we were going to do it. When it came to management tactics, the only thing we could say for sure back then was that much of what the two of us had learned in the twentieth century was wrong, and that it was time to start over.

When astonishing isn't

Today we all live and work in a new era, the Internet Century, where technology is roiling the business landscape and the pace of change is accelerating. This creates unique challenges for all business leaders. To understand those challenges, it helps to step back for a moment and consider just how amazing things are.

Three powerful technology trends have converged to fundamentally shift the playing field in most industries. First, the Internet has made information free, copious, and ubiquitous—practically everything is online. Second, mobile devices and networks have made global reach and continuous connectivity widely available. And third, cloud computing[10] has put practically infinite computing power and storage and a host of sophisticated tools and applications at everyone's disposal, on an inexpensive, pay-as-you-go basis. Today, access to these technologies is still unavailable to much of the world's population, but it won't be long before that situation changes and the next five billion people come online.

From a consumer perspective, the convergence of these three technological waves has made the impossible possible. Taking a flight somewhere? On the day of your departure, your phone will remind you when to leave for the airport, tell you the terminal and gate from which the flight departs, and let you know if you will need an umbrella when you get to your destination, all without you having to ask. Want to track down any piece of information? Type or speak a word or two, and the answer pops up almost instantly, picked from a giant pile of information comprised of most of the world's knowledge. Hear a song you like? Hold up your phone, tap a button, identify the song, buy it, and then listen to it on any device, anywhere in the world. Need to know how to get somewhere? Your phone (or your glasses or watch) will literally tell you how, and show you the traffic along the way. Traveling to a foreign country? Talk into your phone (or your glasses or watch) and see or hear your words translated into practically any language on the planet, or point it at a sign and read it in your native tongue. Like art? You can virtually walk through many of the world's greatest museums

---

10. It's called "cloud computing" because the old programs to draw network schematics surrounded the icons for servers with a circle. A cluster of servers in a network diagram had several overlapping circles, which resembled a cloud.

and see their paintings in far greater detail than anyone ever has, except perhaps the artists who created them. Want to know if that restaurant you picked for tonight's date has the right ambience or easy parking? Virtually drive there, walk through the front door, and take a tour inside. Table 14 looks perfect!

When we went to college in the late 1970s and early '80s, we called home once a week, on Sundays, always before five p.m. because that's when the rates went back up. When Jonathan's son was studying in Australia a couple years ago, he occasionally joined the family back home in California for dinner, via video Hangout, on a laptop that sat at his place at the table. For free.

What's most astonishing is that these astonishing things aren't astonishing at all. It used to be that the most powerful computers and the best electronics were at the office, and once you left work you had to get by on phones attached to walls, maps on paper, music from radio stations that played what they felt like playing, and televisions brought in by two big guys and attached to cables or antennae. These aspects of life remained practically unchanged for years. Today, though, wow innovations are commonplace.

Speed

As much as technology has affected consumers, it has had an even bigger impact on businesses. In economic terms, when the cost curves shift downward on a primary factor of production in an industry, big-time change is in store for that industry.[11] Today, *three* factors of production have become cheaper—information, connectivity, and computing power—affecting any cost curves in which those factors are involved. This can't help but have disruptive effects. Many incumbents—aka pre-Internet companies—built their businesses based on assumptions of

---

11. For those of you who don't speak economist, "downward shifting cost curve" means "stuff that was expensive is now cheap."

scarcity: scarce information, scarce distribution resources and market reach, or scarce choice and shelf space. Now, though, these factors are abundant, lowering or eliminating barriers to entry and making entire industries ripe for change.[12] We saw this first in the media business, whose entire product can now be rendered digitally and sent around the world for free. But practically every industry is, at some level, information-driven. Media, marketing, retail, health care, government, education, financial services, transportation, defense, energy... We can't think of an industry that will escape this era unchanged.

The result of all this turmoil is that product excellence is now paramount to business success—not control of information, not a stranglehold on distribution, not overwhelming marketing power (although these are still important). There are a couple of reasons for this. First, consumers have never been better informed or had more choice.[13] It used to be that companies could turn poor products into winners by dint of overwhelming marketing or distribution strength. Create an adequate product, control the conversation with a big marketing budget, limit customer choice, and you could guarantee yourself a good return. Ever eat at a Bennigan's? A Steak and Ale? In their heyday in the 1980s, these chains had hundreds of locations in the United States, all of them offering perfectly decent food and service.

Things are different today. Cities and suburbs have unique

---

12. Technology visionary George Gilder has observed that every economic era is based on a key abundance and a key scarcity. (When horsepower was scarce, for example, land was abundant—but the opposite was true in the industrial era, when the cost of horsepower fell to just pennies per kilowatt hour.) The result of cheap bandwidth, as Gilder wrote in a remarkably prescient 1996 essay, is "a completely different computer architecture and information economy.... Feeding on low power and high bandwidth, the most common computer of the new era will be a digital cellular phone with an IP address." See George Gilder, "The Gilder Paradigm" (*Wired*, December 1996), reprinted from an issue of the *Gilder Technology Report*.

13. Peter Drucker anticipated this development back in 2001, when he wrote that the center of power has shifted from the supplier to the distributor, and that "in the next thirty years, it will certainly shift to the customer—for the simple reason that the customer now has full access to information worldwide." See Peter Drucker, *The Essential Drucker* (HarperBusiness, 2011), page 348.

restaurants for every taste—locally owned as well as chains—and prospective diners have access to a wealth of information about their quality, from both professional critics and citizen reviewers, on sites ranging from Chowhound to Yelp. With so much information and so many good choices, it's harder for an incumbent, crummy restaurant (chain or not) to survive, regardless of the size of its marketing budget, and easier for a new, high-quality place to gain a word-of-mouth foothold.[14] The same is true of cars, hotels, toys, clothes, and any other product or service that people can research online. The customer has abundant choice, with practically infinite digital shelf space (YouTube has well over a million channels; Amazon sells over fifty thousand books about business leadership alone). And the customer has a voice; provide a bad product or lousy service at your peril.

We've experienced this phenomenon firsthand several times in the Internet Age. When Jonathan worked at Excite@Home and wanted to strike up a search partnership with Google, his CEO decided not to do the deal, telling Jonathan that "Google's search engine is better, but we'll out-market them." Excite@Home is gone, so that obviously didn't work out very well. (On the plus side, the "@" symbol has gone on to be a huge sensation!) Excite@Home's management wasn't unique in its belief in the power of brand and marketing to carry less-than-brilliant products. Have you ever heard of Google Notebook? How about Knol? iGoogle? Wave? Buzz? PigeonRank?[15] These were all Google products that, while they had some merit, never caught on with users. They weren't good enough, and so they died a deserved death. The tailwind of Google's marketing and PR engine and brand wasn't nearly strong

---

14. An economist at the Harvard Business School studied the impact of Yelp on restaurant revenues, finding that positive reviews boost sales in independent restaurants (as opposed to chains). As a result, in markets with a high level of Yelp use, chain restaurants have lost customers. See Michael Luca, "Reviews, Reputation, and Revenue: The Case of Yelp.com" (Harvard Business School Working Paper, September 2011).

15. PigeonRank utilized "pigeon clusters (PCs)" to compute the relative value of web pages. Its demise was particularly quick: It launched on the morning of April 1, 2002, and was shut down at midnight that same day.

enough to overcome a headwind of mediocrity. As Jeff Bezos, founder and CEO of Amazon, says: "In the old world, you devoted 30 percent of your time to building a great service and 70 percent of your time to shouting about it. In the new world, that inverts."[16]

The second reason product excellence is so critical is that the cost of experimentation and failure has dropped significantly. You see this most dramatically in high-tech industries, where a small team of engineers, developers, and designers can create fabulous products and distribute them online globally for free. It's ridiculously easy to imagine and create a new product, try it out with a limited set of consumers, measure precisely what works and what doesn't, iterate the product, and try again. Or throw it out and start over, that much smarter for the experience.

But experimentation costs are lower for manufactured goods as well. One can model prototypes digitally, build them with a 3-D printer, market test them online, adjust their design based on the resulting data, and even raise production funds online with a prototype or slick video. Google[x], a team working on some of Google's most ambitious projects, built the first prototype of Google Glass, a wearable mobile computer as light as a pair of sunglasses, in just ninety minutes. It was quite crude, but served a powerful purpose: Don't tell me, show me.

Product development has become a faster, more flexible process, where radically better products don't stand on the shoulders of giants, but on the shoulders of lots of iterations. The basis for success then, and for continual product excellence, is speed.

Unfortunately, like Jonathan's failed gate-based product development framework, most management processes in place at companies today are designed with something else in mind. They were devised over a century ago, at a time when mistakes were expensive and only

16. Quoted in George Anders, "Jeff Bezos's Top 10 Leadership Lessons" (*Forbes*, April 23, 2012).

the top executives had comprehensive information, and their primary objectives are lowering risk and ensuring that decisions are made only by the few executives with lots of information. In this traditional command-and-control structure, data flows up to the executives from all over the organization, and decisions subsequently flow down. This approach is *designed* to slow things down, and it accomplishes the task very well. Meaning that at the very moment when businesses must permanently accelerate, their architecture is working against them.

The "smart creative"

The good news is that those same economics of abundance that are roiling industries are churning up workplaces too. Today's work environment is radically different than it was in the twentieth century. As already noted, experimentation is cheap and the cost of failure—if done well—is much lower than it used to be. Plus, data used to be scarce and computing resources precious; today both are abundant, so there's no need to hoard them. And collaboration is easy, across a room, a continent, or an ocean. Put these factors together, and you suddenly have an environment where employees, from individual contributors to managers to executives, can have an inordinately big impact.

The default term today for these employees—the ones working in information-based jobs who, to put it way too simplistically, think for a living—is "knowledge workers." This is a label that management guru Peter Drucker first coined in 1959 in a book called *Landmarks of Tomorrow*.[17] Much of Drucker's subsequent work talked about how to make these knowledge workers more productive, and use of the term has risen steadily since the 1960s. Typically, the most valuable knowledge workers are the ones who thrive in the straitjacketed world of corporate process, by building deep expertise in a narrow set of skills. ("Morty? He's our spreadsheet guy. Vicki? She's our warehouse go-to.

17. Peter F. Drucker, *Landmarks of Tomorrow* (Harper, 1959).

Pete? He runs the basketball pool.") They don't seek mobility; organizational status quo is where they excel. Great companies such as IBM, General Electric, General Motors, and Johnson & Johnson offer management tracks for people with the greatest potential, whereby these stars rotate in and out of different roles every two years or so. But this approach emphasizes the development of management skills, not technical ones. As a result, most knowledge workers in traditional environments develop deep technical expertise but little breadth, or broad management expertise but no technical depth.

When we contrast the traditional knowledge worker with the engineers and other talented people who have surrounded us at Google over the past decade-plus, we see that our Google peers represent a quite different type of employee. They are not confined to specific tasks. They are not limited in their access to the company's information and computing power. They are not averse to taking risks, nor are they punished or held back in any way when those risky initiatives fail. They are not hemmed in by role definitions or organizational structures; in fact, they are encouraged to exercise their own ideas. They don't keep quiet when they disagree with something. They get bored easily and shift jobs a lot. They are multidimensional, usually combining technical depth with business savvy and creative flair. In other words, they are not knowledge workers, at least not in the traditional sense. They are a new kind of animal, a type we call a "smart creative," and they are the key to achieving success in the Internet Century.

The primary objective of any business today must be to increase the speed of the product development process and the quality of its output. Since the industrial revolution, operating processes have been biased toward lowering risk and avoiding mistakes. These processes, and the overall management approach from which they were derived, result in environments that stifle smart creatives. Now, though, the defining characteristic of today's successful companies is the ability to continually deliver great products. And the only way to do that is to attract smart creatives and create an environment where they can succeed at scale.

And who, exactly, is this smart creative?

A smart creative has deep technical knowledge in how to use the tools of her trade,[18] and plenty of hands-on experience. In our industry, that means she is most likely a computer scientist, or at least understands the tenets and structure of the systems behind the magic you see on your screens every day. But in other industries she may be a doctor, designer, scientist, filmmaker, engineer, chef, or mathematician. She is an expert in doing. She doesn't just design concepts, she builds prototypes.

She is analytically smart. She is comfortable with data and can use it to make decisions. She also understands its fallacies and is wary of endless analysis. Let data decide, she believes, but don't let it take over.

She is business smart. She sees a direct line from technical expertise to product excellence to business success, and understands the value of all three.

She is competitive smart. Her stock-in-trade starts with innovation, but it also includes a lot of work. She is driven to be great, and that doesn't happen 9-to-5.

She is user smart. No matter the industry, she understands her product from the user or consumer's perspective better than almost anyone. We call her a "power user," not just casual but almost obsessive in her interest. She is the automotive designer who spends her weekends fixing up that '69 GTO, the architect who can't stop redesigning her house. She is her own focus group, alpha tester, and guinea pig.

A smart creative is a firehose of new ideas that are genuinely new. Her perspective is different from yours or ours. It's even occasionally different from her own perspective, for a smart creative can play the perspective chameleon when she needs to.

She is curious creative. She is always questioning, never satisfied

---

18. The English language requires that we choose a gender when using pronouns, and we find that using pronouns makes the task of authorship easier. In this section, we describe our smart creative as a she. In others, she's a he.

with the status quo, seeing problems to solve everywhere and thinking that she is just the person to solve them. She can be overbearing.

She is risky creative. She is not afraid to fail, because she believes that in failure there is usually something valuable she can salvage. Either that, or she is just so damn confident she knows that even in the event that she does fail, she can pick herself up and get it right the next time around.

She is self-directed creative. She doesn't wait to be told what to do and sometimes ignores direction if she doesn't agree with it. She takes action based on her own initiative, which is considerable.

She is open creative. She freely collaborates, and judges ideas and analyses on their merits and not their provenance. If she were into needle-point, she would sew a pillow that said, "If I give you a penny, then you're a penny richer and I'm a penny poorer, but if I give you an idea, then you will have a new idea but I'll have it too." Then she would figure out a way to make the pillow fly around the room and shoot lasers.

She is thorough creative. She is always on and can recite the details, not because she studies and memorizes, but because she knows them. They are *her* details.

She is communicative creative. She is funny and expresses herself with flair and even charisma, either one-to-one or one-to-many.

Not every smart creative has all of these characteristics, in fact very few of them do. But they all must possess business savvy, technical knowledge, creative energy, and a hands-on approach to getting things done. Those are the fundamentals.

Perhaps the best thing about smart creatives is that they are everywhere. We have worked with plenty of smart creatives who boast computer science degrees from elite universities, but plenty more who don't. In fact, smart creatives can be found in every city, in every school, in every class and demographic, and in most businesses, non-profits, and government organizations: the ambitious ones of all ages who are eager (and able) to use the tools of technology to do a lot more. Their common characteristic is that they work hard and are willing to question the status quo and attack things differently. This is why they can have such an impact.

It is also why they are uniquely difficult to manage, especially under old models, because no matter how hard you try, you can't tell people like that how to think. If you can't tell someone how to think, then you have to learn to manage the environment *where* they think. And make it a place where they want to come every day.

A fun project for the two of us

Which brings us back to our journey at Google. By the time we delivered that business plan to the board back in 2003, we knew that we had to do what so many business leaders are faced with today: reinvent our rules for management and create and maintain a new kind of work environment where our amazing smart-creative employees could thrive, in our case in a company growing by leaps and bounds. While we were brought into Google to provide "adult supervision," to succeed we ended up having to relearn everything we thought we knew about management, and our best teachers were the people who surrounded us every day at the Googleplex.

We've been working on this ever since, and along the way, like all good students, we kept notes. Whenever we heard something interesting in a staff meeting or product review, we scribbled it down. When Eric wrote his periodic memos to Googlers about the company's priorities, Jonathan would note its best sections and stow them away for later use. When Jonathan sent emails to the product team, lauding a practice that was working well or calling out one that wasn't, Eric would add his own opinions and analysis. Over time, we started to create a framework for how to manage in this new world.

Then, a few years ago, Nikesh Arora, who heads Google global sales and business operations, asked Jonathan to give a talk to a group of Google sales leaders from around the world. Nikesh is himself a prototypical smart creative. He holds a degree in electrical engineering from the Indian Institute of Technology and joined Google in 2004 to run sales in Europe, despite not having much experience leading a sales organization of that size. He came to California in 2009 to run the global business team. Nikesh always excels, so Jonathan knew the bar was set very high for this particular talk. Google had passed its first decade and was growing like crazy, and Nikesh wanted Jonathan to pass some of the tribal wisdom that he and Eric had accumulated about managing at Google to our next generation of leaders. This was a perfect opportunity to pull together all of those notes on what the "students" had learned from the "teachers" over the years.

The talk was very well received, so we turned it into a management seminar for Google directors, meeting with small groups of Google leaders to review our principles and swap stories about managing smart creatives. Finally, Eric did what all great managers do when they want something to happen: He proposed an idea. His email read:

```
I'm sufficiently impressed with the work here that
I propose that Jonathan and I write a book on
management.
     Of course due to the principles we will espouse in
the book Jonathan will do all the work and I will get
all the credit :) that was a joke.
     In any case I think it would be a fun project for
the two of us.
     Jonathan what do you say?
```

Eric was inspired by a John Chambers talk he once heard. Chambers, the highly respected CEO of Cisco, said that in the early 1990s he had often met with Hewlett Packard CEO Lew Platt to talk strategy and management. At one point an appreciative John asked Lew why he was investing so much of his valuable time to help out a young executive at a different company. "This is the way Silicon Valley works," Mr. Platt replied. "We're here to help you."

Steve Jobs, the late founder and CEO of Apple, who often provided his neighbor Larry Page with advice, had a more colorful way of expressing this same spirit. Our friend Leslie Berlin, the Silicon Valley historian, was researching a biography on Intel cofounder Bob Noyce, and asked Steve during an interview why he had spent so much time with Noyce early in his career. "It's like what Schopenhauer said about the conjurer," Steve replied. He retrieved a book of essays by nineteenth-century German philosopher Arthur Schopenhauer, and read her a passage from one with the chipper title of "On the Sufferings of the World": "He who lives to see two or three generations is like a man who sits some time in the conjurer's booth at a fair, and witnesses the performance twice or thrice in succession. The tricks were meant to be seen only once, and when they are no longer a novelty and cease to deceive, their effect is gone."[19] (We suspect that the ability to pull out a Schopenhauer quote during an interview was precisely one of those tricks.)

We both came to Google as seasoned business executives who were pretty confident in our intellects and abilities. But over the humbling course of a decade, we came to see the wisdom in John Wooden's observation that "it's what you learn after you know it all that counts."[20] We had a front-row seat as we helped our founders and colleagues create a magnificent company—you might say that we saw the conjurers at work—and used it to relearn everything we thought we knew about management. Today we see all sorts of companies and organizations, big and small, from all industries and all over the world, come to

---

19. Arthur Schopenhauer, *Essays and Aphorisms* (Penguin, 1970).

20. Coach Wooden, who died in 2010 at the age of ninety-nine, won ten national championships while coaching men's basketball at UCLA. But he coached there for fifteen years before winning the first of those championships, so he knew something about learning. See John Wooden and Steve Jamison, *Wooden on Leadership* (McGraw-Hill, 2005), page 34.

Silicon Valley to see if they can soak up the insights and energy that make it such a special place. People are eager for change, and that's what this book is about: In the spirit of our forefathers here in Silicon Valley, we'd like to share some of the conjurers' secrets and translate them into lessons that anyone can use.

Our book is organized to mirror the development stages of a successful, growing business or new venture, which can become a self-perpetuating virtuous cycle, sort of like a snowball rolling down the hill, getting bigger as it picks up momentum. We prescribe a series of steps businesses can follow to attract and motivate smart creatives, each of which propels the business to the next step. The steps build and depend on each other, but none of them is ever completed and all of them are dynamic.

We open by discussing how to attract the best smart creatives, which starts with culture, because culture and success go hand in hand, and if you don't believe your own slogans you won't get very far. We then cover strategy, because smart creatives are most attracted to ideas that are grounded in a strong strategic foundation. They know that business plans aren't nearly as important as the pillars upon which they are built. Then, hiring, which is the most important thing a leader does. Hire enough great people, and the resulting intellectual mixture will inevitably combust into creativity and success.

The team is hired, the business grows, now the time comes to make hard decisions. This is where we talk about consensus and how to get there. Our following chapter is about communications, which become vital (and harder) as the organization grows. Innovation is up next, since the only way to achieve sustained success is through continuous product excellence, and an environment of innovative primordial ooze is the only way to get there. We conclude with some thoughts on incumbents and how to imagine the unimaginable.

Pyramids unbuilt

None of this is easy, and many of our lessons we learned the hard way, through long meetings, contentious struggles, and errors. We also humbly acknowledge our great luck in having joined a spectacular company, run by brilliant founders, at the unique moment in history when the Internet was taking off. We weren't quite born on third base thinking we had hit a triple, but first or second sounds about right.

We certainly don't have all the answers, but we have learned a lot about this new world where technology reigns supreme and employees are uniquely empowered to make a big difference. We believe that these lessons could perhaps provide insights and ideas for leaders of all types of organizations, from large enterprises to new start-ups, from non-profits to NGOs to governments, or at least provoke informed discussions of how our experiences at Google might apply in other companies and realms. But mostly, our hope is that we can give you—along with a good read—the ideas and tools to go build something new.

And when we say "you," we mean you, entrepreneur. You are out there. You may not think of yourself as an entrepreneur yet, but you are. You have an idea you're sure will change everything; you might have a prototype, or even a first version of a product. You're smart, ambitious, and hunkered down in a conference room, garage, office, café, apartment, or dorm room, alone or with your small team. You think about your idea even when you're supposed to be doing something else, like studying, performing your day job, or spending time with your kids and partner. You are about to launch a new venture, and we'd like to help.

And when we say "venture," we aren't restricting ourselves to the technology start-ups that surround us here in Silicon Valley. Employees expect much more from their companies now, and they are often not getting it. This is an opportunity: The principles that we talk about apply to anyone who is trying to start a new venture or initiative, either from scratch or from within an existing organization. They aren't just for start-ups, and they aren't just for high-tech businesses. In fact, when skilled leaders can harness all of the great assets of an ongoing organization, that organization can have a far greater impact than a start-up. So just because you don't have a hoodie and a seven-figure check from a venture capitalist, that doesn't mean you can't create the next big thing. All you need is the insight that your industry is transforming at a rapid pace, the guts to take a risk and be part of that transformation, and the willingness and ability to attract the best smart creatives and lead them to make it happen.

Is that you? Are you ready? As Peter Drucker pointed out, the Egyptian who conceived and built the pyramids thousands of years ago was really just a very successful manager.[21] The Internet Century brims with pyramids yet unbuilt. Let's get started.

And this time, with no slave labor.

---

21. Peter F. Drucker, *The Essential Drucker* (HarperBusiness, 2011), pages 312–13. Drucker writes, "Management as a *practice* is very old. The most successful executive in all history was surely that Egyptian who, forty-seven hundred years or more ago, first conceived the pyramid—without any precedent—and designed and built it, and did so in record time."

Culture—Believe Your Own Slogans

One Friday afternoon in May 2002, Larry Page was playing around on the Google site, typing in search terms and seeing what sort of results and ads he'd get back. He wasn't happy with what he saw. He would enter a query for one thing, and while Google came back with plenty of relevant organic results, some of the ads were completely unrelated to the search.[22] A search for something like "Kawasaki H1B" would yield lots of ads for lawyers offering to help immigrants get H-1B US visas, but none related to the vintage motorcycle to which the search query referred. Or a search for "french cave paintings" delivered ads that said "buy french cave paintings at...," with the name of an online retailer that obviously did not stock French cave paintings (or even facsimiles of them). Larry was horrified that the AdWords engine, which figured out which ads worked best with which queries, was occasionally subjecting our users to such useless messages.

At that point, Eric still thought Google was a fairly normal start-up. But what happened over the next seventy-two hours completely shifted that perception. In a normal company, the CEO, seeing a bad product, would call the person in charge of the product. There would be a meeting or two or three to discuss the problem, review

---

22. When you do a Google search, there are two types of results that come back: organic and paid. Organic results are the "natural" search results returned by Google's search engine, while paid results are placed by the ads engine.

potential solutions, and decide on a course of action. A plan would
come together to implement the solution. Then, after a fair amount of
quality assurance testing, the solution would launch. In a normal company, this would take several weeks. This isn't what Larry did.

Instead, he printed out the pages containing the results he didn't
like, highlighted the offending ads, posted them on a bulletin board on
the wall of the kitchen by the pool table, and wrote THESE ADS SUCK in
big letters across the top. Then he went home. He didn't call or email
anyone. He didn't schedule an emergency meeting. He didn't mention
the issue to either of us.

At 5:05 a.m. the following Monday, one of our search engineers,
Jeff Dean, sent out an email. He and a few colleagues (including
Georges Harik, Ben Gomes, Noam Shazeer, and Olcan Sercinoglu)
had seen Larry's note on the wall and agreed with Larry's assessment
of the ads' relative suckiness. But the email didn't just concur with the
founder and add some facile bromide about looking into the problem. Rather, it included a detailed analysis of why the problem was
occurring, described a solution, included a link to a prototype implementation of the solution the five had coded over the weekend, and
provided sample results that demonstrated how the new prototype was
an improvement over the then-current system. While the details of the
solution were geeky and complex (our favorite phrase from the note:
"query snippet term vector"), the gist of it was that we would compute
an "ad relevance score" that would assess the quality of the ad relevant
to the query, and then determine whether and where the ad would
be placed on the page based on that score. This core insight—that
ads should be placed based on their relevancy, not just how much the
advertiser was willing to pay and the number of clicks they received—
became the foundation upon which Google's AdWords engine, and a
multibillion-dollar business, was built.

And the kicker? Jeff and team weren't even on the ads team. They
had just been in the office that Friday afternoon, seen Larry's note, and

understood that when your mission is to organize the world's information and make it universally accessible and useful, then having ads (which are information) that suck (which isn't useful) is a problem. So they decided to fix it. Over the weekend.

The reason a bunch of employees who had no direct responsibility for ads, or culpability when they were lousy, spent their weekends transforming someone else's problem into a profitable solution speaks to the power of culture. Jeff and gang had a clear understanding of their company's priorities, and knew they had the freedom to try to solve any big problem that stood in the way of success. If they had failed, no one would have chastised them in any way, and when they succeeded, no one—even on the ads team—was jealous of their progress. But it wasn't Google's culture that turned those five engineers into problem-solving ninjas who changed the course of the company over the weekend. Rather it was the culture that attracted the ninjas to the company in the first place.

Many people, when considering a job, are primarily concerned with their role and responsibilities, the company's track record, the industry, and compensation. Further down on that list, probably somewhere between "length of commute" and "quality of coffee in the kitchen," comes culture. Smart creatives, though, place culture at the top of the list. To be effective, they need to *care* about the place they work. This is why, when starting a new company or initiative, culture is the most important thing to consider.

Most companies' culture just happens; no one plans it. That can work, but it means leaving a critical component of your success to chance. Elsewhere in this book we preach the value of experimentation and the virtues of failure, but culture is perhaps the one important aspect of a company where failed experiments hurt. Once established, company culture is very difficult to change, because early on in a company's life a self-selection tendency sets in. People who believe in the same things the company does will be drawn to work there, while people who don't, won't.[23] If a company believes in a culture where everyone gets a say and decisions are made by committee, it will attract like-minded employees. But if that company tries to adopt a more autocratic or combative approach, it will have a very hard time getting employees to go along with it. Change like that not only goes against what the company stands for, it goes against its employees' personal beliefs. That's a tough road.

The smart approach is to ponder and define what sort of culture you want at the outset of your company's life. And the best way to do that is to ask the smart creatives who form your core team, the ones who know the gospel and believe in it as much as you do. Culture stems from founders, but it is best reflected in the trusted team the founders form to launch their venture. So ask that team: What do we care about? What do we believe? Who do we want to be? How do we want our company to act and make decisions? Then write down their responses. They will, in all likelihood, encompass the founders' values, but embellish them with insights from the team's different perspectives and experiences.

Most companies neglect this. They become successful, and *then* decide they need to document their culture. The job falls to someone in the human resources or PR department who probably wasn't a member of the founding team but who is expected to draft a mission statement that captures the essence of the place. The result is usually a set of corporate sayings that are full of "delighted" customers, "maximized" shareholder value, and "innovative" employees. The difference, though,

---

23. One of the most important academic expressions of this idea appeared in a 1987 journal article by organizational psychologist Benjamin Schneider, "The People Make the Place" (*Personnel Psychology*, September 1987). In this influential paper, Schneider lays out an attraction-selection-attrition model (ASA model) of how organizational cultures evolve from the traits and choices of individuals. "Attraction" refers to the tendency of job seekers to flock to organizations with which they sense a good fit; "selection" means that a company's current employees tend to hire people who are like them; "attrition," too, isn't random, as employees tend to leave organizations with which they are no longer compatible. As attraction, selection, and attrition processes play out over time, an organization becomes increasingly homogeneous in its culture.

between successful companies and unsuccessful ones is whether employees believe the words.

Here's a little thought experiment for you: Think about someplace where you've worked. Now, try to recite its mission statement. Can you do it? If so, do you believe in it? Does it strike you as authentic, something that honestly reflects the actions and culture of the company and its employees? Or does it seem like something a group of marketing and communications people conjured up one night with a six-pack and a thesaurus? Something like: "Our mission is to build unrivaled partnerships with and value for our clients, through the knowledge, creativity, and dedication of our people, leading to superior results for our shareholders."[24] Boy, that sure checks all the boxes, doesn't it? Clients—check; employees—check; shareholders—check. Lehman Brothers was the owner of that mission statement—at least until its bankruptcy in 2008. Surely Lehman stood for something, but you couldn't tell from those words.

In contrast to Lehman Brothers' leaders, David Packard, a founding member of our all-time Smart Creative Hall of Fame, took culture seriously. He noted in a 1960 speech to his managers that companies exist to "do something worthwhile—they make a contribution to society.... You can look around and still see people who are interested in money and nothing else, but the underlying drives come largely from a desire to do something else—to make a product, to give a service, generally to do something which is of value."[25]

People's BS detectors are finely tuned when it comes to corporate-speak; they can tell when you don't mean it. So when you put your mission into writing, it had better be authentic. A good litmus test is to ask what would happen if you changed the statements that describe culture. Take "Respect, Integrity, Communication and Excellence," which was Enron's motto. If execs at Enron had decided to replace

---

24. Susan Reynolds, *Prescription for Lasting Success* (John Wiley and Sons, 2012), page 51.
25. The full text of Packard's March 8, 1960, speech appears in David Packard's *The HP Way: How Bill Hewlett and I Built Our Company* (HarperCollins, 2005).

those concepts with something different—perhaps Greed, Greed, Lust for Money, and Greed—it might have drawn a few chuckles but otherwise there would have been no impact. On the other hand, one of Google's stated values has always been to "Focus on the User." If we changed that, perhaps by putting the needs of advertisers or publishing partners first, our inboxes would be flooded, and outraged engineers would take over the weekly, company-wide TGIF meeting (which is hosted by Larry and Sergey, and where employees are welcome to—and often do—voice their disagreement with company decisions). Employees always have a choice, so belie your values at your own risk.

Think about your culture, either what you want it to be or what it already is. Imagine, months or years from now, an employee working late, unable to make up his mind about a tough decision.[26] He walks to the kitchen for a cup of coffee, and thinks back on the cultural values he heard expressed at company meetings, talked about with colleagues over lunch, saw demonstrated by that company veteran whom everyone respects. For this employee—for all employees—those values should clearly and plainly outline the things that matter most to the company, the things you care about. Otherwise they are meaningless, and won't be worth a damn when it comes to helping that smart creative make the right call. What values would you want that bleary-eyed employee to consider? Write them down in a simple, concise way. Then share them, not in posters and guides, but through constant, authentic communications. As former General Electric CEO Jack Welch said in *Winning*: "No vision is worth the paper it's printed on unless it is communicated constantly and reinforced with rewards."[27]

---

26. Culture theorists going back to at least Émile Durkheim have argued that through shared beliefs, values, and norms, culture shapes people's thoughts and behaviors. Contemporary social scientists, most notably the social psychologist Hazel Markus, have used controlled experiments to show that even when people aren't aware of it, their culture (such as Japanese vs. American, working-class vs. professional) sways the everyday choices they make. For a popular account of this research, see Hazel Rose Markus and Alana Conner, *Clash!: 8 Cultural Conflicts That Make Us Who We Are* (Hudson Street Press/Penguin, 2013).

27. Jack Welch with Suzy Welch, *Winning* (HarperCollins, 2005), page 69.

When Google went public in 2004, Sergey and Larry recognized the IPO as the perfect opportunity to codify the values that would guide the company's actions and decisions. And not just the most important actions and decisions and not just management's actions and decisions, but *everyone's* actions and decisions, big and small, every day. These values had guided how the company had run since its founding six years earlier, and were deeply grounded in the founders' personal experiences. Inspired by the annual letter Warren Buffett writes to Berkshire Hathaway shareholders, they drafted a "letter from the founders" to include in the IPO prospectus.

The Securities and Exchange Commission initially ruled that the letter did not contain information that would be relevant to investors, and so didn't belong in the company's investment prospectus. We argued and eventually won the right to include it. Still, some of the statements in the letter gave the lawyers and bankers heartburn, and at one point Jonathan found himself in a conference room facing a battalion of them picking at this point or that. He steadfastly defended the text of the letter, using two main arguments: (1) Larry and Sergey had written the letter themselves, with input only from a small group of Googlers, and wouldn't change a thing (it's easy to hold the line in a negotiation when you are, in fact, completely unable to get your side to budge!), and (2) everything the letter said was heartfelt and true.

When it was published in April 2004, the letter generated a lot of curiosity and some criticism. What most people didn't understand, though, was exactly why the company's founders had spent so much time getting the letter exactly right (and why Jonathan dug his heels in every time one of the bankers or lawyers tried to change something). The letter was not primarily about Dutch auctions, voting rights, or showing off a blatant disregard for everything Wall Street. In fact, if we Wall Street have offended, think but this, and all is mended:[28] The founders didn't care about maximizing the short-term value and

---

28. With apologies to that notable smart creative, Puck.

marketability of their stock, because they knew that recording the company's unique values for future employees and partners would be far more instrumental to long-term success. As we write this today, the arcane details of that IPO a decade ago are a matter of history, but phrases like "long term focus," "serving end users," "don't be evil," and "making the world a better place" still describe how the company is run.

There are other aspects of Google culture—about things like crowded offices, hippos, knaves, and Israeli tank commanders—that didn't make the letter. But these, as we shall see, would become integral to creating—and sustaining—a culture where a simple statement like "These ads suck" is all that's needed to make things happen.

Keep them crowded

A new visitor to the Googleplex will immediately notice the dazzling array of amenities available to employees: volleyball courts, bowling alleys, climbing walls and slides, gyms with personal trainers and lap pools, colorful bikes to get from building to building, free gourmet cafeterias, and numerous kitchens stocked with all sorts of snacks, drinks, and top-of-the-line espresso machines. These things usually leave visitors with the correct impression that Googlers are awash in luxuries, and the mistaken impression that luxury is part of our culture. Giving hardworking employees extra goodies is a Silicon Valley tradition dating back to the 1960s, when Bill Hewlett and David Packard bought a few hundred acres of land in the Santa Cruz Mountains and turned it into Little Basin[29]—a camping and recreational retreat

---

29. In 2007, HP sold the Little Basin campsite to a pair of nonprofits, Sempervirens Fund and Peninsula Open Space Trust, who then sold it to the California state parks department. Today it is part of Big Basin Redwoods State Park and open for public use. See Paul Rogers, "Former Hewlett Packard Retreat Added to Big Basin Redwoods State Park" (*San Jose Mercury News*, January 14, 2011).

for employees and their families.[30] In the 1970s, companies such as ROLM started bringing the amenities closer to work, with full gymnasiums and subsidized cafeterias that served gourmet food, and Apple chipped in with its legendary (at least among the hookup-hopeful geek set) Friday afternoon beer busts. In Google's case, our approach to facilities was grounded in the company's beginnings in a Stanford dorm room. Larry and Sergey set out to create an environment similar to a university, where students have access to world-class cultural, athletic, and academic facilities . . . and spend most of their time working their butts off. What most outsiders fail to see when they visit Google is the offices where employees spend the bulk of their time. Follow your typical Googler (and probably LinkedIn, Yahoo, Twitter, or Facebook employee, although the last time we tried we got stopped by security) from the volleyball court, café, or kitchen back to their workspace and what will you find? A series of cubicles that are crowded, messy, and a petri dish for creativity.

Are you in your office right now? Are your coworkers nearby? Spin around and wave your arms. Do you hit anyone? If you have a quiet conversation on your phone while sitting at your desk, can your coworkers hear you? We're guessing no. Are you a manager? If so, can you close your door and have private conversations? We're guessing yes. In fact, your company's facilities master plan was most likely specifically designed to maximize space and quiet (while minimizing cost). And the higher you are on the corporate hierarchy, the more space and quiet you get. Entry-level associates are shoehorned into interior cubicles, while CEOs get the big corner office with lots of space outside the door to house assistants and act as a barrier against everyone else.

---

30. Decades before Google hired its own chef, Bill Hewlett and Dave Packard seemed to understand how much employees and customers prize free food. HP employee John Minck noted: "Some production line donut and Danish trays were set over the top of several soldering irons, set up with variable power transformers to heat them up without burning them. Those breaks were all company furnished and used to amaze customers [whom] we were touring through the plants." Quoted in Michael Malone, *Bill & Dave: How Hewlett and Packard Built the World's Greatest Company* (Portfolio/Penguin, 2007), page 130.

Humans are by nature territorial, and the corporate world reflects this. In most companies the size of your office, the quality of your furniture, and the view from your window connote accomplishment and respect. Conversely, nothing reduces smart people to whiny complainers as quickly as a new office floor plan. It's not uncommon for interior design to become a passive-aggressive means of literally keeping people "in their place." When Eric was at Bell Labs, he had a boss whose office was chronically cold, so he bought a carpet for his cement floor. HR made him take it out because he wasn't a high-enough-level employee to have such a fine amenity. That was a place where all privileges were accorded by tenure, not need or merit.

Silicon Valley is not immune to this syndrome. After all, it's the place that turned the Aeron chair into a status symbol. ("It's because of my back," a legion of dot-com CEOs claimed. Really? At over $500 a pop, those chairs had better fix your front and sides too.) But the facilities-first culture needs to be killed, shot dead before it gains an insidious foothold in the building. Offices should be designed to maximize energy and interactions, not for isolation and status. Smart creatives thrive on interacting with each other. The mixture you get when you cram them together is combustible, so a top priority must be to keep them crowded.

When you can reach out and tap someone on the shoulder, there is nothing to get in the way of communications and the flow of ideas. The traditional office layout, with individual cubicles and offices, is designed so that the steady state is quiet. Most interactions between groups of people are either planned (a meeting in a conference room) or serendipitous (the hallway / water cooler / walking through the parking lot meeting). This is exactly backward; the steady state should be highly interactive, with boisterous, crowded offices brimming with hectic energy. Employees should always have the option to retire to a quiet place when they've had it with all the group stimulation, which is why our offices include plenty of retreats: nooks in the cafés and microkitchens, small conference rooms, outdoor terraces and spaces, and even nap pods. But when they go back to their desk, they should be surrounded by their teammates.

When Jonathan worked at Excite@Home, the company's facilities team leased a second building to house customer support. But when the time came to move everyone to the new space, the management team overruled facilities and kept the support staff crowded in its original offices for a few more months. The new building was used to host lunchtime soccer games (making the new corner offices corner-kick offices). The soccer games brought people together, whereas putting people in that uncrowded space would have pulled them apart. Keeping people crowded also has the collateral benefit of killing facilities envy. When no one has a private office, no one complains about it.

Work, eat, and live together

And who should be in those jam-packed cubicles? We think it's particularly important for teams to be functionally integrated. In too many places, employees are segregated by what they do, so product managers might sit here but the engineers are kept in that building across the street. This can work for traditional product managers, who are usually good with PERT and Gantt charts[31] and at making themselves seem critical to the execution of the "Official Plan" that management bought into after seeing a fancy PowerPoint that projected financial returns above the company's cost of capital hurdle rate. They are there to deliver against the defined plan, navigate any obstacles, "think outside the box" (which has to be the most inside-the-box phrase ever uttered), and obsequiously pander to late requests from the CEO and figure out how to push their team to get them done. This means that it's OK, and sometimes better, for product managers to sit in a different location from engineers, as long as they can depend on regular work-process updates and detailed status reports to keep their finger on the pulse of their product. Not that we have any strong opinions on the matter, but

---

31. Hideously complex and highly useful tools of the project management trade.

let's just say this is a twentieth-century product manager's job, not a twenty-first-century one.

In the Internet Century, a product manager's job is to work together with the people who design, engineer, and develop things to make great products. Some of this entails the traditional administrative work around owning the product life cycle, defining the product roadmap, representing the voice of the consumer, and communicating all that to the team and management. Mostly, though, smart-creative product managers need to find the technical insights that make products better. These derive from knowing how people use the products (and how those patterns will change as technology progresses), from understanding and analyzing data, and from looking at technology trends and anticipating how they will affect their industry. To do this well, product managers need to work, eat, and live with their engineers (or chemists, biologists, designers, or whichever other types of smart creatives the company employs to design and develop its products).

Your parents were wrong—messiness is a virtue

When offices get crowded, they tend to get messy too. Let them. When Eric first arrived at Google in 2001, he asked the head of facilities, George Salah, to clean up the place. George did, and was rewarded with a note the next day from Larry Page saying, "Where did all my stuff go?" That random collection of stuff was an icon of a busy, stimulated workforce.[32] When she was at Google, Facebook COO Sheryl Sandberg gave people in her sales and support team fifty dollars apiece to decorate their space, while Jonathan ran a worldwide "Googley Art Wall" contest that had teams decorating office walls with Google logos fashioned from Rubik's Cubes, photomosaics, and paint shot from paintball guns (the Chicago office, decorating Al Capone–style).

---

32. *Xooglers* blog, April 9, 2011, http://xooglers.blogspot.com/2011/04/photo-of-pre-plex .html.

The late Carnegie Mellon professor Randy Pausch, in his notable *Last Lecture*,[33] showed off photos of his childhood bedroom with walls covered with his handwritten formulas. He told parents in the room, "If your kids want to paint their bedrooms, as a favor to me, let 'em do it." Messiness is not an objective in itself (if it was, we know some teens who would be great hires), but since it is a frequent by-product of self-expression and innovation, it's usually a good sign.[34] And squashing it, which we've seen in so many companies, can have a surprisingly powerful negative effect. It's OK to let your office be one hot mess.

But while offices can be crowded and messy, they need to provide employees with everything they need to get the job done. In our case, Google is a computer science company, so the thing that our smart creatives need most is computing power. That's why we give our engineers access to the world's most powerful data centers and Google's entire software platform. This is another way to kill facilities envy among smart creatives: Be very generous with the resources they need to do their work. Be stingy with the stuff that doesn't matter, like fancy furniture and big offices, but invest in the stuff that does.

There is a method to this madness, and it's not profligacy. We invest in our offices because we expect people to work there, not from home. Working from home during normal working hours, which to many represents the height of enlightened culture, is a problem that—as Jonathan frequently says—can spread throughout a company and

---

33. Randy Pausch, *The Last Lecture* (Hyperion, 2008), page 30.

34. A 2003 study concluded that "the members of our study groups displayed the most creativity when the other group members individuated them and offered them verification for their self-views." (At least we *think* that supports our point. It's hard to tell when a study uses "individuate" as a verb.) A 2013 study shows the creativity-enhancing effects of messy desks: "Orderliness seemed to encourage a general mind-set for conservatism and tradition, and disorder had the effect of stimulating the desire for the unknown." 2003 study: William B. Swann Jr., Virginia S. Y. Kwan, Jeffrey T. Polzer, and Laurie P. Milton, "Fostering Group Identification and Creativity in Diverse Groups: The Role of Individuation and Self-Verification" (*Personality and Social Psychology Bulletin*, November 2003). 2013 study: Kathleen D. Vohs, Joseph P. Redden, and Ryan Rahinel, "Physical Order Produces Healthy Choices, Generosity, and Conventionality, Whereas Disorder Produces Creativity (*Psychological Science*, September 2013).

suck the life out of its workplace. Mervin Kelly, the late chairman of the board of Bell Labs, designed his company's buildings to promote interactions between employees.[35] It was practically impossible for an engineer or scientist to walk down the long halls without running into a colleague or being pulled into an office. This sort of serendipitous encounter will never happen when you are working at home. Google's AdSense[36] product, which developed into a multibillion-dollar business, was invented one day by a group of engineers from different teams who were playing pool in the office. Your partner or roommate is probably great, but the odds of the two of you coming up with a billion-dollar business during a coffee break at home are pretty small, even if you do have a pool table. Make your offices crowded and load them with amenities, then expect people to use them.

Don't listen to the HiPPOs

Hippopotamuses are among the deadliest animals, faster than you think and capable of crushing (or biting in half) any enemy in their path. Hippos are dangerous in companies too, where they take the form of the Highest-Paid Person's Opinion. When it comes to the quality of decision-making, pay level is intrinsically irrelevant and experience is valuable only if it is used to frame a winning argument. Unfortunately, in most companies experience *is* the winning argument. We call these places "tenurocracies," because power derives from tenure, not merit. It reminds us of our favorite quote from Jim Barksdale, erstwhile CEO of Netscape: "If we have data, let's look at data. If all we have are opinions, let's go with mine."[37]

When you stop listening to the hippos, you start creating a meritocracy, which our colleague Shona Brown concisely describes as a place where

---

35. Jon Gertner, "True Innovation" (*New York Times*, February 25, 2012).

36. The ads product where Google places ads on a large network of publisher sites.

37. Bob Lisbonne, a former SVP at Netscape, compiled a list of Jim Barksdale's witticisms, which Lisbonne had jotted down at meetings with the boss, and posted them on his personal website. See lisbonne.com/jb.html.

"it is the quality of the idea that matters, not who suggests it." Sounds easy, but of course it isn't. Creating a meritocracy requires equal participation by both the hippo, who could rule the day by fiat, and the brave smart creative, who risks getting trampled as she stands up for quality and merit.

Sridhar Ramaswamy, one of Google's ads leaders, told a story at a Google meeting that illustrates this nicely. It was early in the days of AdWords, Google's flagship ads product, and Sergey Brin had an idea for something he wanted Sridhar's engineering team to implement. There was no doubt Sergey was the highest-paid person in the room, but he didn't make a compelling argument as to why his idea was the best, and Sridhar didn't agree with it. Sridhar wasn't a senior executive at the time, so as the hippo, Sergey could have simply ordered Sridhar to comply. Instead, he suggested a compromise. Half of Sridhar's team could work on what Sergey wanted, and the other half would follow Sridhar's lead. Sridhar still disagreed, and after much debate about the relative merits of the competing ideas, Sergey's idea was discarded.

This outcome was possible only because Sergey, as a smart creative, deeply understood the data being presented, the technology of the platform, and the context of the decision. The hippo who doesn't understand what's going on is more apt to try to intimidate her way to success. If you are in a position of responsibility but are overwhelmed by the job, it's easier to try to bluster your way through with a "because I said so" approach. You need to have confidence in your people, and enough self-confidence to let them identify a better way.

Sergey also didn't mind ceding control and influence to Sridhar, because he knew that in Sridhar he had hired someone who was quite likely to have ideas better than his own. His job as the hippo was to get out of the way if he felt his idea wasn't the best. Sridhar also had a job to do: He had to speak up. For a meritocracy to work, it needs to engender a culture where there is an "obligation to dissent".[38] If

---

38. We heard this phrase from Shona Brown, who picked it up from her years at McKinsey & Company. McKinsey's website says it quite well: "All McKinsey consultants are obligated to dissent if they believe something is incorrect or not in the best interests of

someone thinks there is something wrong with an idea, they must raise that concern. If they don't, and if the subpar idea wins the day, then they are culpable. In our experience, most smart creatives have strong opinions and are itching to spout off; for them, the cultural obligation to dissent gives them freedom to do just that. Others, though, may feel more uncomfortable raising dissenting views, particularly in a public forum. That's why dissent must be an obligation, not an option. Even the more naturally reticent people need to push themselves to take on hippos.

Meritocracies yield better decisions and create an environment where all employees feel valued and empowered. They demolish the culture of fear, the murky, muddy environment in which hippos prefer to wallow. And they remove biases that can hamper greatness. Our colleague Ellen West related a story to us that was told to her by a member of the Gayglers (Google's diversity group for lesbian, gay, bisexual, and transgender employees). He told Ellen that the Gayglers had discussed whether or not Google could be considered the first "post-gay" company at which they had worked. The consensus was that it was close, since at Google "it doesn't matter who you are, just what you do." Bingo.

The rule of seven

Reorganization is one of the most despised phrases in the corporate lexicon, perhaps matched only by "outsourcing" and "eighty-slide presentation." An executive decides that the way the company is structured is the source of its problems, and if the company was organized differently everything would be puppies and sunshine. So the company lurches from centralized organization to decentralized, or from functional to divisional. Some execs "win" and others "lose." Meanwhile,

---

the client. Everyone's opinion counts. While you might be hesitant to disagree with the team's most senior member or the client, you're expected to share your point of view."

most employees remain in limbo, wondering if they still have jobs, and if so, who their new boss will be and whether they'll get to keep their nice cube next to the window. Then a year or two later some other executive (or quite possibly the same one) realizes the company still has problems and orders another reorganization. Such is the glorious "for loop"[39] of corporate life.

Organizational design is hard. What works when you're small and in one location does not work when you get bigger and have people all over the world. This is why there are so many reorgs: If there is no perfect answer, companies lurch between the less-than-optimal alternatives. To help avoid this dance, the best approach is to put aside preconceived notions about how the company should be organized, and adhere to a few important principles.

First, keep it flat. In most companies, there is a basic underlying tension: People claim that they want a flat organization so they can be closer to the top, but in fact they usually long for hierarchy. Smart creatives are different: They prefer a flat organization, less because they want to be closer to the top and more because they want to get things done and need direct access to decision-makers. Larry and Sergey once tried to accommodate this need by abolishing managers altogether; they called it a "dis-org." At one point the head of engineering, Wayne Rosing, had 130 direct reports. But smart creatives aren't *that* different; like any other employee, they still need a formal organization structure. The no-manager experiment ended and Wayne got to see his family again.

The solution we finally hit upon was slightly less draconian but just as simple. We call it the rule of seven. We've worked at other companies with a rule of seven, but in all of those cases the rule meant that managers were allowed a *maximum* of seven direct reports. The Google version suggests that managers have a *minimum* of seven direct reports

---

39. Computer science inside joke proudly written by Jonathan Rosenberg, economics major. Next footnote.

(Jonathan usually had fifteen to twenty when he ran the Google product team). We still have formal organization charts, but the rule (which is really more of a guideline, since there are exceptions) forces flatter charts with less managerial oversight and more employee freedom. With that many direct reports—most managers have a lot more than seven—there simply isn't time to micromanage.

Every tub (not) on its own bottom

When Eric was at Sun and the company was growing quickly, the business was getting complex enough that the powers-that-be decided to reorganize into business units. The new units were called "planets," because they revolved around Sun's core business of selling computer servers, and each of them had its own profit-and-loss structure. (People within Sun often explained the separate P&L structure by saying "every tub has its own bottom," probably because planets don't have bottoms, tubs don't rotate around the sun, or just saying "it's how most big companies do it" wasn't sufficient.)

The problem with this approach was that almost all of the company's revenue came from the hardware business (the sun, not the planets), so it required a team of accountants to look at that revenue and allocate it among the planets. The structure of how this was all supposed to run was itself a secret, so much so that leaders of the business units were not allowed to have their own copy of the document that codified it. It was read aloud to them.

We believe in staying functionally organized—with separate departments such as engineering, products, finance, and sales reporting directly to the CEO—as long as possible, because organizing around business divisions or product lines can lead to the formation of silos, which usually stifle the free flow of information and people. Having separate P&Ls seems like a good way to measure performance, but it can have the unfortunate side effect of skewing behavior: The leaders of a business unit are motivated to prioritize their unit's P&L over the company's. If you do have P&Ls, make sure they are driven by real external customers and partners. At Sun, the formation of the planets led to a huge loss of productivity, as leaders (and accountants) became focused not on creating great products that generate actual revenue, but on optimizing a number at the end of an accounting formula.

And whenever possible, avoid secret organizational documents.

Do all reorgs in a day

There are times when a reorganization actually does make sense. When that day comes, we have a couple of rules. First, beware of the tendencies of different groups: Engineers add complexity, marketing adds management layers, and sales adds assistants. Manage this (and being aware of it is a big first step). Second, do all reorgs in a day. This may seem impossible to accomplish, but there is a counterintuitive point working in its favor. When you have a company of smart creatives, you can tolerate messiness. In fact, it helps, because smart creatives find it empowering, not confusing.

When Nikesh Arora reorganized Google's business organization—a team of thousands of people spanning sales, operations, and marketing—in 2012, he moved quickly, announcing the changes to his team before all the details were worked out. Google's product line had expanded from just one main product, AdWords, to several offerings (including YouTube ads, Google Display Network, and Mobile Ads) in just a few years, spawning new sales teams and leading to some confusion in the field. Nikesh wanted—like many sales leaders with multiple products—to create a "One Google" organization that would return its focus to the customer. But unlike most sales leaders, Nikesh planned and executed the reorganization in just a few weeks (OK, it wasn't a day, but as Clarence Darrow might point out, sometimes a day doesn't literally mean twenty-four hours),[40] knowing that his team would jump in and finish the job. Over the next few months, the business team did make several adjustments, staying true to the intent of the changes while making them work better. The key was doing the reorg quickly and launching it before it was complete. As a result, the organization design was stronger than initially conceived, and the team was more invested in its success because it helped create the end result. Since there is no perfect organizational design, don't try to find one. Get as close as you can and let your smart creatives figure out the rest.

The Bezos two-pizza rule

The building block of organizations should be *small* teams. Jeff Bezos, Amazon's founder, at one point had a "two-pizza team" rule,[41] which stipulates that teams be small enough to be fed by two pizzas. Small teams get more done than big ones, and they spend less time politicking and worrying about who gets credit. Small teams are like families: They can bicker and fight, or even be downright dysfunctional, but they usually pull together at crunch time. Small teams tend to get bigger as their products grow; things built by only a handful of people eventually require a much bigger team to maintain them. This is OK, as long as the bigger teams don't preclude the existence of small teams working on the next breakthroughs. A scaling company needs both.

---

40. In case you dozed off that day in American history class, or grew up elsewhere, we're alluding to the Scopes Trial of the summer of 1925, in which Clarence Darrow, the renowned lawyer, defended high-school teacher John Scopes for teaching evolution in violation of a Tennessee state law. Darrow argued that the Biblical "days" of creation might not have been twenty-four hours long, and could have actually been longer, so therefore evolution was not incompatible with the teachings of the Bible.

41. Richard L. Brandt, "Birth of a Salesman" (*Wall Street Journal*, October 15, 2011).

Organize the company around the people whose impact is the highest

One last organizational principle: Determine which people are having the biggest impact and organize around them. Decide who runs the company not based on function or experience, but by performance and passion. Performance should be relatively easy to measure, but passion can be trickier to gauge. It is native in the best leaders—the sort of people who are elected captain of the team without even volunteering—and it draws others to them like iron filings to a magnet. Bill Campbell, the former Intuit CEO and ongoing coach and mentor to us both, often quotes Debbie Biondolillo, Apple's former head of human resources, who said, "Your title makes you a manager. Your people make you a leader."

Eric once chatted with Warren Buffett about what he looks for when acquiring companies. His answer was: a leader who doesn't need him. If the company is run by a person who is performing well because she is committed to its success, and not just by making a bundle by selling to Berkshire Hathaway, then Warren will invest. Internal teams work in much the same way: You want to invest in the people who are going to do what they think is right, whether or not you give them permission. You'll find that those people will usually be your best smart creatives.

This does not mean you should create a star system, in fact the best management systems are built around an ensemble, more like a dance troupe than a set of coordinated superstars. This approach creates long-term consistency, with a deep bench of high-performance talent ready to lead when the opportunity appears.

At the most senior level, the people with the greatest impact—the ones who are running the company—should be product people. When a CEO looks around her staff meeting, a good rule of thumb is that at least 50 percent of the people at the table should be experts in the company's products and services and responsible for product development. This will help ensure that the leadership team maintains focus on product excellence. Operational components like finance, sales, and legal are obviously critical to a company's success, but they should not dominate the conversation.

You also want to select as your leaders people who don't place their own interests above the company's. We see this a lot in companies with business units or divisions, where the success of the unit, as we noted before, can take precedence over that of the company as a whole. Once, when he was at Sun, Eric needed a new server. It was during the holidays, so rather than ordering one through the internal purchasing system he just went down to the warehouse and pulled a system from the shelves. He opened the box and found six "Read me first" documents, each one representing a division whose hippo felt its message was the most important.

A lot of government websites are guilty of this. (TV remotes too. At least, that's the only explanation we can conceive for why they are so horrible. Seriously, why is the mute button tiny and hidden, while the "on demand" button is big and a different color? Because the exec who runs the on-demand business unit has a number to hit, and no one gets paid when viewers mute ads.) You should never be able to reverse engineer a company's organizational chart from the design of its product. Can you figure out who reigns supreme at Apple when you open the box for your new iPhone? Yes. It's you, the customer; not the head of software, manufacturing, retail, hardware, apps, or the Guy Who Signs the Checks. That is exactly as it should be.

Once you identify the people who have the biggest impact, give them more to do. When you pile more responsibility on your best people, trust that they will keep taking it on or tell you when enough is enough. As the old saying goes: If you want something done, give it to a busy person.

Exile knaves but fight for divas

Remember the childhood riddle about knights and knaves? You are on an island with knights, who always tell the truth, and knaves, who always lie. You stand at a fork in a road. One way leads to freedom, the other to death. There are two people standing there, one a knight and the other a knave, but you don't know which is which. You get to ask one yes/no question to determine which way to go. What do you do?[42]

Life is something like that island, only more complicated. For not only are knaves in real life devoid of integrity, they are also sloppy, selfish, and have a sneaky way of working their way into virtually any company. Arrogance, for example, is a knavish tendency that is a natural by-product of success, since exceptionalism is fundamental to winning. Nice humble engineers have a way of becoming insufferable when they think they are the sole inventors of the world's next big thing. This is quite dangerous, as ego creates blind spots.

There are other things that classify people as knaves. Jealous of your colleague's success? You're a knave. (Remember that famous knave Iago, warning the smart creative Othello to "beware, my lord, of jealousy. It is the green-eye'd monster, which doth mock the meat it feeds on."[43]) Taking credit for someone else's work? Knave. Selling a customer something she doesn't need or won't benefit from? Knave. Blowing up a Lean Cuisine in the company microwave and not cleaning it up? Knave. Tagging the wall of a nave? Knave.

The character of a company is the sum of the characters of its people, so if you strive for a company of sterling character, that is the standard you must set for your employees. There is no room for knaves. And generally, in our experience, once a knave, always a knave. (Tom Peters: "There is no such thing as a minor lapse of integrity.")

Fortunately, employee behavior is socially normative. In a healthy culture of knightish values, the knights will call out the knaves for their

---

42. There are a few correct answers. You could point in one direction and ask either person, "If I were to ask you, 'Is that the road to freedom?' would you say yes?" If the answer is yes, then it's the road to freedom. If the answer is no, then it's the road to death. You could ask one of them, "If I ask the other person which way to go, what would he say?" Then do the opposite. Or you could act like some American presidents, and order an invasion.

43. Shakespeare, William.

poor behavior until they either shape up or leave. (This is another argument for crowded offices: Humans are at their best when surrounded by social controls, and crowded offices have lots of social controls!) This is pretty effective for most knavish offenses, since knaves are generally more motivated by personal success than knights, and if they sense that their behavior is not a route to success they are more apt to leave. As a manager, if you detect a knave in your midst it's best to reduce his responsibility and appoint a knight to assume it. And for more egregious offenses, you need to get rid of the knave, quickly. Think about the baby elephant seals (knaves) who try to steal milk from other baby seals' mothers; they are bitten not only by the nursing mother but also by other female seals (knights).[44] You *must* always be firm with the people who violate the basic interests of the company. Don't bite them, but do act swiftly and decisively. *Nip crazy in the bud.*

There are tipping points in knave density. It approaches a critical mass—which is smaller than you think[45]—and people start to believe they need to be knave-like to succeed, which only exacerbates the problem. Smart creatives may have a lot of good traits, but they aren't saints, so it's important to watch your knave quotient.

Knaves are not to be confused with divas. Knavish behavior is a product of low integrity; diva-ish behavior is one of high exceptionalism. Knaves prioritize the individual over the team; divas think they

---

44. Elephant seals mean business: "These bites sometimes resulted in serious injuries. If a weaner cried out as it fled, it attracted the attention of neighboring females who often joined in attempting to bite the fleeing animal. The result was that weaners caught trying to steal milk were usually chased out of the harem." See Joanne Reiter, Nell Lee Stinson, and Burney J. Le Boeuf, "Northern Elephant Seal Development: The Transition from Weaning to Nutritional Independence" (*Behavioral Ecology and Sociobiology*, Volume 3, August 1978), pages 337–67.

45. One of the most robust findings in psychology, true across a wide range of human experience, is that, as a famous paper puts it, "bad is stronger than good." In organizations it often takes only a few bad apples to spoil the barrel. See Roy F. Baumeister, Ellen Bratslavsky, Catrin Finkenauer, and Kathleen D. Vohs, "Bad Is Stronger Than Good" (*Review of General Psychology*, Volume 5, Issue 4, December 2001). For the bad-apple effect in organizations, see Will Felps, Terence R. Mitchell, and Eliza Byington, "How, When, and Why Bad Apples Spoil the Barrel: Negative Group Members and Dysfunctional Groups" (*Research in Organizational Behavior*, Volume 27, January 2006).

are better than the team, but want success equally for both. Knaves need to be dealt with as quickly as possible. But as long as their contributions match their outlandish egos, divas should be tolerated and even protected. Great people are often unusual and difficult, and some of those quirks can be quite off-putting. Since culture is about social norms and divas refuse to be normal, cultural factors can conspire to sweep out the divas along with the knaves. As long as people can figure out any way to work with the divas, and the divas' achievements outweigh the collateral damage caused by their diva ways, you should fight for them. They will pay off your investment by doing interesting things. (And if you have been reading this paragraph thinking "she" every time we mention diva, remember that Steve Jobs was one of the greatest business divas the world has ever known!)

Overworked in a good way

Work-life balance. This is another touchstone of supposedly "enlightened" management practices that can be insulting to smart, dedicated employees. The phrase itself is part of the problem: For many people, work is an important part of life, not something to be separated. The best cultures invite and enable people to be overworked in a good way, with too many interesting things to do both at work and at home. So if you are a manager, it's your responsibility to keep the work part lively and full; it's *not* a key component of your job to ensure that employees consistently have a forty-hour workweek.

We've both worked with young moms who go completely dark for a few hours in the evening, when they are with their families and putting their kids to bed. Then, around nine, the emails and chats start coming and we know we have their attention. (Dads too, but the pattern is especially true for the working moms.) Are they overworked? Yes. Do they have too much to do at home too? Yes. Are they sacrificing their family and life for work? Yes and no. They have made their lifestyle decisions. There are times when work overwhelms everything and they have to make sacrifices, and they accept that. But there are also those times when they sneak away for an afternoon to take the kids to the beach or—more likely—have the gang drop by the office for lunch or dinner. (Google's main campus courtyard on a summer evening looks like family camp, there are so many children running around while their parents enjoy a nice dinner.) The intense stretches may last for weeks or even months, especially in start-ups, but they never last forever.

Manage this by giving people responsibility and freedom. Don't order them to stay late and work or to go home early and spend time with their families. Instead, tell them to own the things for which they are responsible, and they will do what it takes to get them done. Give them the space and the freedom to make it happen. Marissa Mayer, who became one of Silicon Valley's most famous working mothers not long after she took over as Yahoo's CEO in 2012, says that burnout isn't caused by working too hard, but by resentment at having to give up what really matters to you.[46] Give your smart creatives control, and they will usually make their own best decisions about how to balance their lives.[47]

Keeping them in small teams can help too. In small teams, teammates are more apt to sense when one member is burning out and needs to go home early or take a vacation. A big team may think someone who takes a vacation is slacking off; a small team is happy to see that empty seat.

We encourage people to take real vacations, although not to promote "work-life balance." If someone is so critical to the company's

---

46. Marissa Mayer, "How to Avoid Burnout" (*Bloomberg Businessweek*, April 12, 2012).

47. There is no question that work overload can cause burnout—obviously, people's time and energy are finite. But the research on burnout shows that lack of control is a major culprit too. (Other culprits include insufficient reward, breakdown in community, absence of fairness, and conflicting values.) The leading researcher on burnout, psychologist Christina Maslach, sees burnout as a symptom of a mismatch between people and their jobs, and she places the burden on organizations to create more humane work environments. See Christina Maslach and Michael P. Leiter, *The Truth About Burnout: How Organizations Cause Personal Stress and What to Do About It* (Jossey-Bass, 1997).

success that he believes he can't unplug for a week or two without things crashing down, then there is a larger problem that must be addressed. No one should or can be indispensable. Occasionally you will encounter employees who create this situation intentionally, perhaps to feed their ego or in the mistaken belief that "indispensability" equals job security. Make such people take a nice vacation and make sure their next-in-line fills in for them while they are gone. They will return refreshed and motivated, and the people who filled their shoes will be more confident. (This is a huge hidden benefit of people taking maternity and paternity leaves too.)

Establish a culture of Yes

We are both parents, so we understand through years of firsthand experience the dispiriting parental habit of the reflexive no. "Can I have a soda?" No. "Can I get two scoops of ice cream instead of one?" No. "Can I play video games even though my homework isn't done?" No. "Can I put the cat in the dryer?" NO!

The "Just Say No" syndrome can creep into the workplace too. Companies come up with elaborate, often passive-aggressive ways to say no: processes to follow, approvals to get, meetings to attend. No is like a tiny death to smart creatives. No is a signal that the company has lost its start-up verve, that it's too corporate. Enough no's, and smart creatives stop asking and start heading to the exits.

To keep this from happening, establish a culture of Yes. Growing companies spawn chaos, which most managers try to control by creating more processes. While some of these processes may be necessary to help the company scale, they should be delayed for as long as possible. Set the bar high for that new process or approval gate; make sure there are very compelling business reasons for it to be created. We like this quote from American academic and former University of Connecticut president Michael Hogan: "My first word of advice is this: Say yes. In fact, say yes as often as you can. Saying yes begins things.

Saying yes is how things grow. Saying yes leads to new experiences, and new experiences will lead you to knowledge and wisdom....An attitude of yes is how you will be able to go forward in these uncertain times."[48]

A few years ago the former head of YouTube, Salar Kamangar, had his own "attitude of yes" moment. It came during his weekly staff meeting, at which the testing of a new feature—high-definition playback—was being discussed. The testing was going well. So well, in fact, that Salar asked if there was any good reason the feature couldn't be launched right away. "Well," someone replied, "the schedule says it's not supposed to be released for several more weeks, so we can test it further and make sure it works." "Right," Salar replied, "but besides the schedule is there any good reason we can't launch it now?" No one could think of one, and high-def YouTube launched the next day. Nothing blew up, nothing broke, and millions of happy YouTube users benefited weeks early from one man's commitment to saying yes.

fun, not Fun

Every week, at Google's TGIF all-hands meeting, all the new hires are seated in one section and provided with multicolored propeller hats to identify them. Sergey warmly welcomes them, everyone applauds, then he says "Now get back to work." It's not the greatest joke, but delivered in Sergey's deadpan tone and slightly Russian accent it always gets a hearty laugh. Among his other great talents, one of Sergey's strengths as a leader of smart creatives is his sense of humor. When he hosts TGIF, his constant ad-libbed one-liners generate a lot of laughs—not laugh-at-the-founder's-jokes-or-else laughs, but real laughs.

A great start-up, a great project—a great job, for that

---

48. Steve Friess, "In Recession, Optimistic College Graduates Turn Down Jobs" (*New York Times*, July 24, 2009).

matter—should be fun, and if you're working your butt off without deriving any enjoyment, something's probably wrong. Part of the fun comes from inhaling the fumes of future success. But a lot of it comes from laughing and joking and enjoying the company of your coworkers.

Most companies try to manufacture Fun, with a capital F. As in: We are having the annual company picnic / holiday party / off-site on Friday. There will be Fun music. There will be Fun prizes. There will be a Fun contest of some sort that will embarrass some of your coworkers. There will be Fun face painting / clowns / fortune-tellers. There will be Fun food (but no Fun alcohol). You will go. You will have Fun. There's a problem with these Fun events: They aren't fun.

This doesn't have to be the case. There's nothing wrong with organized company events, as long as they are done with flair. In fact, it's not hard to throw a fun company party. The formula is exactly the same as fun weddings: great people (and you did hire great people, didn't you?) + great music + great food and drink. While the fun factor can be endangered by those guests who are congenitally unfun (Aunt Barbara from Boca Raton, Craig from accounting), there's nothing a good '80s cover band and a fine brew can't fix. Everyone's fun when they're dancing to Billy Idol and swigging an Anchor Steam.

Then there are group or company off-sites. These are often justified as "team building" events that will help the group learn how to work together better. You go to the ropes course or chef's class, take a personality test or solve a group problem, and just like that you will coalesce into a fine-tuned machine. Or not. Here's our idea for off-sites: Forget "team building" and have fun. Jonathan's criteria for his excursions included doing outdoor group activities (weather permitting) in a new place far enough from the office to feel like a real trip, but still doable in a day, and providing an experience that people couldn't or wouldn't have on their own.

These rules have led Jonathan to take his teams on trips all over

Northern California: to Muir Woods, Pinnacles National Park, Año Nuevo to see the famous elephant seals, and the Santa Cruz Beach Boardwalk. These events don't cost much—fun can be cheap (Fun, usually not). The price of admission to Larry and Sergey's roller hockey games in Google's early days was nothing more than a stick, a pair of skates, and the willingness to be hip-checked by a founder. Sheryl Sandberg ran a book club for her sales team that was so popular in our India office that every single person participated. Eric led the entire Seoul team in dancing "Gangnam Style" with Korean pop star PSY, who had come by the office for a visit. (Eric doesn't adhere to Satchel Paige's advice to "dance like nobody's watching." When you're a leader, everyone is watching, so it doesn't matter that you dance poorly, it matters that you dance.)

Jonathan once made a bet with head of marketing Cindy McCaffrey on whose team would have higher participation in the company's annual employee feedback survey, Googlegeist. The loser had to wash the winner's car. When Jonathan lost, Cindy rented a stretch Hummer, caked it in as much mud as possible (to this day we don't know how), and then gathered her team so they could watch Jonathan wash the behemoth SUV and pelt him with water balloons while he was at it. Another time, Jonathan got the company basketball court built by bringing in a couple of hoop sets and challenging a few engineering teams to see who could put them together first. Some of these guys didn't know a dunk from a dongle, but they knew an engineering challenge when they saw it.

A defining mark of a fun culture is identical to that of an innovative one: The fun comes from everywhere. The key is to set the boundaries of what is permissible as broadly as possible. Nothing can be sacred. In 2007, a few of our engineers discovered that Eric's profile photo in our intranet system was in a public folder. They altered the background of the photo to include a portrait of Bill Gates, and, on April Fools' Day, posted the updated image on Eric's page. Any Googler who looked up Eric saw this:

Eric kept it as his profile photo for a month.

Smart-creative humor is often not quite as gentle as a photo of Bill Gates on a wall, which is where the loose boundaries come in. In October 2010, a couple of Google engineers named Colin McMillen[49] and Jonathan Feinberg launched an internal site called Memegen, which lets Googlers create memes—pithy captions matched to images—and vote on each other's creations. Memegen created a new way for Googlers to have fun while commenting acerbically on the state of the company. It has succeeded wildly on both fronts. In the fine tradition of Tom Lehrer and Jon Stewart, Memegen can be very funny while cutting to the heart of controversies within the company. To wit:

---

49. Before coming to Google, Colin was a cofounder of reCAPTCHA, which makes a software application that helps websites ensure their users are people and not bots. It's that thing where you read distorted text and enter it into a box. But certainly his greatest accomplishment is Memegen.

Eric is apparently popular with the memegeners:

Because a constant Google complaint is how things at the company used to be so much better:

An idea for a new Google Glass app:

After Project Loon (which we explain in more detail later in the book) was announced, one Googler felt that his OKRs (quarterly performance goals—they are also explained further on) needed revising:

Seoul dancing with Korean pop star PSY:

This isn't Fun—it couldn't possibly be created by fiat. It's fun, and can only occur in a permissive environment that trusts its employees and doesn't defer to the "what happens if this leaks?" worrywarts. It's impossible to have too much of that kind of fun. The more you have, the more you get done.

You must wear something

Not long after he became the CEO of Novell, Eric heard a good piece of advice from an acquaintance. "When you are in a turnaround," the man told him, "find the smart people first. And to find the smart people, find one of them." A few weeks later, Eric was on a flight from San Jose to Utah (where the company is based) with a Novell engineer who impressed him. Eric remembered the advice he had received about turnarounds, stopped the smart engineer practically mid-sentence, and asked him to produce a list of the ten smartest people he knew at Novell. A few minutes later Eric had his list. He set up one-on-one meetings with each of the ten.

A couple of days later the first person on the list showed up in Eric's office, white as a sheet. "Have I done something wrong?" he asked. The next few meetings started off in similar fashion. Each of the smart people arrived at the meeting defensive and fearful. Eric soon figured out that the way people were let go at Novell was in one-on-one meetings with the CEO. He had inadvertently scared some of the best people in the company into thinking they were being fired.

This was one of our early lessons in how difficult it can be to change the culture of an ongoing enterprise. The advice to find the smart people was sound, but its execution was disrupted by an incumbent culture that Eric hadn't anticipated. While establishing a culture in a start-up is relatively easy, changing the culture of an ongoing enterprise is extraordinarily difficult, but even more critical to success: A stagnant, overly "corporate" culture is anathema to the average smart creative.

We have some recent hands-on experience with this scenario in our work at Motorola Mobility, which Google acquired in 2012.[50] There are a couple of important steps to take. First, recognize the problem. What is the culture that defines your company today (not the one described by the mission or value statements, the real one that people live in every day)? What problems has this culture caused with the business? It is important not to simply criticize the existing culture, which will just insult people, but rather to draw a connection between business failures and how the culture may have played a hand in those situations.

Then articulate the new culture you envision—to borrow Nike's advertising phrase from the 2010 World Cup, "write the future"— and take specific, high-profile steps to start moving that way. Promote transparency and sharing of ideas across divisions. Open up everyone's calendar so that employees can see what other employees are doing. Hold more company-wide meetings and encourage honest questions without reprisal. And when you get those tough questions, answer them honestly and authentically. When Motorola was the topic one week at a TGIF meeting, several Googlers asked challenging questions about the company's products, which were answered as well as possible. Later Jonathan overheard a few Motorolans wondering if the questioners would be fired. No, he told them.

Sometimes, when looking to redefine a culture, it can be useful to look at the original one. Lou Gerstner, who helped engineer a turnaround at IBM, notes in his book *Who Says Elephants Can't Dance?*, "It's been said that every institution is nothing but the extended shadow of one person.[51] In IBM's case, that was Thomas J. Watson, Sr."[52] Gerstner goes on to talk about rebuilding IBM based on Watson's core

---

50. Google announced that it was selling Motorola to Lenovo in 2014.

51. This quote is originally from Ralph Waldo Emerson, who wrote, "An institution is the lengthened shadow of one man." See Ralph Waldo Emerson, *Self-Reliance and Other Essays* (Dover Thrift Editions, 1993), page 26.

52. Louis V. Gerstner Jr., *Who Says Elephants Can't Dance?: Inside IBM's Historic Turnaround* (HarperBusiness, 2002), page 183.

beliefs: excellence in everything they do, superior customer service, and respect for the individual. But while building on the legacy of that founder, don't be afraid to scrap its obsolete trappings. Gerstner abolished the famous blue-suit, white-shirt dress code that Watson established, because it no longer served its purpose of showing respect for the customer. "We didn't replace one dress code with another. I simply returned to the wisdom of Mr. Watson and decided: Dress according to the circumstances of your day and recognize who you will be with."[53]

(Eric was once asked at a company meeting what the Google dress code was. "You must wear something" was his answer.)

This all takes a lot of time. The most important lesson from our Moto experience is something that many of you who work at incumbents may already know: Practicing what we preach in this book in the effort to change a culture takes a lot more time than expected.

Ah'cha'rye

As someone launching a new venture (or reinventing an established one), you are signing up for long days, sleepless nights, and maybe some missed birthday parties. You will hire people who need to believe in you and your idea enough to be willing to make the same sacrifices. To do all this, you have to be crazy enough to think you will succeed, but sane enough to make it happen. This requires commitment, tenacity, and most of all, single-mindedness. When Israeli tank commanders head into combat, they don't yell "Charge!" Rather, they rally their troops by shouting "Ah'cha'rye," which translates from Hebrew as "Follow me." Anyone who aspires to lead smart creatives needs to adopt this attitude.

Eric once had a meeting with Mark Zuckerberg at Facebook headquarters in Palo Alto. At the time, it was already clear that Facebook and Mark were going to be massively successful. The two men chatted

---

53. Ibid., pages 184–85.

for a couple of hours, wrapping up around seven p.m. As Eric was leaving, an assistant brought Mark's dinner and placed it next to his computer. Mark sat down and got back to work. There was no doubt where his commitment lay.

One of our early engineers, Matt Cutts, recalls how he would often see Urs Hölzle, the engineering executive who led the creation of Google's data center infrastructure, picking up small bits of trash in the hallway as he walked through the office. This is a common refrain you hear in Silicon Valley: the CEO who picks up the stack of newspapers outside the front door, the founder who wipes the counters. With these actions, the leaders demonstrate their egalitarian natures—we're all in this together and none of us are above the menial tasks that need to get done. Mostly, though, they do it because they care so much about the company. Leadership requires passion. If you don't have it, get out now.

Don't be evil

Eric had been at Google for about six months. By then he knew all about the company's "Don't be evil" mantra, which had been coined by engineers Paul Buchheit and Amit Patel during a meeting earlier in the company's life. But he completely underestimated how much this simple phrase had become a part of the company's culture. He was in a meeting in which they were debating the merits of a change to the advertising system, one that had the potential to be quite lucrative for the company. One of the engineering leads pounded the table and said, "We can't do that, it would be evil." The room suddenly got quiet; it was like a poker game in an old Western, when one player accuses another of cheating and everyone else backs away from the table, waiting for someone to draw. Eric thought, Wow, these guys take these things seriously. A long, sometimes contentious discussion followed, and ultimately the change did not go through.

The famous Google mantra of "Don't be evil" is not entirely what it seems. Yes, it genuinely expresses a company value and aspiration that is deeply felt by employees. But "Don't be evil" is mainly another way to empower employees. The experience Eric had was not unusual (except for the fist pounding): Googlers do regularly check their moral compass when making decisions.

When Toyota invented its famous kanban system of just-in-time production, one of its quality control rules was that any employee on the assembly line could pull the cord to stop production if he noticed a quality problem.[54] That same philosophy lies behind our simple three-word slogan. When the engineer in Eric's meeting called the proposed new feature "evil," he was pulling the cord to stop production, forcing everyone to assess the proposed feature and determine if it was consistent with the company's values. Every company needs a "Don't be evil," a cultural lodestar that shines over all management layers, product plans, and office politics.

This is the ultimate value of having a well-established and well-understood company culture. It becomes the basis for everything you and the company do; it is the safeguard against something going off the rails, because it *is* the rails. The best cultures are aspirational. For each of the components we discuss in this chapter, we have given examples where we have lived up to our ideals. But we could have just as easily talked about cases where we fell short. There will be failures, but there will be more cases where people overdeliver, and when that happens the bar gets set even higher. That is the power of a great culture: It can make each member of the company better. And it can make the company ascendant.

---

54. David Magee, *How Toyota Became #1: Leadership Lessons from the World's Greatest Car Company* (Portfolio/Penguin, 2007).

Strategy—Your Plan Is Wrong

We have no idea what your venture is or even your industry, so we won't presume to tell you how to create a business plan. But we can tell you with 100 percent certainty that if you have one, it is wrong. MBA-style business plans, no matter how well conceived and thought out, are *always* flawed in some important way. Faithfully following that flawed plan will result in what entrepreneur Eric Ries calls "achieving failure."[55] This is why a venture capitalist will always follow the maxim of investing in the team, not the plan. Since the plan is wrong, the people have to be right. Successful teams spot the flaws in their plan and adjust.

So how can a new venture attract great people and other important things (like financing) without having a plan? In fact, it's fine to have a plan, but understand that it will change as you progress and discover new things about the products and market. This rapid iteration is critical to success, but equally important is the foundation upon which the plan is built. The tectonic, technology-driven shifts that characterize the Internet Century have rendered some of the commonly accepted strategic fundamentals we learned in school and on the job incorrect.[56]

---

55. Ries defines "achieving failure" as successfully executing a plan that leads nowhere because the plan was utterly flawed. See Eric Ries, *The Lean Startup* (Crown Business/ Random House, 2011), pages 22, 38.

56. Or it could be that we weren't learning the right fundamentals. For example, Peter Drucker wrote back in 1974 that "ten years is a rather short time span these days," noting that every major management decision takes years before it is really effective. Yet he

So although your plan might change, it needs to be based on a foundational set of principles that are grounded in how things work today and that guide your plan as it shape-shifts its way to success. The plan is fluid, the foundation stable.

Some prospective team members may be turned off by this flexibility; most people don't like uncertainty. Smart creatives, on the other hand, relish the "we'll figure it out" approach—they have, as Jonathan wrote in one person's review, the "pliancy to roll with the punches in this vertiginous environment."[57] In fact, they won't trust a plan that claims to have all the answers, but will jump at one that doesn't, as long as it is built on the right foundation.

Jonathan's team taught him this lesson not long after he joined the company in 2002. Back then the company had a very well thought-out strategic foundation. It just wasn't very well *written* out. In fact, no one had taken the time to fully document the Google strategy since the company's founding in 1998. Jonathan set out immediately to rectify this glaring oversight. He wanted to build the traditional, doomed-for-obsolescence-before-the-ink-dries type of business plan to which he was accustomed, but his team of deputies—Marissa Mayer, Salar Kamangar, and Susan Wojcicki—stopped him.[58] The company didn't need to document its plan (or even have one), they argued, but in order to hire new people and keep everyone moving in the same direction, it did need to document the foundation for that plan. Give Googlers

---

hastened to explain that the idea of long-range planning is often misunderstood: " 'Short range' and 'long range' are not determined by any given time span. A decision is not short range because it takes only a few months to carry it out. What matters is the time span over which it is effective. A decision is not long range because in the early 1970s we resolve on making it in 1985; this is not a decision but an idle diversion. It has as much reality as the eight-year-old boy's plan to be a fireman when he grows up." See Peter F. Drucker, *Management: Tasks, Responsibilities, Practices* (Harper & Row, 1974).

57. Jonathan borrowed this line from his former boss at Apple, James Isaacs, who once used it in a review of one of his favorite employees (or so we like to think), one Jonathan Rosenberg.

58. Jonathan took to calling the Marissa/Salar/Susan trio a "pack of camels," because they always had their own ideas and generally refused to follow him. Eventually this came to be a term of endearment. ;)

those foundational elements, Salar, Marissa, and Susan said, and they would figure out the rest.

The result was a presentation entitled "Google Strategy: Past, Present, and Future." We delivered it to the board in October 2002 (setting the stage for Mike Moritz's request for a more comprehensive plan the following summer), and components of it continued to be used to describe Google's approach for years thereafter. The principles that it describes were quite different from those of the normal late-'90s dotcom, and today they stand as a foundational blueprint for how to create an Internet Century success story: Bet on technical insights that help solve a big problem in a novel way, optimize for scale, not for revenue, and let great products grow the market for everyone.

Bet on technical insights, not market research

In the mid-'90s, when Larry and Sergey began to research the PhD thesis project that would become Google, the leading search engines ranked their results based on the content of a website. If you typed in a query such as "university," you were just as likely to get a link to the website of a bookstore or a bike shop as you were to get one to an actual university. In fact, during a visit to one of those search companies, Larry complained about the poor results he got when he used the "university" query with their product. The fault was his, he was told. He should have been more precise with his query.

So Larry and Sergey discovered a better way. They figured out that they could determine the quality of a web page—how relevant its content would be in answering the user's query—by figuring out which other pages linked to it. Find a page that a lot of other pages point to, and you have probably found a page with higher-quality content.[59]

---

59. This method is the PageRank algorithm on which Google Search was based, named after Larry Page and described in Lawrence Page, Sergey Brin, Rajeev Motwani, and Terry Winograd, "The PageRank Citation Ranking: Bringing Order to the Web" (Stanford InfoLab Technical Report, 1999).

There are a lot of other factors that made Google Search so much better than the competition when it launched—for example, it placed more faith in results found on academic websites—but the heart of the product's advantage consisted of this single technical insight about using the web's link structure as a roadmap to the best answer.

Since then, most of Google's successful products have been based on strong technical insights, while most of the less successful ones lacked them. AdWords, the Google ads engine that generates most of the company's revenue, was based on the insight that ads could be ranked and placed on a page based on their value as information to users, rather than just by who was willing to pay more.[60] Google News, the site that aggregates news headlines from thousands of media outlets, was based on the insight that we could algorithmically group stories by topic, not source. Chrome, Google's open-source browser, was founded on the insight that as websites grew more complex and powerful, browsers needed to be reengineered for speed. Pick an innovative, successful Google product, and you are likely to find at least one significant technical insight behind it, the sort of idea that could have appeared in a technical journal. Knowledge Graph in search is based on organizing the Internet's vast amount of unstructured data about a particular person, place, or thing into structured data, and presenting it in an easy-to-consume format. YouTube Content ID creates a unique data representation for every audio and video clip and matches that fingerprint against a global rights database, thereby giving content rights owners the ability to find (and sometimes monetize) their content on YouTube. Translate gets help from a vast multilingual user base to continuously improve translation quality.

---

60. One of Google's competitors in the early 2000s was Overture, a pioneer in using an auction system to place ads. The problem with Overture's approach was that it didn't reward advertisers for creating better ads, or penalize them for bad ads. Advertisers started deliberately placing their ads on totally unrelated user queries (such as a car ad on a search for a restaurant). Users rarely clicked on these ads, so advertisers didn't get charged, but they would still see the advertiser's name and message, generating a free impression. The more advertisers started to do this, the *worse* ads quality got. Google's approach of ranking ads by quality torpedoed this practice (the bad ads weren't shown), leading to better ads and more clicks.

Hangouts (live video chat with one or more people) transcodes various video formats in the cloud rather than at the device level, making it one-click easy to conduct a global video conference from any device.

Product leaders create product plans, but those product plans often (usually!) lack the most important component: What is the technical insight upon which those new features, products, or platforms will be built? A technical insight is a new way of applying technology or design that either drives down the cost or increases the functions and usability of the product by a significant factor. The result is something that is better than the competition in a fundamental way. The improvement is often obvious; it doesn't take a lot of marketing for customers to figure out that this product is different from everything else.

Sometimes developing technical insights is simple—OXO built a business by ergonomically redesigning kitchen tools—but more often it's hard, which is perhaps why most companies don't make it a foundation of their strategy. Rather, they follow the conventional MBA approach of figuring out what they are best at (their competitive advantage, per Michael Porter),[61] and then leveraging that to expand into adjacent markets. This approach can be very effective if you are an incumbent that measures success in percentage points, but not if you are trying a new venture. You will never disrupt an industry or transform your business, and you'll never get the best smart creatives on board, if your strategy is narrowly based on leveraging your competitive advantage to attack related markets.

Companies can also rely on smart tactics in pricing, marketing, distribution, and sales to squeeze out more market share and higher

---

61. Economist Michael Porter, a professor at Harvard Business School and a founder of the consulting firm Monitor, is a highly influential expert on strategy and how companies, regions, and nations get an edge over their competition. In his landmark book, *Competitive Strategy: Techniques for Analyzing Industries and Competitors* (Free Press, 1980), Porter lays out the five forces that determine a company's capacity to remain competitive and profitable. In his equally influential follow-up, *Competitive Advantage: Creating and Sustaining Superior Performance* (Free Press, 1985), Porter explains the activities necessary to gain an edge over rival companies, arguing that this competitive advantage stems from either cost leadership, differentiation, or a focus on a specific niche.

profits. Think of all the products in a grocery aisle slapped with a "new, improved" label, when in fact the only discernible improvement is in packaging and advertising. These tactics are often informed by market research, which involves a set of consultants slicing and dicing the company's prospective customer base into narrowly defined segments— digital millennials here, Generation X there, tweens, bleens, spleens— leading the product designers to end up creating 31 flavors of mediocrity (no offense, Baskin-Robbins). The best thing about market research consultants? They are easy to blame and fire when they are wrong.

Excite@Home, where Jonathan ran the product team in the late '90s, was a company founded on a set of technical insights that turned the coaxial cables carrying TV shows into people's homes into broadband pipelines. The cable modem Excite@Home developed was a breakthrough product, but it ran headlong into an intractable enemy: market research. The cable operators had data showing that their customers mostly had personal computers (PCs) with Intel 80286 and 80386 processors, so Excite@Home's modems needed to support those systems. But Excite@Home's engineers knew that those older processors didn't have the horsepower to do anything interesting with a broadband connection, and that customers with those computers who bought their service would have a bad experience. The cable operators pushed hard on this point, trying to force Excite@Home to offer a useless service for outmoded PCs because that is what their market research said to do. But the market research failed to see that PC performance was following Moore's Law by doubling roughly every two years, and that pretty soon all those slow PCs would be gone.[62]

While Excite@Home ultimately prevailed in this particular

---

62. Moore's Law is the prediction, made by Intel cofounder Gordon Moore, that the number of transistors on a chip—and hence computing power—would double every two years. (In his original 1965 article, he actually predicted a doubling every year, switching to the more conservative rate later.) See Gordon E. Moore, "Cramming More Components onto Integrated Circuits" (*Electronics*, April 19, 1965), pages 114–17. So far, the prediction has been correct. However, Moore's Law is bound to hit a limit at some point, either because of the physics of chip manufacturing or its economics. See Karl Rupp and Siegfried Selberherr, "The Economic Limit to Moore's Law" (*Proceedings of the IEEE*,

argument, the company was not immune to making market research–driven mistakes. When it asked potential customers what they cared most about, the top answer was speed, so that's what Excite@Home highlighted in its marketing. But even though cable broadband was indeed fast, the feature users really loved once they got the service was that it was "always on"; they didn't have to wait for the dialing and hissing of modems and servers consummating their cyberspace connection to access the web. Jonathan and colleagues marketed to what users said they wanted, but market research can't tell you about solving problems that customers can't conceive are solvable. Giving the customer what he wants is less important than giving him what he doesn't yet know he wants.

There's nothing wrong with continuous improvement and smart business tactics, but the tail is wagging the dog when market research becomes more important than technical innovation. Most incumbents get their start through technical insights, but then they stray (as tail-wagged dogs often do). The suits become more important than the lab coats. This may or may not be a fashion mistake, but it's certainly a mistake for the incumbent—and an opportunity for the attacker.

Basing products on technical insights has always been a core principle of Google, but its importance became even more clear to us in 2009, when we reviewed our product line and started to see a pattern emerging: The best products had achieved their success based on technical factors, not business ones, whereas the less stellar ones lacked technical distinction. Our brand had gotten strong enough that any product we launched would gain a certain amount of market momentum just by virtue of coming from Google. If we measured success by number of users, we could (and did) trick ourselves into believing that the products were successful. Sometimes they weren't, though; momentum for many of these offerings flat-out stalled. And in virtually every case, the flat-lining products were the ones that lacked technical insights.

March 2010), and Rick Merritt, "Moore's Law Dead by 2022, Expert Says" (*EE Times*, August 27, 2013).

For example, at that time Google was experimenting in applying some of our expertise from online advertising to other advertising markets, including print, radio, and TV. These were clever efforts, supported by smart people, but they lacked that fundamental technical insight that would shift the cost-performance curve nonincrementally and provide significant differentiation. All three ultimately failed. And when we look back at other Google products that didn't make it (iGoogle, Desktop, Notebook, Sidewiki, Knol, Health, even the popular Reader), they all either lacked underlying technical insights from the outset, or the insights upon which they were based became dated as the Internet evolved.

A period of combinatorial innovation

So where do you find these magical insights? In the Internet Century, all companies have the opportunity to apply technology to solve big problems in new ways. We are entering what lead Google economist Hal Varian calls a new period of "combinatorial innovation." This occurs when there is a great availability of different component parts that can be combined or recombined to create new inventions. For example, in the 1800s, the standardization of design of mechanical devices such as gears, pulleys, chains, and cams led to a manufacturing boom. In the 1900s, the gasoline engine led to innovations in automobiles, motorcycles, and airplanes. By the 1950s, it was the integrated circuit proliferating in numerous applications. In each of these cases, the development of complementary components led to a wave of inventions.

Today the components are all about information, connectivity, and computing. Would-be inventors have all the world's information, global reach, and practically infinite computing power. They have open-source software and abundant APIs[63] that allow them to build easily on each other's work. They can use standard protocols and languages. They can

---

63. Application Programming Interfaces, which enable software applications to interact with other systems.

access information platforms with data about things ranging from traffic to weather to economic transactions to human genetics to who is socially connected with whom, either on an aggregate or (with permission) individual basis. So one way of developing technical insights is to use some of these accessible technologies and data and apply them in an industry to solve an existing problem in a new way.

Besides these common technologies, each industry also has its own unique technical and design expertise. We have always been involved in computing companies, where the underlying technical expertise is computer science. But in other industries the underlying expertise may be medicine, mathematics, biology, chemistry, aeronautics, geology, robotics, psychology, logistics, and so on. Entertainment businesses are built on a different form of technical expertise—storytelling, performing, composing, and creating—while consumer product companies combine technology and design to develop breakthrough products. Financial services companies use technical insights to create new securities and trading platforms (and get seriously rich, until the bubble bursts or the indictments hit). So regardless of your business, there is a robust corpus of technical knowledge upon which the industry is based. Who are the geeks in your company? The guys in the labs and studios working on new, interesting stuff? Whatever that stuff is, that's your technology. Find the geeks, find the stuff, and that's where you'll find the technical insights you need to drive success.

Another potential source of technical insights is to start with a solution to a narrow problem and look for ways to broaden its scope. This is in keeping with a long and fine tradition in the world of innovation. New technologies tend to come into the world in a very primitive condition, often designed for very specific problems. The steam engine was used as a nifty way to pump water out of mines long before it found its calling powering locomotives.[64] Marconi sold radio as a

---

64. The idea that new technologies come into the world in a primitive state was an observation of Jonathan's father, Nathan Rosenberg, a distinguished economic historian. See Nathan Rosenberg, *Perspectives on Technology* (Cambridge University Press, 1976).

means of ship-to-shore communications, not as a place to hear phrases like "Baba Booey!" and "all the children are above average." Bell Labs was so underwhelmed by the commercial potential of the laser when it was invented in the '60s that it initially put off patenting it. Even the Internet was initially conceived as a way for scientists and academics to share research. As smart as its creators were, they could never have imagined its future functionality as a place to share pictures and videos, stay in touch with friends, learn anything about anything, or do the other amazing things we use it for today.

Our favorite example of building upon a solution developed for a narrow problem has to do with those clever early adopters of technology, the adult entertainment industry. When Google search started to ramp up, some of our most popular queries were related to adult-oriented topics. Porn filters at the time were notoriously ineffective, so we put a small team of engineers on the problem of algorithmically capturing Supreme Court Justice Potter Stewart's definition of porn, "I know it when I see Google it." They were successful by combining a couple of technical insights: They got very good at understanding the *content* of an image (aka skin), and could judge its *context* by seeing how users interacted with it. (When someone searches for a pornography-related term and the image is from a medical textbook, they are unlikely to click on it, and if they do, they won't stay on that site for long.) Soon we had a filter called SafeSearch that was far more effective in blocking inappropriate images than anything else on the web—a solution (SafeSearch) to a narrow problem (filtering adult content).

But why stop there? Over the next couple of years we took the technology that had been developed to address the porn problem and used it to serve broader purposes. We improved our ability to rate the relevance of images (any images, not just porn) to search queries by using the millions of content-based models (the models of how users react to different images) that we had developed for SafeSearch. Then we added features that let users search for images similar to the ones they find in their search results ("I like that shot of Yosemite—go find me more that look just like that"). Finally, we developed the ability to start a search not with a written query ("half dome, yosemite"), but a photograph (that snapshot you took of Half Dome when you visited Yosemite). All of these features evolved from technology that had initially been developed for the SafeSearch porn filter. So when you are looking at screen upon screen of Yosemite photos that are nearly identical to the ones you took, you can thank the adult entertainment industry for helping launch the technology that is bringing them to you.

Don't look for faster horses

When you base your product strategy on technical insights, you avoid me-too products that simply deliver what customers are asking for. (Henry Ford: "If I had listened to customers, I would have gone out looking for faster horses.")[65] That sort of incremental innovation can work very well for incumbents who are concerned with maintaining the status quo and quibbling over percentage points of market share. But if you are starting a new venture or trying to transform an existing enterprise, it's not enough.

Basing products on technical insights seems like a fairly obvious approach, but it is a lot more difficult to practice than to preach. Back in 2009, after we conducted the product review that demonstrated just how important it was to follow this strategy, we asked the product managers for all of our major products in the pipeline to describe in a few sentences the technical insight upon which they were building their plan. Some of them could, but many of them couldn't. "What is your technical insight?" turns out to be an easy question to ask and a

---

65. We love this quote, although it may be apocryphal. In Ford's book, *My Life and Work*, he says nothing about faster horses—and, in fact, writes that before he had ever built a car, people had already been discussing the idea of a horseless carriage for many years. Karl Benz built the first gasoline-powered car in 1885, which Ford later saw and disparaged for having "no features that seemed worth while." So perhaps Henry Ford wasn't looking for faster horses, but rather a faster Benz.

hard one to answer. So for your products, ask the question. If you can't articulate a good answer, rethink the product.

Optimize for growth

It used to be that companies got big slowly and methodically. Create a product, achieve success locally or regionally, then grow a step at a time by building sales, distribution, and service channels, and ramping up manufacturing capability to match your progress. Everything took its time. The acorn, after long, slow decades, grew into the oak.

We called this "growth," and there may still be industries where it is good enough. As in "top-line growth this quarter was 8 percent"— and that's good enough for a bonus or promotion. Well, enjoy those days, because they are short-lived. If you are trying to do something big, it's not enough to just grow, you need to *scale*. Not scale as in that thing you step on in the morning to see how the diet's going, or the verb that means to climb something (although scaling things is good exercise, which leads to a better outcome when you scale the scale). No, this is a new type of scale; it means to grow something very quickly and globally.

In the Internet Century, this sort of global growth is within anyone's reach. We have the democratization of just about everything— information, connectivity, computing, manufacturing, distribution, talent—so it no longer takes a phalanx of people and a widespread network of offices to create a company with global reach and impact. That doesn't mean that your strategy can ignore the question of how to scale, just the opposite. Scaling needs to be a core part of your foundation. Competition is much more intense and competitive advantages don't last long, so you have to have a "grow big fast" strategy.

The ecosystem matters a lot. The most successful leaders in the Internet Century will be the ones who understand how to create and quickly grow platforms. A platform is, fundamentally, a set of products and services that bring together groups of users and providers to form multisided markets.[66] Platforms are increasingly (if not exclusively) technology based. For example, YouTube is a platform that lets anyone create videos and distribute them to a global audience (or, in most cases, just a familial one). Or a classic example is the telephone, whose platform (the network of wires and switches that connects devices and lets people talk to each other) was pretty worthless when the first phone was connected to it, as there was no one to call. But as each additional phone was added, the network became more useful to everyone who used it (since there were more people they could call).

Talking about landline phones seems downright quaint now. Back then, scaling meant reaching millions: It took the global phone network eighty-nine years to reach 150 million phones.[67] Today, platforms can grow to support billions, and in a much shorter time. Facebook, which broke out from a host of social networking sites when it turned itself into an application platform, hit a billion users not long after its eighth birthday.[68] Android, the leading mobile operating system, activated its billionth device in its fifth year.[69] While financial analysts anguish over its profitability, Amazon always focuses on growth. Now it is one of the most disruptive forces in at least three different industries: retail, media, and computing.

When Jonathan first met Larry Page one day in 1999, they were walking across the Google parking lot to Jonathan's car when Larry mentioned, almost in passing, that he knew there had to be a way, eventually, to monetize search. After all, Larry reasoned, when someone did

---

66. And what is a multisided market? A place where two or more distinct user groups can connect and provide each other with beneficial services. Newspapers are a good example (connecting readers and advertisers), as are credit cards (consumers and merchants). For a more detailed description of platforms and multisided markets, see Thomas Eisenmann, Geoffrey Parker, and Marshall W. Van Alstyne, "Strategies for Two-Sided Markets" (*Harvard Business Review*, October 2006).

67. Jessi Hempel, "How Facebook Is Taking Over Our Lives" (*Fortune*, February 17, 2009).

68. Helen A. S. Popkin, "Facebook Hits One Billion Users" (*NBCNews.com*, October 4, 2012).

69. "Mobile Makeover" infographic (*MIT Technology Review*, October 22, 2013).

a search they were telling Google exactly what they were interested in. At the time, Google's search traffic was ramping up but the company wasn't making much money. Larry and Jonathan were discussing a potential partnership between Google and Excite@Home, which was a well-funded company formed by the merger of @Home, a pioneer in the cable modem business, and Excite, one of the web's early search engines. But while Excite@Home was trying to monetize its traffic in every way possible, Google patiently focused on growth. There were plenty of opportunities to cash in; as traffic to Google.com grew rapidly, the company could have followed the lead of every other commercial website and put ads on the home page. But it didn't. Instead it invested in improving the search engine.

We took a similar approach with our AdWords ads platform. We cut deals with publishing partners such as America Online (AOL) and Ask Jeeves, who used Google's ad system to place ads on their sites. With these partnership deals, one concern was always around the revenue split. Let's say we placed an ad on AOL's or Ask Jeeves's website, and the user clicked on it. The advertiser would then pay Google a certain amount of money, which we would share with the publishing partner. But how much to share? Our approach was usually to try to share as much as possible—remember, the priority was to grow, not to make more money. This kept the partners very happy. They all had ambitious revenue objectives, which were getting harder to meet as Google search gained momentum. So to close the gap and generate more revenue at quarter's end, they always opted to show more ads.

Jonathan went so far as to visit his counterparts at AOL to counsel them against increasing their ads volume. You are hurting your user experience, he told them, and that will eventually impact your traffic. It didn't matter. They prioritized revenue over growth; we did just the opposite.

At the risk of stating the obvious, though, a successful foundation must provide a good basis for revenue generation. The old dot-com mantra of "We have no idea how we're going to make money (but look at our sock puppet!)" didn't cut it then and still doesn't. The Google founders knew that they would make money from advertising. Initially they didn't know exactly how, and they were biding their time while scaling their platform, but they were very clear about the general revenue model.

There's another important benefit of platforms: As they grow and get more valuable, they attract more investment, which helps to improve the products and services the platform supports. This is why, in the technology industry, companies always think "platforms, not products."

Coase and the nature of the firm

One very compelling—and underappreciated—aspect of the Internet is how it has greatly expanded the potential to build platforms not just in the technology business, but in *any* industry.

Companies have always built networks, but historically those networks were internal and designed to reduce costs. In this way, they followed the tenets of University of Chicago economist and Nobel laureate Ronald Coase, who argued that it often makes sense for firms to do things internally rather than externally, because the transaction costs of finding vendors, negotiating contracts, and making sure the work gets done right are high. As Coase put it, "a firm will tend to expand until the costs of organizing an extra transaction within the firm become equal to the costs of carrying out the same transaction by means of an exchange on the open market or the costs of organizing in another firm."[70] Many smart twentieth-century companies ran the numbers and found that for much of what they wanted to get done, Coase was right: The internal management costs were lower than the transaction costs of outsourcing. This led them to do as much as they could within the organization, and, when they did go outside their four

---

70. Ronald Coase, "The Nature of the Firm" (*Economica*, November 1937).

walls, they worked with a small group of tightly controlled partners. So the twentieth century was dominated by corporations that were large hierarchies—or, at their most expansive, closed networks.

Today, Coase's framework still holds true—but it leads to radically different outcomes than it did in much of the twentieth century. Rather than growing the biggest possible closed networks, companies are outsourcing more functions and working with a bigger and more diverse network of partners. Why? Don Tapscott put it well in *Wikinomics*, when he wrote that "the Internet has caused transaction costs to plunge so steeply that it has become much more useful to read Coase's law, in effect, backward: Nowadays firms should shrink until the cost of performing a transaction internally no longer exceeds the cost of performing it externally."[71] Most companies have taken this approach purely for operational and cost-cutting reasons: They save money by outsourcing jobs to lower-wage markets.

But they miss an important point. In the Internet Century, the objective of creating networks is not just to lower costs and make operations more efficient, but to create fundamentally better products. Lots of companies build networks to lower their costs, but fewer do so to transform their products or business model. This is a massive missed opportunity for incumbents in numerous industries, creating a giant opening for new competitors.

Twitter is not a technology company, it is a publishing company. Airbnb is a platform for the lodging industry, while Uber is one for personal transportation services. 23andMe is a platform play as well as a consumer service company. For a fee, it will map a customer's personal genetic code; if it aggregates all of that data it could create a powerful data platform. Pharmaceutical companies, for example, could potentially use 23andMe's data to identify participants in new studies, and when they do, contribute any additional data they create back into the platform.

---

71. Don Tapscott and Anthony D. Williams, *Wikinomics: How Mass Collaboration Changes Everything* (Portfolio/Penguin, 2006), page 56.

The list goes on: Square for small-business payments, Nike FuelBand for physical fitness, Kickstarter for financing, MyFitnessPal for weight loss, Netflix for video entertainment, Spotify for music. These companies assembled existing technology components in new ways to reimagine existing businesses. They set up platforms for customers and partners to interact, and use those platforms to create highly differentiated products and services. This model can apply just about anywhere: travel, automobiles, apparel, restaurants, food, retail—there are ways to make products in virtually every industry better as more people use them.[72]

This is the difference between twenty-first- and twentieth-century economies. Whereas the twentieth century was dominated by monolithic, closed networks, the twenty-first will be driven by global, open ones. There are platform opportunities all around us. The successful leaders are the ones who discover them.

Specialize

Another approach is to find ways to specialize; sometimes the best way to grow a platform is to find a specialty that has the potential to expand.[73] To grow its search platform in the late '90s, Google focused on one thing: being great at search, which we measured along five axes—speed (fast is always better than slow), accuracy (how relevant

---

72. Nathan Rosenberg pointed out the valuable role that such companies play in applying existing technologies in new ways. He proposed that a good definition of innovation is something that "establishes a new framework for the working out of incremental innovations," which often leads to an entirely new industry.

73. Borrowing an image from an essay by the philosopher Isaiah Berlin, Jim Collins calls the idea of specializing "the Hedgehog Concept." (Berlin himself was expounding on a cryptic line from the Greek poet Archilochus: "The fox knows many things but the hedgehog knows one big thing.") Collins found that of the firms he analyzed in *Good to Great*, the great ones were all hedgehogs. Academics have taken Collins to task for concluding that the Hedgehog Concept must be a key to success, since specializing is a risky strategy that can lead to either great gains or great losses. See, for example, Phil Rosenzweig, *The Halo Effect* (Free Press/Simon & Schuster, 2007). Nonetheless, we like the Hedgehog Concept, even if we have no idea what is the one big thing that the hedgehog knows.

are the results to the user's query?), ease of use (can everyone's grand-parents use Google?), comprehensiveness (are we searching the entire Internet?), and freshness (how fresh are the results?). The company was so intent on getting users the right answers, that Google search results often included links to Yahoo, AltaVista, and Ask Jeeves at the bottom of the page so users could easily try those sites if they didn't like Google's results.

At the time, most competitive sites were intent on becoming "portals," multifunctional media sites that catered to a wide variety of interests and needs. Some of these companies—Netscape, Yahoo, America Online (AOL)—weren't that interested in search, and were happy to cut partnerships with Google to let us handle that task.[74] While Google certainly believed that search was one of the most important applications in the burgeoning Internet business, we didn't choose to specialize in that area because our crystal ball told us it would ultimately be more lucrative and impactful than the alternate, more popular portal business model. Rather, we focused on search because it was something we felt we were better at than anyone else.[75] So in those early days of the Internet, while these leaders of the industry were busy tending to their business of building Internet portals, Google search got better and better at providing great answers for users.

(Improving Google search also had the beneficial effect of increasing traffic to publishers' sites, since it made it easier for users to find

---

74. The first partnership deal, with Netscape in 1999, generated so much traffic when we first flipped the switch that we had to temporarily disable our own site, Google.com, in order to keep serving Netscape users. According to our colleague Craig Silverstein, the code we wrote to turn off Google.com still resides in Google's programs, rendered dormant by the comment line "#ifdef MAKE_GOOGLE_UNAVAILABLE_BECAUSE_DISASTERS_ARE_HAPPENING".

75. Unbeknownst to Larry and Sergey, they were building on a key idea from Michael Porter, who wrote: "An effective strategy for achieving above-average results can be to specialize on a tightly constrained group of products. . . . It may also allow the enhancement of product differentiation with the customer as a result of the specialist's perceived expertise and image in the particular product area." Michael Porter, *Competitive Strategy: Techniques for Analyzing Industries and Competitors* (Free Press, 1980), pages 208–9.

the news, information, and entertainment offered on those sites. This helped spur the migration of more content online.)

Default to open, not closed

Platforms generally scale more quickly when they are open. Look at the biggest platform of them all, the Internet. In the early '70s, when Vint Cerf and Robert Kahn[76] developed TCP/IP (Transmission Control Protocol / Internet Protocol), which enabled disparate computer networks (such as the Internet's forefather, ARPANET) to be connected and communicate, they weren't quite sure of the size of the networks they were connecting, or how many there were. So they didn't set an upper limit on the number of networks that could be connected, and in fact decided to let any network connect to any other using their protocol. This singular decision to keep the Internet open (which was not a foregone conclusion at the time), directly led to the remarkable web we use every day. (Hal Varian calls the Internet "a lab experiment that got loose.")

Or look again at the classic example of the landline telephone. Conceived as a single-application platform—voice communications— growth of the AT&T network in the United States eventually tapered off. There was practically no innovation, and the only growth came from population increases and baby-boom teenagers ordering second lines. But then, under government mandate, AT&T opened up its network to new devices and other carriers, and innovation took off. New types of phones, fax machines, data modems, cheap long-distance calling—Remember "long-distance call"? That was a thing, once—all innovations that became possible only after the platform went from closed to open.[77]

---

76. Vint, considered one of the founders of the Internet and a prime example of a smart creative, is currently Google's Chief Internet Evangelist.

77. Phil Lapsley, *Exploding the Phone: The Untold Story of the Teenagers and Outlaws Who Hacked Ma Bell* (Grove/Atlantic, 2013), pages 298–99.

Another example is the IBM PC, which launched in 1981 with an architecture that allowed software developers and manufacturers to build applications and add-on components, and even their own "clone" PCs, without paying IBM licensing fees. This decision helped establish the IBM PC as the definitive standard in the emerging "microcomputer" market, giving a huge boost to a couple of small companies called Microsoft and Intel.[78] It also drew flocks of applications, accessories, and competitive manufacturers into the ecosystem, and ultimately created the dominant computing platform for the next twenty-five years. None of this would have happened if the PC had been a closed platform.[79]

"Open" can be a rather Rashomon-like term—different companies will define it in different ways to meet their own objectives. But generally it means sharing more intellectual property such as software code or research results, adhering to open standards rather than creating your own, and giving customers the freedom to easily exit your platform. This can seem heretical to traditional, MBA-style thinking, which dictates that you build up a sustainable competitive advantage over rivals and then close the fortress and defend it with boiling oil and flaming arrows. Like most things heretical, open is terrifying to the establishment mindset. It's a lot easier to compete by locking customers into your nice, closed world than it is by venturing out into the open wild and competing on innovation and merit. With open, you trade control for scale and innovation.[80] And trust that your smart creatives will figure it out.

---

78. James M. Utterback, *Mastering the Dynamics of Innovation* (Harvard Business School Press, 1994), page 15.

79. By contrast, the Apple Macintosh, which launched in 1984, was a closed system. Bill Gates noted in a memo to then–Apple CEO John Sculley in 1985: "The IBM architecture, when compared to the Macintosh, probably has more than 100 times the engineering resources applied to it when investment of compatible manufacturers is included." See Jim Carlton, "They Coulda Been a Contender" (*Wired*, November 1997).

80. A leading scholar of "open innovation" is economist Henry Chesbrough, author of *Open Innovation: The New Imperative for Creating and Profiting from Technology* (Harvard

If you are attacking an entrenched incumbent, you can use its very entrenchedness to your advantage. Your porcine competitor is probably feasting at a closed trough, and you can take it on by matching your disruptive product with a disruptive business model. Open can play that part very effectively. It drives innovation into the ecosystem (new features for the platform, new applications from partners) and drives down the cost of complementary components. All of this leads to more value for users and more growth for the new ecosystem, usually at the expense of the incumbent's (presumably) closed platform. Look, for example, at how organizations like Khan Academy, Coursera, and Udacity are trying to gain a foothold in the education market.[81] They combine Internet Century technologies (online video, interactive and social tools) with an open business model (anyone can take any classes for free) that is radically different from how the entrenched incumbents operate (high tuitions to cover a high cost basis). No one can predict which, if any, of these disrupters will grow and thrive, or if some of the more nimble incumbents will fend them off. But what does seem certain is that this combination of technology + open will lead to a better learning ecosystem that provides, as Khan's mission states, "a free world-class education for anyone anywhere."

Open also allows you to harness the talents of thousands of people, because, as Sun cofounder Bill Joy noted, "no matter who you are, most of the smartest people work for someone else."[82] It spurs greater innovation, since people don't have to reinvent work that's already been done and can instead focus on pushing the entire system forward with new inventions. Netflix is a case in point: In 2006, the movie-rental company wanted to improve its recommendation algorithm, but internal efforts had plateaued. So they took a previously proprietary data set

Business School Press, 2003), and *Open Business Models: How to Thrive in the New Innovation Landscape* (Harvard Business School Press, 2006).

81. Eric is a member of the Khan Academy Board of Directors.

82. Karim Lakhani and Jill A. Panetta, "The Principles of Distributed Innovation" (*Innovations*, Volume 2, Number 3, Summer 2007).

of a hundred million anonymized user movie ratings and published it, while announcing that the first person or team who could use that data to beat the current algorithm's accuracy by at least 10 percent would win a $1-million prize. Even the contest was open: Netflix reported top teams' progress on a public leaderboard, and within three years a winning solution emerged.[83]

There is another, less obvious but equally important benefit to open source. Putting all your information online shows that there are no hidden agendas. In software, when we open source code, everyone can see whether or not that code delivers any particular benefit to one company, and if it does, take action to rectify that advantage. Open-sourcing something says, in effect, that we are committed to growing a platform, an industry, and an ecosystem as a whole. It lets everyone see that the playing field is level, with no unfair advantages conferred upon any particular player. Removing this suspicion of unfair advantages helps growth.[84]

A final thought on defaulting to open is the concept of user freedom, a practice that is the opposite of customer lock-in: Make it easy for customers to leave. At Google we have a team whose job it is to make it as easy as possible for users to leave us. We want to compete on a level playing field and win users' loyalty based on merit. When customers have low barriers to exit, you have to work to keep them.

Default to open, except when...

Open is not a moral argument. Defaulting to open is usually the best way to drive innovation and lower costs in an ecosystem, so view it

---

83. Steve Lohr, "Netflix Awards $1 Million Prize and Starts a New Contest" (*Bits* blog, *New York Times*, September 21, 2009).

84. Even small businesses and incubators can go open source. Y Combinator, which provides seed funding for promising start-ups, publishes, for anyone's free use, term sheets and other legal documents originally used by YC-funded companies in raising capital from angel investors. The stated purpose in open-sourcing these documents is to make financing easier (and cheaper) for both sides. See Michael Arrington, "Y Combinator To Offer Standardized Funding Legal Docs" (*TechCrunch*, August 13, 2008), and "Series AA Equity Financing Documents" (ycombinator.com/seriesaa).

as another strategic tactic at your disposal: Will going open help you achieve scale and profitability? Open's virtuous halo can help attract smart creatives, mostly because, as the poet once sang, nothing can change the world like a global platform. (Well, the poet should have sung that, anyway.)

With a few exceptions, Google defaults to open, and for these exceptions we are often criticized as being hypocritical, since we preach open in some areas but then sometimes ignore our own advice. This isn't hypocritical, merely pragmatic. While we generally believe that open is the best strategy, there are certain circumstances where staying closed works as well. When you have a product that is demonstrably better (usually because it is based on strong technical insights) and you are competing in a new, rapidly growing market, you can grow quickly without opening up the platform. This was the case with Google's search and ads engines in our early days, but it is a fairly rare circumstance.

Plus, there are situations when open platforms do *not* work on behalf of users and innovation. Most incumbents who keep their platforms closed employ the argument that opening up their systems will hurt quality, so by keeping their closed platform closed they are just being good corporate citizens, looking out for the interests of their customers. In some cases, like ours, this argument is actually true. Opening up our search and ads algorithms would severely compromise quality, since there are many parties in the search world who profit from a worse user experience. They don't want users to view and click on the most relevant results and ads, they want users to see and view *their* results and ads, even if it is a crummier experience for the user. So the search ecosystem is best served, we believe, by keeping secret the algorithms by which we match results to user queries.

In 2005, when we bought what was then a small mobile operating system called Android, there was some debate among our management team about whether or not we should keep it open. Andy Rubin and the Android team initially thought it should be closed, but Sergey suggested the opposite: Why not make it open? Keeping Android open would help us scale quickly in the highly fragmented mobile operating system space. So that's what we did. Meanwhile, Apple launched the iPhone, built on a closed iOS, opting for control over scalability. Android stayed open, grew extraordinarily, and helped Google smoothly navigate the platform shift from PC to mobile by giving us a platform that was highly complementary to search (more people online with smartphones means more people searching more often). iOS stayed closed and achieved both massive scale and profitability. From the perspective of a new venture, either path is a win, but keep in mind that Apple's success with the iPhone, just like Google's with search, was based on an unusual set of technical insights that yielded an obviously superior product in a rapidly growing space. If you can achieve that sort of extreme impact with a closed system, then give it a shot. Otherwise, default to open.

Don't follow competition

We are constantly amazed by how much business leaders obsess about their competition. When you get in a room with a bunch of senior execs from large companies, their attention can often wander as they check smartphones and think about the rest of their day, but bring up the topic of their competition and suddenly you'll have everyone's full attention. It's as if, once you get to a particular level in an organization, you worry as much about what your competition is doing as how your own organization is performing. At the highest echelons of business, the default mentality is, too often, siege.

This fixation leads to a never-ending spiral into mediocrity. Business leaders spend much of their time watching and copying the competition, and when they do finally break away and try something new, they are careful risk-takers, developing only incremental, low-impact changes. Being close to your competition offers comfort; it's like covering tactics in match race sailing, when the lead boat tacks whenever the follower does, to ensure that the follower doesn't go off in a different direction and find stronger wind. Incumbents clump together so that no one finds a fresher breeze elsewhere. But as Larry Page says, how exciting is it to come to work if the best you can do is trounce some other company that does roughly the same thing?[85]

If you focus on your competition, you will never deliver anything truly innovative. While you and your competitors are busy fighting over fractions of a market-share point, someone else who doesn't care will come in and build a new platform that completely changes the game. Larry again: "Obviously we think about competition to some extent. But I feel my job is mostly getting people not to think about our competition. In general I think there's a tendency for people to think about the things that exist. Our job is to think of the thing you haven't thought of yet that you really need. And by definition, if our competitors knew that thing, they wouldn't tell it to us or anybody else."[86]

This isn't to say you should ignore competition. Competition makes you better. It keeps you sharp. We are all human and subject to complacency, no matter how often we tell ourselves to stay on our toes. Nothing lights a fire like a competitor. When Microsoft launched the Bing search engine in 2009, we were concerned enough to kick off an all-hands-on-deck process to intensify our efforts on search. This planted seeds that led to new features such as Google Instant (search results as you type) and Image Search (drag an image into the search box and Google figures out what it is and uses it as the query). You can draw a line from the launch of Bing to these great new features.

As Nietzsche wrote in *Thus Spake Zarathustra*: "You must be proud of your enemy; then your enemy's successes are also your successes."[87] Be proud of your competitors. Just don't follow them.

---

85. Steven Levy, "Google's Larry Page on Why Moon Shots Matter" (*Wired.com*, January 17, 2013).

86. Miguel Helft, "Larry Page on Google" (*Fortune*, December 11, 2012).

87. Friedrich Nietzsche, edited and translated by Stanley Appelbaum, *Thus Spake Zarathustra (Selections)* (Dover Publications, 2004).

Eric's Notes for a Strategy Meeting

We have spent countless hours working on strategy with our teams. This is an experience you will get to enjoy at some point, once you have gathered a coterie of smart creatives and are ready to write down the fundamentals of your new venture. So when you are on your way to that first strategy jam session, consider these pearls of (we hope) wisdom that we have collected from our own strategy sessions over the years, culled from conference-room whiteboards, Post-its stuck on walls, scribbled notes, and emails to ourselves.

The right strategy has a beauty to it, a sense of many people and ideas working in concert to succeed.

Start by asking what will be true in five years and work backward. Examine carefully the things you can assert will change quickly, especially factors of production where technology is exponentially driving down cost curves, or platforms that could emerge.

In a five-year timeline there are disrupters—and opportunities—in many markets. What will be the disrupters affecting you?

There is now almost perfect market information and broad availability of capital, so you need to win on product and platform. Spend the vast majority of your time thinking about product and platform.

When there is disruption in a market, there are two possible scenarios. If you are the incumbent, you can acquire, build, or ignore a disruptive challenger. Ignoring the challenger will work for only a short while. If you opt to acquire or build, you must viscerally understand the technical insights and options the challenger will use to attack.

If you are the challenger, you need to invent a new product and build a business around it, and understand the tools (business relationships, regulations, and lawsuits) and obstacles incumbents will use to stop you.

Consider the role of other players whose incentives can be aligned to help you. Your strategy should include a way you can have people outside the existing business framework (division, company, team) thinking about innovation along with the people inside.

Growth matters most. All big successes in the Internet Century will embody large platforms that get better and stronger as they grow.

Articulate a rough time frame and the end point you want to achieve.

Don't use market research and competitive analyses. Slides kill discussion. Get input from everyone in the room.

Iteration is the most important part of the strategy. It needs to be very, very fast and always based on learning.

Many large, successful companies started with the following:

1. They solved a problem in a novel way.
2. They used that solution to grow and spread quickly.
3. That success was based largely on their products.

And the coterie you gather to work on this strategy? Choose it wisely. It shouldn't just comprise the people who have been around the longest or those with the biggest titles, rather it should include the best smart creatives and the ones who will have a good perspective on the changes to come.

Talent—Hiring Is the Most Important Thing You Do

A s Jonathan headed over to Mountain View one day in February 2000, to interview with Sergey for the role of product leader at Google, he assumed the meeting was a mere formality. As a senior VP at Excite@Home, he was quite happy in his current job and wasn't sure he wanted to jump ship. But if he did, he fancied himself an expert in online search and advertising and he came recommended for the job by John Doerr, a partner at Kleiner Perkins and member of the Google and Excite@Home boards. So the job was certainly his for the asking, and Sergey would probably spend the interview time trying to convince him to take it.

Then he got to the crowded office on Bayshore Parkway, a stone's throw from 101, and followed Sergey into a conference room. After a few pleasantries, Sergey asked one of his favorite interview questions: "Could you teach me something complicated I don't know?" Jonathan was an economics major at Claremont McKenna and the offspring of a Stanford economist, so, after he got over his surprise that he was actually being interviewed, he launched into a whiteboard proof of the economic law that marginal cost bisects average cost at the latter's minimum. From there he figured he could dazzle Sergey by demonstrating how to use cost and revenue functions to find the optimal point of production and profit by maximizing the firm's output quantities.

(For economics majors, this passes for pillow talk.) He soon realized, as Sergey started fiddling with his Rollerblades and looking out the window, that he was failing to address every aspect of the question. He wasn't teaching Sergey anything, the economics law in question wasn't interesting, and, as a math wizard, there was a good chance that Sergey already knew the calculus involved in resolving the economic formulas on the board. Jonathan needed to change tactics now. So he stopped the economics lesson and embarked on a new topic: courtship. It started with an explanation of how to "dangle the hook," using Jonathan's method for hooking a first date, with his wife as a case study.[88] Sergey started paying attention, and Jonathan got the job.[89]

If you asked managers at large companies "What is the single most important thing you do at work?" most would reflexively answer "Go to meetings." If you persisted—"No, not the most *boring* thing you do at work, the most *important*"—they would probably respond by spouting some of the standard principles they learned in business school, something about "devising smart strategies and creating opportunistic synergies to accumulate accretive financial effects in an increasingly competitive market." Now imagine asking the same question of the top sports coaches or general managers. They go to meetings all day too, yet they would probably say that the most important thing they do is *draft, recruit, or trade for the best players they can.* Smart coaches know that no amount of strategy can substitute for talent, and that is as true in business as it is on the field. Scouting is like shaving: If you don't do it every day, it shows.

For a manager, the right answer to the question "What is the single most important thing you do at work?" is *hiring.* When Sergey was interviewing Jonathan that day, he wasn't just going through the paces,

---

88. He sent her roses and a puzzle, the roses to pique her curiosity about this guy she had never met, and the puzzle to determine if she was smart. She was, but went out with Jonathan anyway.

89. Jonathan received an offer to join Google in February 2000 and, for a variety of reasons, none of which were even close to smart, he turned it down. When Eric presented another offer two years later, in February 2002, Jonathan accepted it.

he was intent on doing a great job. At first Jonathan chalked this up to the fact that he would be a senior member of the team and would work closely with Sergey, but once he arrived at Google he realized that the company's leaders pursued interviewing with the same level of intensity for every candidate. It didn't matter if the person would be an entry-level software engineer or a senior executive, Googlers made it a priority to invest the time and energy to ensure they got the best possible people.

You would think this level of commitment would be common. But even though most managers get their own positions through the familiar hiring process—résumé, phone screen, interviews, *more* interviews, offer, haggling, *more* haggling, acceptance—once hired, they seemingly do everything in their power to avoid being involved in hiring anyone else. Recruiting is for recruiters. Reviewing résumés can be delegated to young associates or someone in human resources. Interviewing is a chore. That feedback form is so long and intimidating that the task of filling it out inevitably slides to late Friday afternoon, by which time the details of the interview have faded into a blur. So interviewers dash off a cursory report and hope that their colleagues do a better job with *their* interview feedback. The higher up you go in most organizations, the more detached the executives get from the hiring process. The inverse should be true.

There's another, even more important aspect to hiring well in the Internet Century. The traditional hiring model is hierarchical: The hiring manager decides who gets the job, while other members of the team provide their input and senior executives rubber-stamp whatever decision the manager makes. The problem with this is that once that person starts at the company, the working model is (or should be) collaborative, with high degrees of freedom and transparency and a disdain for rank. So now a single hiring manager has made a decision that directly impacts numerous teams besides her own.

There's another reason that hierarchical hiring doesn't work. Leaders (and management book authors) often say they hire people smarter than themselves, but in practice this rarely happens in a hierarchical hiring process. The rational "let's-hire-this-guy-because-he's-so-smart" decision usually gets usurped by the more emotional "but-then-he-might-be-better-than-me-and-make-me-look-bad-and-then-I-won't-get-promoted-and-my-kids-will-think-I'm-a-loser-and-my-wife-will-run-off-with-that-guy-from-Peet's-Coffee-and-take-my-dog-and-truck" decision. In other words, human nature gets in the way.

From the outset, Google's founders understood that to consistently hire the best people possible, the model to follow wasn't that of corporate America, but that of academia. Universities usually don't lay professors off, so they invest a lot of time in getting faculty hiring and promotion right, normally using committees. This is why we believe that hiring should be peer-based, not hierarchical, with decisions made by committees, and it should be focused on bringing the best possible people into the company, even if their experience might not match one of the open roles. Eric hired Sheryl Sandberg even though he didn't have a job for her. It didn't take long for her to assume the task of building our small business sales team, a role that didn't formally exist until she helped create it. (Of course, Sheryl later left us and became COO of Facebook and a best-selling author. When you hire smart creatives, some of them eventually smartly create opportunities for themselves outside the company. More on that later in the chapter.) In a peer-based hiring process, the emphasis is on people, not organization. The smart creatives matter more than the role; the company matters more than the manager.

"Our people are our most important asset" is a well-worn cliché, but building a team of smart creatives that lives up to that statement requires more than just saying the words: You need to change how the members of the team are hired. The nice thing about these changes is that anyone can make them. Some of the culture recommendations that we made in the earlier chapter may be challenging for ongoing companies to adopt, but anyone can change how they hire. The not-so-nice thing is that hiring well takes a lot of work and time. But it is the best investment you can make.

The herd effect

A workforce of great people not only does great work, it attracts more great people.[90] The best workers are like a herd: They tend to follow each other. Get a few of them, and you're guaranteed that a bunch more will follow. Google is renowned for its fabulous amenities, but most of our smart creatives weren't drawn to us because of our free lunches, subsidized massages, green pastures, or dog-friendly offices. They came because they wanted to work with the best smart creatives.

This "herd effect" can cut both ways: While A's tend to hire A's, B's hire not just B's, but C's and D's too. So if you compromise standards or make a mistake and hire a B, pretty soon you'll have B's, C's, and even D's in your company. And regardless of whether it works to the benefit or detriment of the company, the herd effect is more powerful when the employees are smart creatives and the company is new. In that case, each person's relative importance is magnified; early employees are more conspicuous. Also, when you put great people with great people, you create an environment where they will share ideas and work on them. This is always true, but particularly in an early-stage environment.

A positive people herd effect can be orchestrated. "You're brilliant, we're hiring," the phrase adorning Google's early ads recruiting new employees,[91] was a clever Marxist trick. Not Karl, Groucho, since it was designed to inspire a response along the lines of "Yes, I *do* want to belong to this club that wants me as a member!" The intent was to let

---

90. Remember the ASA model? See Benjamin Schneider, "The People Make the Place" (*Personnel Psychology*, September 1987). Here's the first A in action: the virtuous cycle of great people attracting other great people, building up a culture of greatness.

91. Marissa Mayer originally saw this phrase on a recruiting flyer in the CS building when she was a student at Stanford. The phrase caught her eye and she brought it with her to Google.

the world know that we set the hiring bar quite high, and rather than dissuading applicants, this became a recruiting tool in itself. Jonathan used to keep a stack of résumés of the people he had hired in his desk, and when he was trying to close a candidate, he'd hand over the résumés and show the person the team she'd be joining. These weren't just a cherry-picked group of Jonathan's best hires, they were the entire set. That was a club our smart-creative Grouchos usually wanted to join. So set the bar high from the very beginning, and then shout it from the rafters.

This is especially important for product people, because they can have such a big impact. Pay close attention to hiring them, and when your process guarantees excellence at the product core of the company, it will spill over to every other team as well. The objective is to create a hiring culture that resists the siren song of compromise, a song that only gets louder amidst the chaotic whirlwind of hypergrowth.

Passionate people don't use the word

A fine marker of smart creatives is passion. They care. So how do you figure out if a person is truly passionate, since truly passionate people don't often use the "P-word"? In our experience, a lot of job candidates have figured out that passion is a sought-after trait. When someone begins a sentence with the conspicuously obvious phrase "I'm passionate about..." and then proceeds to talk about something generic like travel, football, or family, that's a red flag that maybe his only true passion is for conspicuously throwing the word "passion" around a lot during interviews.

Passionate people don't wear their passion on their sleeves; they have it in their hearts. They *live* it. Passion is more than résumé-deep, because its hallmarks—persistence, grit, seriousness, all-encompassing absorption—cannot be gauged from a checklist. Nor is it always synonymous with success. If someone is truly passionate about something, they'll do it for a long time even if they aren't at first successful. Failure is often part of the deal. (This is one reason we value athletes, because sports teach how to rebound from loss, or at least give you plenty of opportunities to do so.) The passionate person will often talk at length, aka ramble, about his pursuits. This pursuit can be professional. In our world, "perfecting search" is a great example of something people can spend an entire career on and still find challenging and engaging every day. But it can also be a hobby. Andy Rubin, who started Android, loves robots (and is now spearheading Google's nascent efforts in that area). Wayne Rosing, Google's first head of engineering, loves telescopes. Captain Eric loves planes and flying (and telling stories of flying planes).

More often than not, these seemingly extracurricular passions can yield direct benefits to a company. Android's great Sky Map is an astronomy application that turns a phone into a star chart. It was built by a team of Googlers in their spare time (what we call "20 percent time"—more on that later), not because they love to program computers, but because they were enthusiastic amateur astronomers.[92] We have been just as impressed by one candidate who studied Sanskrit, and another who loved restoring old pinball machines. Their deep interest made them more interesting, which is why in an interview context our philosophy is *not* "Don't get them started." When it comes to the things they care most about, we *want* to get them started.

Once they start, listen very carefully. Pay attention to *how* they are passionate. For example, athletes can be quite passionate, but do you want the triathlete or ultramarathoner who pursues his craft all alone, or someone who trains with a group? Is the athlete solo or social, exclusive or inclusive? When people are talking about their professional experience, they know the right answers to these questions—most people don't like a loner in the work environment. But when you get people

---

92. Sky Map was developed at Google and launched in 2009. The code was converted to open source in 2012.

talking about their passions, the guard usually comes down and you gain more insight into their personalities.

Hire learning animals

Think about your employees. Which of them can you honestly say are smarter than you? Who among them would you not want to face across a chessboard, on *Jeopardy!*, or in a crossword-puzzle duel? The adage is to always hire people who are smarter than you. How well do you follow it?

This adage still holds true, but not for the obvious reasons. Of course smart people know a lot and can therefore accomplish more than others less gifted. But hire them not for the knowledge they possess, but for the things they don't yet know. Ray Kurzweil said that "information technology's growing exponentially...And our intuition about the future is not exponential, it's linear."[93] In our experience raw brainpower is the starting point for any exponential thinker. Intelligence is the best indicator of a person's ability to handle change.

It is not, however, the only ingredient. We know plenty of very bright people who, when faced with the roller coaster of change, will choose the familiar spinning-teacups ride instead. They would rather avoid all those gut-wrenching lurches; in other words, reality. Henry Ford said that "anyone who stops learning is old, whether at twenty or eighty. Anyone who keeps learning stays young. The greatest thing in life is to keep your mind young."[94] Our ideal candidates are the ones who prefer roller coasters, the ones who keep learning. These "learning animals" have the smarts to handle massive change and the character to love it.

---

93. Quoted in "IT Growth and Global Change: A Conversation with Ray Kurzweil" (*McKinsey Quarterly*, January 2011).

94. As is usually the case with aphorisms attributed to Ford, we can't be certain it was he who said this.

Psychologist Carol Dweck has another term for it. She calls it a "growth mindset."[95] If you believe that the qualities defining you are carved in stone, you will be stuck trying to prove them over and over again, regardless of the circumstances. But if you have a growth mindset, you believe the qualities that define you can be modified and cultivated through effort. You can change yourself; you can adapt; in fact, you are more comfortable and do better when you are forced to do so. Dweck's experiments show that your mindset can set in motion a whole chain of thoughts and behaviors: If you think your abilities are fixed, you'll set for yourself what she calls "performance goals" to maintain that self-image, but if you have a growth mindset, you'll set "learning goals"[96]—goals that'll drive you to take risks without worrying so much about how, for example, a dumb question or a wrong answer will make you look. You won't care because you're a learning animal, and in the long run you'll learn more and scale greater heights.[97]

Most people, when they are hiring for a role, look for people who have excelled in that role before. This is not how you find a learning animal. Peruse virtually any job listing and one of the top criteria for a position will be relevant experience. If the job is for chief widget

---

95. At least that's what she calls it when talking with nonacademics. (The term she's used in her research is that these people have an "incremental theory" of intelligence, personality, or other positive qualities.) Her book for a lay audience is Carol S. Dweck, *Mindset: The New Psychology of Success* (Random House, 2006).

96. Elaine S. Elliott and Carol S. Dweck, "Goals: An Approach to Motivation and Achievement" (*Journal of Personality and Social Psychology*, Volume 54, Number 1, January 1988), pages 5–12.

97. For Dweck's pioneering explanation of how different mindsets influence motivation and actual learning in children, see Carol S. Dweck, "Motivational Processes Affecting Learning" (*American Psychologist*, Volume 41, Number 10, October 1986). Learning animals also have a related quality, a combination of passion and perseverance, that psychologists call "grit." The psychologist Angela Duckworth and colleagues have found that "grittier" people are more willing to persevere despite setbacks and temptations—and, as a result, go further toward long-term goals like college graduation, placing high in the National Spelling Bee, and success in West Point's "Beast Barracks" training program. See Angela L. Duckworth, Christopher Peterson, Michael D. Matthews, and Dennis R. Kelly, "Grit: Perseverance and Passion for Long-Term Goals" (*Journal of Personality and Social Psychology*, Volume 92, Number 6, June 2007).

designer, it's a given that high on the list of requirements will be five to ten years of widget design and a degree from Widget U.

Favoring specialization over intelligence is exactly wrong, especially in high tech. The world is changing so fast across every industry and endeavor that it's a given the role for which you're hiring is going to change. Yesterday's widget will be obsolete tomorrow, and hiring a specialist in such a dynamic environment can backfire. A specialist brings an inherent bias to solving problems that spawns from the very expertise that is his putative advantage, and may be threatened by a new type of solution that requires new expertise. A smart generalist doesn't have bias, so is free to survey the wide range of solutions and gravitate to the best one.

Finding learning animals can be a challenge. Jonathan's modus operandi is to ask candidates to reflect on a past mistake. In the early 2000s, he used to ask candidates "What big trend did you miss about the Internet in 1996? What did you get right, and what did you get wrong?" It's a deceptively tricky question. It makes candidates define what they expected, link it to what they observed and explore the revelations, and forces them to admit a mistake—and not in the lame, my-biggest-weakness-is-that-I'm-a-perfectionist sort of way. It's impossible to fake the answer.

The question can be adapted to any big events of the recent past. The point is not to see if someone was prescient, but rather how she evolved her thinking and learned from her mistakes. Few people answer this question well, but when they do, it's a great indication that you're talking to a learning animal. Of course, they could just come out and tell you, "I have no special talents. I am only passionately curious."[98] That's what Albert Einstein claimed, and we would have hired him in an instant (despite his use of the P-word; devising the theory of relativity trumps that).

---

98. Letter to his biographer, Carl Seelig, March 11, 1952, Einstein Archives 39-013 from *The Expanded Quotable Einstein* (Princeton, 2000).

Once you hire those learning animals, keep learning them![99] Create opportunities for every employee to be constantly learning new things—even skills and experiences that aren't directly beneficial to the company—and then expect them to use them. This won't be challenging for true learning animals, who will gladly avail themselves of training and other opportunities. But keep an eye on the people who don't; perhaps they aren't quite the learning animals you thought they were.

The LAX test

So, passion is crucial in a potential hire, as is intelligence and a learning-animal mindset. Another crucial quality is character. We mean not only someone who treats others well and can be trusted, but who is also well-rounded and engaged with the world. Someone who is *interesting*.

Judging character during the interview process used to be fairly easy, since job interviews often included lunch or dinner at a restaurant and perhaps a drink or two, *Mad Men* style. Such a venue allowed the hiring executive to observe how the candidate comported himself "as a civilian." What happens when he lets his guard down? How does he treat the waiter and bartender? Great people treat others well, regardless of standing or sobriety.

Today you usually don't get to get candidates drunk, so you need to be more observant, especially during the before-and-after spaces of the interview. Jonathan interviewed for a job at a big consulting firm his second year in business school. His competition for the position was a fortunate and highly pedigreed fellow—Jonathan is sure his name was Hodsworth Bodsworth III—who was not only far more qualified than Jonathan, but better looking too. Jonathan was certainly doomed: Bodsworth was bound to get the job. But while Jonathan waited for his interview to start, he chatted with the administrative assistant and learned she was planning a trip to California, his home state. Soon he

---

99. Perhaps starting with some basics of grammar.

was giving her travel advice and recommending sites to see. When the firm called the next day to discuss an offer, he figured that either there was a mistake or two people were getting hired. But no. Bodsworth didn't get hired because, according to the interviewer, "He was an asshole to my secretary, and she likes you." We usually ask our assistants what they think of candidates, and listen to their response. Call it the Bodsworth rule.

As important as character, though, is whether or not a candidate is interesting. Imagine being stuck at an airport for six hours with a colleague; Eric always chooses LAX for maximum discomfort (although Atlanta or London will do in a pinch). Would you be able to pass the time in a good conversation with him? Would it be time well spent, or would you quickly find yourself rummaging through your carry-on for your tablet so you can read your latest email or the news or anything to avoid having to talk to this dull person? (TV star Tina Fey has her own version of the LAX test, which she credits to *Saturday Night Live* producer Lorne Michaels: "Don't hire anyone that you wouldn't want to run into by the bathrooms at three in the morning, because you're going to be [in the office] all night.")[100]

We institutionalized the LAX test by making "Googleyness" one of four standard sections—along with general cognitive ability, role-related knowledge, and leadership experience—on our interview feedback form. This includes ambition and drive, team orientation, service orientation, listening & communication skills, bias to action, effectiveness, interpersonal skills, creativity, and integrity.

(Larry and Sergey took the LAX test one step further when they were looking for a CEO: They took candidates away for a weekend. Eric played it a bit more conservatively: "Look, guys, I don't need to go to Burning Man with you. How about dinner?")

---

100. Tina Fey told this quote to Eric when he interviewed her onstage at Google on April 20, 2011.

Insight that can't be taught

A person who passes the LAX/Googleyness/three-a.m.-in-the-*SNL*-bathroom test has to be someone you could have an interesting conversation with and respect. However, he or she is *not* necessarily someone you have to like. Imagine that person with whom you are stuck at LAX has nothing in common with you, and in fact represents the polar opposite of wherever you stand on the political spectrum. Yet if this person is your equal (or more) in intellect, creativity, and these factors we call Googleyness, the two of you would still have a provocative conversation, and your company will be better off having the both of you on the same team.

You often hear people say they only want to work with (or elect as president) someone they would want to have a beer with. Truth be told, some of our most effective colleagues are people we most definitely would *not* want to have a beer with. (In a few rare instances they are people we would rather pour a beer *on*.) You must work with people you don't like, because a workforce comprised of people who are all "best office buddies" can be homogeneous, and homogeneity in an organization breeds failure. A multiplicity of viewpoints—aka diversity—is your best defense against myopia.

We could go off on a politically correct tangent on how hiring a workforce that is diverse in terms of race, sexual orientation, physical challenges, and anything else that makes people different is the right thing to do (which it is). But from a strictly corporate point of view, diversity in hiring is even more emphatically the right thing to do. People from different backgrounds see the world differently. Women and men, whites and blacks, Jews and Muslims, Catholics and Protestants, veterans and civilians, gays and straights, Latinos and Europeans, Klingons and Romulans,[101] Asians and Africans, wheelchair-bound and able-bodied: These differences of perspective generate insights that

---

101. We draw the line at the Borg, since being assimilated doesn't promote diversity.

can't be taught. When you bring them together in a work environment, they integrate to create a broader perspective that is priceless.[102]

Great talent often doesn't look and act like you. When you go into that interview, check your biases at the door[103] and focus on whether or not the person has the passion, intellect, and character to succeed and excel.

The same goes for managing people once they join you. Just like hiring, managing performance should be driven by data, with the sole objective of creating a meritocracy. You cannot be gender-, race-, and color-blind by fiat; you need to create empirical, objective methods to measure people. Then the best will thrive, regardless of where they're from and what they look like.

Expand the aperture

The ideal candidate is out there. She has passion, intellect, integrity, and a unique perspective. Now, how do you find her and get her on board? There are four links in this critical chain: sourcing, interviewing, hiring, and compensation.

Let's start with sourcing, which in turn starts with defining the type of candidate for whom you are looking. Our recruiting partner Martha Josephson calls this "expanding the aperture." The aperture

---

102. Scholars have actually tried to determine the value of diversity. For example, in a study of a sample of for-profit businesses, the sociologist Cedric Herring found an association between racial diversity and increased sales revenue, more customers, greater market share, and greater relative profits. He also found an association between some of these markers of financial performance and gender diversity. See Cedric Herring, "Does Diversity Pay?: Race, Gender, and the Business Case for Diversity" (*American Sociological Review*, Volume 74, Number 2, April 2009). Other scholars, however, point out that diversity creates conflict among coworkers—but in our experience, conflict is a *good* thing, usually leading to more thoughtful decisions.

103. Easier said than done, which is why Google invested in training its employees to spot their own unconscious biases. For more information on these unconscious tendencies, see Anthony G. Greenwald and Mahzarin R. Banaji, "Implicit Social Cognition: Attitudes, Self-Esteem, and Stereotypes" (*Psychological Review*, Volume 102, Number 1, January 1995).

is the opening in a camera through which light flows to the sensors that capture the image. A typical hiring manager will have a narrow aperture, considering only certain people with certain titles in certain fields, those who will undoubtedly do today's job well. But the successful manager sets a wider aperture and rounds up people beyond the usual suspects.

Let's say you like to hire people from a particular company, one that is well known for harboring tremendous talent. Said company knows that you want its employees, and has made it pretty hard to pry people out of there. If you expand the aperture and look for someone who can do the job well tomorrow as well as today, you can find some gems, and you can offer them opportunities their current employer might not be able to. The engineer who wants to move into product management, but is blocked from leaving his team; the product manager who wants to get into sales, but there's no open headcount. You can get great talent if you are willing to take a risk on people by challenging them to do new things. They will join you precisely because you are willing to take that risk. And those willing to take risks introduce the exact self-selection tendency you are looking for.

For example, if you're hiring a software engineer and all your code is written in a certain language, that doesn't necessarily mean you should hire an expert in that language. You should hire the best engineer you can find, regardless of her coding preference, because if she's the best she can down enough Java to C how to make the Python Go.[104] And when the language of choice changes (it inevitably will) she'll be able to adapt better than anyone else. Supercomputer pioneer Seymour Cray used to deliberately hire for *in*experience because it brought him people who "do not usually know what's supposed to be impossible."[105] We do something similar at Google with our Associate Product Manager (APM) program, which was created by Marissa

---

104. Java, C, Python, and Go all being the names of computer languages.
105. Tracy Kidder, *The Soul of a New Machine* (Little, Brown, 1981), page 59.

Mayer back when she was a director on Jonathan's team with a prime directive of hiring the smartest computer scientists we could find straight out of school. This isn't unusual; lots of companies hire smart recent graduates—that's the easy part. The hard part is to give them vital roles in projects with real impact. Smart creatives thrive in these positions, while risk-averse managers cringe. They have no experience! (Good!) What if they screw up? (They will, but they will also succeed in ways you can't imagine.) Brian Rakowski set the tone pretty well as our very first APM, hired straight out of Stanford and immediately given product management responsibility for Gmail, working directly with lead engineer Paul Buchheit. Brian is now a lead on the Android team, and Gmail hasn't done too poorly either.

Of course, sometimes we screw this up ourselves. Once, Salar Kamangar was impressed with one of our young marketing associates and wanted to transfer said young man into the APM program. Unfortunately, the APM program only accepted candidates with degrees in computer science, which this associate didn't have. Although Salar argued that the young associate was a self-taught programmer and had a "history of working closely with engineers and shipping things," several influential execs, including Jonathan, steadfastly refused to expand the aperture, and denied the transfer. The young marketing associate, Kevin Systrom, eventually left Google. He cofounded a company called Instagram, which he later sold to Facebook for a billion dollars.[106] You're welcome, Kevin!

One way to make expanding the aperture work is to judge candidates based on trajectory. Our former colleague Jared Smith notes that the best people are often the ones whose careers are climbing, because when you project their path forward there is potential for great growth and achievement. There are plenty of strong, experienced people who have hit a plateau. With those candidates, you know exactly what you are getting

106. Somini Sengupta, Nicole Perlroth, and Jenna Wortham, "Behind Instagram's Success, Networking the Old Way" (*New York Times*, April 13, 2012).

(which is good) but there is much less potential for the extraordinary (bad). It's important to note that age and trajectory are not correlated, and that there are exceptions to the trajectory guideline, such as people running their own business or those with nontraditional career paths.

Expanding the aperture is much harder as you work your way up the corporate food chain. Hiring senior people is almost always experience-based, and experience is important, but in most industries today technology has rendered the environment so dynamic that having the right experience is only a part of what it takes to succeed. Companies consistently overvalue relevant experience when judging senior candidates. They should be more focused on what talented smart creatives have to offer.

For example, in 2003, when we were looking for a head of human resources to round out our executive team, we interviewed something like fifty candidates, many with great experience in the traditional sense but none who were qualified to do what we knew needed to be done. We were growing a company faster than perhaps any other company in history, so all the standard operating experience that these candidates brought to the table was not going to cut it. We needed executives who understood how to build scalable engines on which a company could run at a fundamentally different pace.

It was a long process. At one point Eric blurted out, "Find me a Rhodes scholar who is also an astrophysicist." We decided after some discussion that an astrophysicist, although probably qualified for the job, wouldn't come to Google to be a business executive. "Alright," Sergey said, "get me a law partner." Jonathan found one of the law partner candidates in Sergey's office one day, furiously writing a contract. Sergey had given him an assignment: Write a contract that is well done, comprehensive, and funny. A half hour later, the candidate delivered contract 666, whereby Mr. Sergey Brin sold his soul to the devil in exchange for one dollar and numerous other considerations. The piece was brilliant and funny but he didn't get the job—not technical enough.

With the lawyer approach not working out, our search partner, Martha Josephson, suggested that the right combination might be

McKinsey partner + Rhodes scholar, and brought us Shona Brown, whom we hired to run business operations even though she had never held a role like that before. It worked out so well that when we needed a new CFO in 2008 to replace the estimable George Reyes, Eric asked Martha to "find another Shona Brown." She found Rhodes scholar and former McKinsey partner Patrick Pichette, who became CFO in 2008.

(Google's preference for talented people goes well beyond senior execs. One year, Jonathan was heading out to our London office, where his agenda included speaking at an event with a group of Rhodes scholars that Shona was hosting. He was trying to determine how to decide which of them would receive offers to interview in Mountain View, when he ran into Sergey in a hallway and explained his problem. "Why decide at all?" Sergey said. "Offer all of them jobs." Which seemed crazy at first, but not so crazy when he thought about it. Some of those Rhodes scholars went on to do very well at Google.)

Expanding the aperture brings risks. It leads to some failures, and the start-up costs for hiring a brilliant, inexperienced person are higher than those of hiring a less-brilliant, experienced one. The hiring manager may not want to bear the costs, but such concerns need to be set aside for the greater good. Hiring brilliant generalists is far better for the company.

Everyone knows someone great

You probably know someone whose résumé is truly exceptional: someone who climbed K2, is an Olympic-class hockey player, published a critically acclaimed novel, worked her way through college and finished cum laude, just had an art exhibit, started a (real) nonprofit, speaks four languages, owns three patents, codes top-100 apps for fun, plays lead guitar in a band, and once danced onstage with Bruno Mars. If you know at least one person like that, then it stands to reason that everyone you work with knows one of them too. Then why do you let only recruiters handle recruiting? If everyone knows someone great, why isn't it *everyone's* job to recruit that great person?

Establishing a successful hiring culture that delivers a steady stream of outstanding people starts with understanding the role of recruiters in sourcing candidates. Hint: It isn't their exclusive realm. Don't get us wrong, we love good recruiters. We work with them all the time and appreciate their insights and their hard work. But the job of finding people belongs to everyone, and this fact needs to be woven into the fabric of the company. Recruiters can manage the process, but everyone should be recruited into recruiting.

This is easy when a company is small, since getting all hands on the recruiting deck is natural. At a certain size, however—in our experience the number is around five hundred employees—managers start worrying about headcount allocation more than about whom they're going to get to fill those allocations. You hear about "fighting for headcount" a lot more than "finding great people," because the latter is what those recruiters are for, right? Not exactly. The problem with overdependence on recruiters is that it becomes tempting for recruiters to stop looking for the cream of the crop and settle for the half-and-half or even the skim milk. They don't have to live with their mistakes, the company does. On the other hand, it is easy for any company to double in size with great people. All it takes, as Larry often told us, is for each employee to refer just one great person. When you completely delegate recruiting, quality degrades.

The simple way to keep recruiting in everyone's job description is to measure it. Count referrals and interviews. Measure how quickly people fill out interview feedback forms. Encourage employees to help with recruiting events, and track how often they do. Then make these metrics count when it comes to performance reviews and promotions. Recruiting is everyone's job, so grade it that way.

Interviewing is the most important skill

The loftier your hiring aspirations, the more challenging and important the interview process becomes. The interview is where you truly learn about a person—it is far more important than the résumé. The résumé tells you that the person got a 3.8 from an elite school while majoring in computer science and running track; the interview tells you that the person is a boring grind who hasn't had an original idea in years.

The most important skill any business person can develop is interviewing. You've probably never read that in any management book or heard it in an MBA course. CEOs, professors, and venture capitalists always (correctly) preach the primacy of people when it comes to success, but they often don't say how to get those great people. They talk in theory, but business is practice and in practice your job is to determine a candidate's merit in the context of an artificial, time-constrained interview. That calls for a unique and difficult skill set, and the simple truth is most people are not good at it.

Go back to the initial response people had in our hypothetical "What is the most important thing you do at work?" exercise, which was "Go to meetings." Meetings are indeed how we spend the majority of our time. The nice thing about meetings is that the higher up you are on the food chain, the less you have to prepare for them. When you're the top dog (or somewhere up there on the canine hierarchy), other people prepare for the meeting while all you have to do is listen and opine. Your colleagues leave with the action items, and you leave with nothing to do but run to the next meeting.

Conducting a good interview requires something different: preparation. This is true regardless of whether you're a senior executive or a fresh associate. Being a good interviewer requires understanding the role, reading the résumé, and—most important—considering your questions.

You should first do your own research on who the interviewee is and why they are important. Look at their résumé, do a Google search, find out what they worked on and do a search on that too. You aren't looking for the drunken Carnival photo, but rather trying to form an opinion of them—is this someone who is interesting? Then, in the interview use your researched knowledge of their projects to dig deeper. You need to ask challenging questions that push the candidate. What was the low point in the project? Or why was it successful? You want to learn if the candidate was the hammer or the egg, someone who caused a change or went along with it.

Your objective is to find the limits of his capabilities, not have a polite conversation, but the interview shouldn't be an overly stressful experience. The best interviews feel like intellectual discussions between friends ("What books are you reading right now?"). Questions should be large and complex, with a range of answers (to draw out the person's thought process) that the interviewer can push back on (to see how the candidate stakes out and defends a position). It's a good idea to reuse questions across candidates, so you can calibrate responses.

When asking about a candidate's background, you want to ask questions that, rather than offering her a chance to regurgitate her experiences, allow her to express what insights she gained from them. Get her to show off her thinking, not just her résumé. "What surprised you about...?" is one good way to approach this, as it is just different enough to surprise a candidate, so you don't get rehearsed responses, and forces her to think about her experiences from a slightly different perspective. "How did you pay for college?" is another good one, as is "If I were to look at the web history section of your browser, what would I learn about you that isn't on your résumé?" Both of these can lead to a far better understanding of the candidate. They are also quite specific, which helps you gauge how well someone listens and parses questions.

Scenario questions are often helpful, but more so when interviewing more senior people, because they can reveal how a person will use or trust their own staff. For example, "When you are in a crisis, or need to make an important decision, how do you do it?" will often reveal if a candidate is of the "if you want something done, do it yourself" ilk, or if they will rely on the people around them. The former is more likely to get frustrated with the people who work for them and thus hang on to control, the latter more likely to hire great people and have faith in them. Generic answers to these questions indicate someone who lacks insight on issues. You want the answers to be interesting or at least specific. If the answers you get are cut and pasted from marketing claims, or are simply the reflection of commonly held wisdom, then you have a generic candidate, one who will not be adept at thinking deeply about things.

Then there are Google's infamous brainteasers. In recent years, we have phased out the practice of asking these puzzling questions during interviews. Many of the questions (and answers) ended up online, so continuing to ask them wouldn't necessarily reveal a candidate's ability to reason out a complex problem as much as her ability to conduct research before an interview and then act as if she hadn't memorized the answers to all of our brainteasers. (A valuable skill, to be sure; just not the one we're looking for.) The brainteasers also became a lightning rod for criticism as an elitist tool. To those critics, let us say once and for all: You are right. We want to hire the best minds available, because we believe there is a big difference between people who are great and those who are good, and we will do everything we can to separate the two. And if you, our critics, still persist in believing that elitism in hiring is wrong, well, we have just one question for you: If you have twelve coins, one of which is counterfeit and a different weight than the others, and a balance, how do you identify the counterfeit coin in just three weighings?[107]

---

107. With the first weighing, pull out four coins and weigh the other two sets of four against each other. If those two sets balance, then the counterfeit coin must be in the third set, the one that you set aside. In this case, pick two coins from among the eight that you just weighed, and two from the unweighed set of four. If these balance, then the counterfeit coin is in the pair of coins that has never been on the balance. If they do not balance, then the counterfeit coin is in the pair that was introduced in the second weighing. In the third weighing, balance one of the coins from the pair with the "bad" coin against a control "good" coin. If they balance, the counterfeit one is the one sitting on the table. If not, it's the one on the scale.

That was the easier scenario. Let's see if you can figure out the harder one, when the first weighing doesn't balance, on your own.

There are two reason we like questions like this one. First, you see if someone has the intellect to deconstruct a complex problem, regardless of whether they get to the answer. Second, do they enjoy the process?

When preparing for an interview, it helps to keep in mind that the interviewee is not the only person being interviewed. A highly qualified candidate is evaluating you as much as you are evaluating her. If you waste the first few minutes of the interview reading her résumé and making small talk, the candidate who is considering several options (and the great candidates always have several options) may not be impressed. First impressions work both ways.

While you want to ask thoughtful questions, you should also identify the *candidates* who ask thoughtful questions. People who ask good questions are curious, smarter, more flexible and interesting, and understand that they don't have all the answers—exactly the type of smart-creative characteristics you want.

The only way to get good at interviewing is to practice. That's why we tell young people to take advantage of every opportunity to interview. Some of them do but most of them don't, preferring to spend their time on things they think are more important. They don't realize what a great gift we are giving them. Come on, we're saying, you can practice the most important skill you can possibly develop, get paid for doing it, and since you will most likely not be the person's manager, you won't have to live with the consequences of a bad hire. They ignore us. Getting people to interview is like pulling teeth.

Of course, not everyone is good at interviewing, and people who don't want to get good at it won't. At Google we implemented a trusted-interviewer program, an elite team of people who were actually good at interviewing and liked to do it, and they got to do the bulk of the work (and were rewarded with higher scores during performance review). Product managers who wanted to be in the program had to go through interview training and shadow a minimum of four interviewers as they met with candidates. Once in the program they were scored on a variety of performance metrics, including how many interviews they conducted, reliability (it's amazing how many people think it's OK to cancel interviews at the last minute, or not even show up), and quality and promptness of their feedback (quality of feedback declines precipitously after forty-eight hours; our best interviewers schedule time to enter their feedback right after the interview). We published these stats and let people not in the program "challenge" the incumbents and replace them if their performance was better. In other words, *not* interviewing was seen as punishment. With this program, interviewing became a privilege, not a chore, and quality increased across the board.

And about that drunken Carnival photo: Unless they demonstrate a serious character flaw, we generally don't hold a candidate's online photos and commentary against her. We are hiring for passion, remember, and passionate people will often have an exuberant online presence. This demonstrates a love of the digital medium, an important characteristic in today's world.

Schedule interviews for thirty minutes

Who decided that an interview should last an hour? Oftentimes, you walk into an interview and know within minutes that a person is wrong for the company and the job. Who says you have to spend the rest of the hour making useless conversation? What a waste of time. That's why Google interviews are a half hour. Most interviews will result in a no-hire decision, so you want to invest less time in them, and most good interviewers can make that negative call in a half hour. If you like the candidate and want to keep talking, you can always schedule another interview or choose to make time in your calendar right then and there (easy to do if you have scheduled the following fifteen minutes to write up your feedback). The shorter interview time forces a conversation that's more protein and less fat; there's no time for small talk or meaningless questions. It forces people, including (especially!) you, into a substantive discussion.

Not only do most companies conduct overlong interviews, they conduct too many of them. One time, in our early days at Google, we interviewed a particular candidate over thirty times and we *still* couldn't decide if we wanted to hire him. That's just wrong. So we declared by fiat that a candidate couldn't be interviewed more than thirty times. Then we did some research and discovered that each additional interviewer after the fourth increased our "decision accuracy" by less than 1 percent. In other words, after four interviews the incremental cost of conducting additional interviews outweighs the value the additional feedback contributes to the ultimate hiring decision. So we lowered the maximum to five, a number with the added benefit (at least for computer scientists) of being prime.

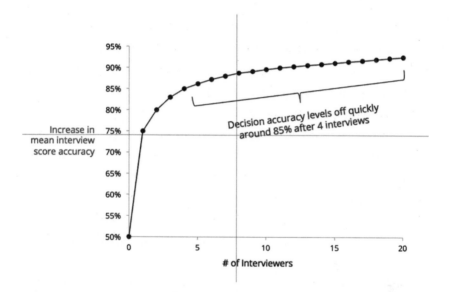

Have an opinion

Remember: From the interviewer's standpoint, *the goal of the interview is to form an opinion.* A strong opinion. A yes or no. At Google we grade interview candidates on a scale of 1 to 4. The average score falls around a 3, which translates to "I'll be okay with this person getting an offer, but someone else should like them a lot." As an average, 3 is fine, but as an individual response it's a cop-out, since what it really means is that the interviewer can't make up his mind and is passing the buck to someone else to decide. We encourage interviewers to take a stand.

For example, on the product management team the score of 4.0 meant "This person is perfect for this role. If you don't hire them, expect to hear from me." This isn't just saying we should hire the person. It's saying, "If someone wants to get in the way of hiring this person, I will hunt you down and...passionately debate the decision based on the objective data included in the packet."

The language assigned to these scores was deliberately emotional—"expect to hear from me"—because smart creatives *care* about who joins their team. It's as if they are inviting someone into their family. They believe every interview must lead to a decision, and that decision is personal. There's no wishy-washy.

When you tell people to have an opinion, though, you need to tell them what to have an opinion about. Whether or not to hire the candidate is obvious, but interviewers also need to be guided in how to form that opinion. At Google we break down candidate evaluations into four different categories, and we keep these categories consistent across functions. From sales to finance to engineering, smart creatives tend to score well on all of these, regardless of what they do or at what level. The categories and descriptions:

• Leadership: We'll want to know how someone has flexed different muscles in various situations in order to mobilize a team. This can include asserting a leadership role at work or with an organization, or even helping a team succeed when they weren't officially appointed as the leader.

• Role-Related Knowledge: We look for people who have a variety of strengths and passions, not just isolated skill sets. We also want to make sure that candidates have the experience and the background that will set them up for success in the role. For engineering candidates in particular, we check out coding skills and technical areas of expertise.

- General cognitive ability: We're less concerned about grades and transcripts and more interested in how a candidate thinks. We're likely to ask a candidate some role-related questions that provide insight into how they solve problems.

- Googleyness: We want to get a feel for what makes a candidate unique. We also want to make sure this is a place they'll thrive, so we look for signs around their comfort with ambiguity, bias to action, and collaborative nature.

Friends don't let friends hire (or promote) friends

Another part of the interviewing process that most companies screw up is letting the hiring manager make the hiring decision. The problem with this is that the hiring manager will probably be the new employee's manager for only a matter of months or a year or two; organizations are highly fungible. Besides, in the most effective organizations, who you work *for* matters a lot less than who you work *with*. Hiring decisions are too important to be left in the hands of a manager who may or may not have a stake in the employee's success a year later.

That's why at Google we set up the process so that the hiring decision is made by committee. With hiring committees, it doesn't matter who you are: If you want to hire someone, the decision needs approval from a hiring committee, whose decisions are based on *data*, not relationships or opinion. The primary criterion for serving on a hiring committee is that you will not be driven by anything other than what is best for the company, period. Committees should have enough members to allow a good range of viewpoints, but should be small enough to allow an efficient process; four or five is a pretty good number. The best composition promotes a wide variety of perspectives, so aim for diversity: in seniority, in skills and strengths (since people will often favor people cut in their own mold), and in background. The hiring manager is not entirely powerless in a committee-based process; she (or her recruiter) can participate in committee meetings, and she gets to decide whether or not to move a candidate from interview process to offer process, meaning she has veto power but not hiring power. The hiring committee ensures that people don't hire their friends, unless those friends happen to be superstars.

In the early 2000s, as Google started adding employees by the thousands, Eric, Larry, and Sergey observed that many of the newer hires were good but not as strong as needed. Perhaps they couldn't control *what* every group was doing, the trio decided, but they could control *whom* they hired. Larry suggested a policy that senior management would review every offer. The resulting hiring committee process, which was developed by Urs Hölzle, entails a hierarchy of committees, culminating with a committee of one: Larry, who for several years reviewed every offer. This made it clear to everyone involved in hiring just how high a priority it was to the company. The process was designed to optimize for quality, not efficiency, and for control, not scale. Over the years, we have done our best to make it scale efficiently anyway, but our original tenet still stands, even as we pass forty-five thousand employees: Nothing is more important than the quality of hiring.

The unit of currency in this system is the hiring packet, a document containing all the known information about a candidate who has progressed through the interview process. A hiring packet needs to be both comprehensive and standardized, so that all members of the hiring committee get the exact same information, and that information comprises a complete picture of the candidate. The Google hiring packet was designed by engineers with this objective in mind (as well as the objective of keeping Larry happy, since he reviewed each one getting an offer). It is based on a template that is standardized across the entire company (functions, countries, levels), with room for flexibility.

When completed, the ideal hiring packet is stuffed to the brim with data, not opinion, and this distinction is critical. If you are the hiring manager or one of the interviewers, it isn't sufficient to express an opinion; you need to support it with data. You can't say, "We should hire Jane because she's smart." You have to say, "We should hire Jane because she's smart and has the MacArthur Fellowship to prove it." Most candidates aren't accommodating enough to win MacArthur Fellowships, so supporting every opinion with data or empirical observations tends to be a lot harder than this example. But when people don't do it, packets get kicked out of the committee.

The other important rule is that the packet is the only source of information for the hiring committee. If something isn't in the packet, it doesn't get considered. This forces people to be thorough in constructing a hiring packet. You can't omit information from the packet and then bring it up in the meeting as a power move; aces up the sleeve get people shot (figuratively... usually). The people who get hired are the ones with the best packets, not the loudest cheerleaders on the committee.

The best packets are like any other great piece of executive communications: a one-page summary with all the key facts, and comprehensive supporting material. The summary consists of hard data and evidence in support of the hiring decision, and the supporting material includes interview reports, résumé, compensation history, reference information (especially if the candidate was sourced via internal reference), and any other relevant material (college transcripts, copy of a candidate's patents or awards, writing or coding samples).

In compiling a hiring packet, details matter. For example, for recent graduates, does their school's GPA comply with a typical American four-point scale, or is it like the University of Geneva, which grades on a six-point scale? Class rank is another important detail for recent grads; because of grade inflation, an A may no longer be worth that much, but a top class ranking is still the best. The packet also needs to be well formatted and easy to read quickly; for example, the candidate's best or worst answers should be highlighted for easy reference. But not everything should be formatted: A candidate's original résumé should be included as is, so everyone can see the typos and formatting errors (or bold or italic fonts). Getting all of these details of the packet right is what enables the committee to get the details of the candidate right.

Even a purely data-based packet can lie, though. Interviewers have natural biases—one person's 3.8 rating is another's 2.9 (and another, more irrational person's π). The solution to this? More data. Stipulate that all packets include statistics on each interviewer's *past* scores—including number of interviews, range of scores, and mean—so committee members can factor into their decision-making which interviewers grade higher and which clump their scores in the middle of the bell curve. (Interviewers, knowing that this data is part of the packet, will often be more conscientious in grading tougher and providing more opinionated scores.)

Some managers want absolute control over building their teams. When we instituted the committee system, some people hated it and even threatened to leave. That's OK. If someone cares that much about having absolute control over their team, perhaps you don't want them around. Dictatorial tendencies rarely contain themselves to just one aspect of work. The good managers will realize that hiring by committee is actually better for the company as a whole.

Similarly, deciding who gets promoted should also be via a committee rather than a top-down management decision. Our managers can nominate their people for promotion and act as advocates throughout the process, but the decision itself is out of their hands. The reasons are the same as they are for hiring: Promotions have a company-wide impact, so they are too important to be left in the hands of individual managers. But with promotions, there is an additional factor favoring a committee-based process. Many smart creatives (a majority, in our experience) are conflict-averse and have a hard time saying no. With committees, the rejection doesn't come from an individual but from the more faceless committee. This small detail can have a surprisingly big calming effect on promotion rates.

(There's a lot more to how Google hires people than we can get into here. If you want to learn more and get the science behind not just recruiting but all of our people practices, read our colleague Laszlo Bock's upcoming book, *Work Rules!* Laszlo runs people operations at Google, and in his book he details how the principles we established in the early days grew into a system that any team or business can emulate.)

Urgency of the role isn't sufficiently important to compromise quality in hiring

Our emphasis on quality hiring does not mean the process has to be slow. In fact, everything that we've described about our method is set up to make it faster. We keep interviews at a half hour and limit ourselves to five per candidate. We tell interviewers that once they finish meeting with a candidate they should *immediately* tell the recruiter thumbs-up or -down. We design candidate packets so that the hiring committees making final decisions on candidates can review a packet within 120 seconds. (Literally. We timed it.) These steps make the hiring process scalable and force clarity. They're good for candidates too, because piling on interviews and stringing out a decision is unfair. After all, if they're the kind of people you want to hire, they want to move fast too.

But there is a golden rule to hiring that cannot be violated: *The urgency of the role isn't sufficiently important to compromise quality in hiring.* In the inevitable showdown between speed and quality, quality must prevail.

Disproportionate rewards

Once you get your smart creatives on board, you need to pay them; exceptional people deserve exceptional pay. Here again we can look to the sports world for guidance: Outstanding athletes get paid outstanding amounts. It's not uncommon for the best player on a professional team to be compensated with deals worth hundreds of millions, while the deal the rookie at the end of the bench gets is only in the hundreds of thousands. Are those stars worth it? Baseball great Babe Ruth, when asked if he thought it was right that his salary was higher than President Herbert Hoover's, answered, "Why not? I had a better year than he did." We have a more reasoned response. Yes, they are worth it (when they perform up to expectations), because successful athletes possess rare skills that are tremendously leverageable. When they do well, they have a disproportionate impact. They help teams win, and winning drives huge business benefits: more fans, more viewers, more jerseys and hats sold. Hence, the big money.

Smart creatives today may not share many characteristics with professional athletes, but they do share one important thing: the potential for disproportionate impact. Top performers get paid well in athletics, and they should in business too. If you want better performance from the best, celebrate and reward it disproportionately.

This doesn't mean you should give new hires a blank check. In fact, the compensation curve should start low. You can attract the best smart creatives with factors *beyond* money: the great things they can do, the people they'll work with, the responsibility and opportunities they'll be given, the inspiring company culture and values, and yes, maybe even free food and happy dogs sitting desk-side. (One of the early engineers at Google wanted to bring his ferret to the office. We said yes. He didn't haggle over salary.) But when those smart creatives become employees and start performing, pay them appropriately. The bigger the impact, the bigger the comp.

At the opposite end of the scale, managers should reward people greatly only when they do a great job. They are managing *professionals*, not coaching Little League, where everyone gets a standing ovation and a trophy, even the dreamer in right field who spends the game picking daisies and hunting for four-leaf clovers. All men and women are created equal in that they are all endowed with certain inalienable rights, but that decidedly does *not* mean they are all equally good at what they do. So don't pay or promote them as if they are. The business world traditionally rewards people for being closer to the top (case in point: outrageous CEO salaries) or for being closer to the transactions (investment bankers, salespeople).[108] But what's most important in the Internet Century is product excellence, so it follows that big rewards should be given to the people who are closest to great products and innovations. This means that yes, the lower-level employee who helps create a breakthrough product or feature should be very handsomely rewarded. Pay outrageously good people outrageously well, regardless of their title or tenure. What counts is their impact.[109]

Trade the M&Ms, keep the raisins

You have done all this work to create a hiring process that brings in all these awesome smart creatives, and how do they pay you back? By leaving!! That's right. News flash: When you hire great people, some of them may come to realize that there is a world beyond yours. This isn't a bad thing, in fact it's an inevitable by-product of a healthy, innovative team. Still, fight like hell to keep them.

The best way to retain smart creatives is to not let them get too comfortable, to always come up with ways to make their jobs interesting. When Georges Harik, who was part of the team that created AdSense and who helped solve the "ads suck" problem we discussed

---

108. Economists usually explain this phenomenon through "tournament theory," which starts with the observation that many fields are set up as long-running contests for the top slots, with outsize pay as the winners' prize. The original theory is laid out by economists Edward Lazear and Sherwin Rosen, in "Rank-Order Tournaments as Optimum Labor Contracts" (*Journal of Political Economy*, Volume 89, Number 5, October 1981).

109. We are as puzzled as economists are by egalitarian pay systems, in which people making vastly different contributions are nonetheless paid more or less the same amount. Doesn't the use of narrow pay bands reward low effort and demoralize the highest performers? For an academic discussion of this question, see George P. Baker, Michael C. Jensen, and Kevin J. Murphy, "Compensation and Incentives: Practice vs. Theory" (*Journal of Finance*, July 1988). One possible explanation is that widely varying wages are bad for team morale, and can reduce team productivity. See, for example, David I. Levine, "Cohesiveness, Productivity, and Wage Dispersion" (*Journal of Economic Behavior and Organization*, Volume 15, Number 2, March 1991). We believe this trade-off is well worth making: In our experience, getting great work out of the best performers outweighs any team problems from perceived unfairness. Mostly, people are happy for their colleagues and strive to do something great themselves, so they can earn a similar payday.

earlier in the book, was thinking about leaving the company, Eric suggested that he might be interested in sitting in on his staff meetings. So it came to be that Eric's staff meetings included the founders, all the execs who reported to Eric...and Georges, who was also added to the staff's email distribution list. Eric and the rest of the company's leaders got more perspective from the engineering trenches, and Georges learned a lot about business. He was intrigued enough by what he heard that he ended up joining the product management team and stayed at the company for two more years. That's two years of contribution from Georges we otherwise would not have gotten.

Jonathan employed the same approach when he was looking for help in managing his staff meetings. Typically, senior execs may bring in a chief of staff to play this role, but having a full-time chief of staff just encourages politics. Jonathan's solution was to rotate a series of APMs through the job in six-month stints, serving as his de facto chief of staff and working directly for Jonathan while still holding down their day jobs. Other APMs were encouraged to sign up for so-called chain-gang tasks, which were side projects posted on an internal site for which anyone could volunteer. For example, one task, created in September 2003, was to help Larry Page learn more about how projects got done at Google. Maybe not the most exciting assignment, but several young APMs jumped at the chance to work with the company's cofounder. The point of these assignments wasn't to spice up our staff meetings or to take advantage of cheap labor, it was to make the lives of our talented employees more interesting and challenging.

But often it takes more than interesting side projects to keep people engaged and prevent them from leaving. You need to prioritize the interests of the highly valued individual over the constraints of the organization. Salar Kamangar, whom the founders hired straight out of Stanford, is a great example of this. Salar helped invent AdWords and spent several years in the product organization, but when he was ready to expand his responsibilities and become a general manager, we didn't have a role for him. So we created one, appointing him the head of YouTube. There are numerous other cases like this, where smart creatives need or want to do something new and the company figures out a way to make it happen. Do the best thing for the person and make the organization adjust.

Encouraging people to take on new roles can be institutionalized in the form of rotations, but it needs to be done properly or it will backfire. Google's APM program (and its spin-offs in marketing and people operations) forces rotation every twelve months. This works great in a small program with entry-level employees, but it is difficult to create a structured rotation program across bigger segments of the company. So our approach has always been to encourage job movement, to make it as easy as possible, and to make it a standard part of the management discussion. We discuss it in our staff meetings and one-on-ones: Who on your team is a good candidate for rotation? Where do they want to go? Do you think that is the best thing for them?

Make sure as you have these discussions that the employees in question are the good ones. Managers are like kids trading goodies after a night of Halloween trick-or-treating: When you push them to rotate people off their teams, their inclination is to hang on to the Reese's cups and M&Ms and get rid of the boxes of raisins. This may be good for them, but it's bad for the company. It keeps the very best people, the ones you want to keep challenged and inspired, locked up on one team. When Eric let Georges Harik sit in on his staff meetings, he didn't do it because Georges was a mediocre performer whom he was trying to improve, but rather because Georges was a superior performer he was trying to keep. Make managers trade away their M&Ms; let them keep their raisins.

If you love them, let them go (but only after taking these steps)

Even if you keep your best people challenged and engaged, some of them will still consider leaving for greener pastures. When that happens, focus your retention efforts on the stars, the leaders, and the innovators (not necessarily the same people), and do whatever it takes to keep them around. The loss of these people can have a big ripple effect, as they often inspire their followers to leave too. Because people seldom leave over compensation, the first step to keeping them is to listen. They want to be heard, to be relevant and valued.

In these conversations, the leader's role is not to be the advocate of the organization ("Please stay!") but the advocate of the smart creative who is thinking about leaving. Many employees, particularly the younger ones, tend to think in terms of shorter time frames (perhaps still attached to the rhythms of a school year). They can overreact when they hit a bump in the road, and relish the days when they could start each semester with a clean notebook and no grades yet recorded. Help them take a longer-term perspective. How could staying at the company ultimately position them for much greater success when they do decide to leave? Have they considered the financial ramifications of leaving? Do they have a clear financial plan and a good sense of what they might be leaving behind? Listen to why they want to leave, and help them find a way to perhaps recharge their dilithium crystals while sticking around. Then, if they want to continue the conversation, have a plan for how they can develop their career while staying. This demonstrates your commitment to their success, not just the company's.

The best smart creatives often want to leave so they can go start something on their own. Don't discourage this, but do ask them for their elevator pitch. ("Elevator pitch" is venture capital–speak for "you have thirty seconds to impress me with your business idea.") What is your strategic foundation? What sort of culture do you envision? What would you tell me if I were a prospective investor? If they don't give good answers, then they obviously aren't ready to go. In that case, we usually advise them to stick around and continue to contribute at the company while they are working on their idea, and tell them that when they actually can convince us to invest, we'll let them go with our best wishes (if not a check!). This is a hard-to-resist offer, and it has helped us retain numerous talented people.

Then there is the case when the valued smart creative has an attractive offer in hand from another company. Sometimes that person will negotiate with an either/or threat: "Either do this, or else I'm out of here." When that happens, the game is usually already over, since someone who operates that way is not emotionally attached to the company anymore and is unlikely to rebuild that commitment. But if there is a bond still there and you want to make a counteroffer, do it very quickly—within an hour if possible. After that, the employee has started to settle into the new company in her mind.

And of course, if it truly is in the best interest of the person to go, then let her go. As Reid Hoffman, Jonathan's former colleague at Apple and founding CEO of LinkedIn notes, "Just because a job ends, your relationship with your employee doesn't have to. . . . The first thing you should do when a valuable employee tells you he is leaving is try to change his mind. The second is congratulate him on the new job and welcome him to your company's alumni network."[110]

We had one talented young product manager, Jessica Ewing, who helped us launch iGoogle (which let users customize the Google home page and was retired in 2013) and had a very bright future at the company. But she also had a burning desire to try her hand at writing. Think about your career trajectory, we advised. Think about those stock units you still have to vest. She did and left anyway. Jessica, we haven't heard from you in a while! Why don't you write?

Firing sucks

Not as much as *getting* fired, to be sure, but it's still plenty bad. If you've ever had to do it, you know how difficult it is to pull some poor soul aside and tell him it's not working out. Maybe the employee will see it coming and take it well; maybe he won't and will start throwing things.

---

110. Reid Hoffman, Ben Casnocha, and Chris Yeh, "Tours of Duty: The New Employer-Employee Compact" (*Harvard Business Review*, June 2013).

And maybe he'll use labor laws as silver bullets in a vindictive quest to make your life miserable. All the factors that make the right smart creatives great hires can make the wrong ones hell to fire: their intensity, their confidence, their fearlessness. So always keep in mind, from the outset, that the best way to avoid having to fire underperformers is not to hire them. This is why we would rather our hiring process generate more false negatives (people we should have hired but didn't) than false positives (we shouldn't have hired, but did).

Test yourself: If you could trade the bottom 10 percent of your team for new hires, would your organization improve? If so, then you need to look at the hiring process that yielded those low performers and see how you can improve it. Another test: Are there members of your team whom, if they told you they were leaving, you would not fight hard to keep? If there are employees you would let go, then perhaps you *should*.

One last note: There are some people who actually enjoy firing. Beware of them. Firing instills a culture of fear that will inevitably fail, and "I'll just fire them" is an excuse for not investing the time to execute the hiring process well.

Google's Hiring Dos and Don'ts

Hire people who are smarter and more knowledgeable than you are.
Don't hire people you can't learn from or be challenged by.

Hire people who will add value to the product *and* our culture.
Don't hire people who won't contribute well to both.

Hire people who will get things done.
Don't hire people who just think about problems.

Hire people who are enthusiastic, self-motivated, and
  passionate.
Don't hire people who just want a job.

Hire people who inspire and work well with others.
Don't hire people who prefer to work alone.

Hire people who will grow with your team and with the
  company.
Don't hire people with narrow skill sets or interests.

Hire people who are well rounded, with unique interests
  and talents.
Don't hire people who only live to work.

Hire people who are ethical and who communicate
  openly.
Don't hire people who are political or manipulative.

Hire only when you've found a great candidate.
Don't settle for anything less.

Career—Choose the F-16

We are frequently asked for career advice. Budding entrepreneurs, Nooglers fresh out of school, emerging superstars—they all want to know what they should do to manage their path. And if we are ever fortunate enough to be invited to give another graduation speech, say at one of our alma maters (are you paying attention, Princeton and Claremont McKenna?), it might sound something like this:

Treat your career like you are surfing

When Jonathan was in business school and interested in product management, he went to a couple of presentations given by prospective employers. One was from a company that was a leader in consumer packaged goods, stuff like shampoo and household cleaners. They described product management in their business as a science, driven by precise data garnered from focus groups and product performance. "It's like driving forward by looking in your rearview mirror," they said, and they meant that as a good thing.

Then he went to a presentation by one of the leading high-tech firms in Silicon Valley. They said that product management in Silicon Valley was like "flying an F-16 at Mach 2 over a boulder-strewn landscape, two meters off the ground. Plus, if you crash it's just like a video game at the arcade, and we have lots of quarters." Cool! The best industries are the ones where you're flying the F-16, your pocket full of quarters, trying not to crash.

In business, and particularly in high tech, it's not enough to be great at what you do, you have to catch at least one really big wave and ride it all the way in to shore. When people are right out of school, they tend to prioritize company first, then job, then industry. But at this point in their career that is exactly the wrong order. The right industry is paramount, because while you will likely switch companies several times in your career, it is much harder to switch industries. Think of the industry as the place you surf (in Northern California the most rad waves are at Mavericks, dude) and the company as the wave you catch. You always want to be in the place with the biggest and best waves.

If you choose the wrong company or you have bad luck with an aggro boss who drops in on your first wave, you'll still have a killer time if you're surfing in an industry with boda-cious waves. (Alright, Mr. Spicoli, that's enough surfer lingo.) Conversely, if you choose the wrong industry early in your career, then growth opportunities within your company will be limited. Your boss won't move, and you'll be stuck without much leverage when you're ready to look for jobs at other companies.

Fortunately, the tectonic forces driving the Internet Cen-tury mean that a *lot* of industries are great places to surf. It's not just the Internet companies that have a big upside, but also energy, pharmaceuticals, high-tech manufacturing, advertising, media, entertainment, and consumer electronics. The most interesting industries are those where product cycle times are accelerating, because this creates more chances for disruption and so more opportunities for fresh talent. But even businesses like energy and pharmaceuticals, where product cycle times are long, are ripe for massive transforma-tion and opportunity.

From a compensation standpoint, stock options and other forms of equity are quite limited early in your career, so it's more lucrative to develop expertise in the right industry than to bet on a particular company. Later, as you gain experi-ence (and age!), it becomes more important to pick the right wave. At that point you can start to earn compensation pack-ages with much more equity, so the priority flips.

Always listen for those who get technology

After you pick the industry, then it's time to pick the com-pany. When you do, listen for the people who truly get tech-nology. These are the genius-level smart creatives who see, before the rest of us, where technology is going and how it will transform industries. Bill Gates and Paul Allen saw that chips and computers were getting cheap and that software would be the key to the future of computing, so they started Microsoft. Chad Hurley saw that cheap video cameras, bandwidth, and storage would transform how video entertainment is created and consumed, so he cofounded YouTube. Reid Hoffman knew that the connecting power of the web would be vital to professionals, so he started LinkedIn. Marc Benioff believed that powerful software would live in the cloud, so he based Salesforce.com on that principle and didn't waver during the dot-com meltdown. Steve Jobs foresaw computers as consumer accessories and it took over two decades for the technology and market to catch up to him.

How do you know if someone gets it? It helps to look at their history. Often, they are playing with technology and entrepreneurship long before they think of it as a career. Reid Hoffman got his first job (at age twelve) by presenting a copy of a computer game's manual marked up with his suggestions for product improvements to one of the game's developers.[111] He wasn't looking for a job—he wanted to make the game better. Marc Benioff sold his first computer program ("How To Juggle") and started a company making games for the Atari 800 when he was fifteen. Larry Page built a printer out of Legos. (It was dot matrix, but still.)

These are the famous examples, but there are many others, people who may not be as well known but brim with insights. They are the ones navigating the best waves in the best places. Find them, hook in, and hang on.

---

111. Evelyn Rusli, "A King of Connections Is Tech's Go-To Guy" *(New York Times*, November 5, 2011).

Plan your career

Career development takes effort and forethought—you need to plan it. This is such an obvious point, yet it's astonishing how many people who have come to us over the years have failed to do it. Jonathan usually gives these folks a set of career exercises, accompanied with his favorite Tom Lehrer line—"Life is like a sewer: What you get out of it depends on what you put into it"[112]—and a promise that if they put real effort into the exercises, he will help them.

Here are some simple steps to creating a plan:

Think about your ideal job, not today but five years from now. Where do you want to be? What do you want to do? How much do you want to make? Write down the job description: If you saw this job on a website, what would the posting look like? Now fast forward four or five years and assume you are in that job. What does your five-years-from-now résumé look like? What's the path you took from now to then to get to your best place?

Keep thinking about that ideal job, and assess your strengths and weaknesses in light of it. What do you need to improve to get there? This step requires external input, so talk to your manager or peers and get their take on it. Finally, how will you get there? What training do you need? What work experience?

By the way, if your conclusion is that you are ready for your ideal job today, then you aren't thinking big enough. Start over and make that ideal job a stretch, not a gimme.

If you follow these steps, it will work. If you don't follow them, you will likely prove Yogi Berra's point that "You've got

112. Tom Lehrer, "We Will All Go Together When We Go," *An Evening Wasted with Tom Lehrer* (Marathon Media, 2010).

to be careful if you don't know where you're going 'cause you might not get there."[113]

Statistics is the new plastics

Stats are sexy. Deal with it. The sexiest jobs in the Internet Century will involve statistics, and not just in a parallel geeky fantasy world. Hal Varian notes that it is always a good idea for individuals to build expertise in areas that complement things that are getting cheap, and data, along with computing power to crunch it, is definitely getting cheap. We are in the era of big data, and big data needs statisticians to make sense of it. The democratization of data means that those who can analyze it well will win. Data is the sword of the twenty-first century, those who wield it well, the samurai. So start sharpening that blade, *uruwashii*,[114] and take statistics.

"But I'm not a numbers person!" we hear some of you whining, especially you in the back with the magenta shirt. Don't worry, there is hope. Asking the questions and interpreting the answers is as important a skill as coming up with the answers themselves. No matter your business, learn how the right data, crunched the right way, will help you make better decisions. Learn which questions to ask the people who *are* good with numbers and how to make the best use of their replies. Even if you aren't a numbers person, you can learn how to use the numbers to get smarter.

---

113. Yogi Berra, *The Yogi Book: I Really Didn't Say Everything I Said!* (Workman Publishing, 1998), page 102.

114. "cultured warrior"

Read

Most organizations have an impressive archive of written information. Find the best of it and read it. At Google, we always tell people who come to us seeking advice to ingest the founders' letter from our 2004 IPO and all the internal strategy memos that Eric and Larry subsequently wrote. These are the clearest, most concise explanations of our values and strategy that can be found, yet many people are too busy to read them. Don't make that mistake.

And don't stop at your company's borders. The web has a *lot* of written information, and while much of it is drivel, there is a lot of great stuff too. Figure out how to use the various tools at your disposal to tap into the sites and authors you respect. Create circles of other like-minded smart people and swap books and articles. One of the best, easiest ways to get ahead in a field is to know more about it. The best way to do that is to read. People always say they don't have the time to read, but what they are really saying is that they aren't making it a priority to learn as much as they can about their business. You know who reads a lot about their business? CEOs. So think like a CEO and read.

Know your elevator pitch

Let's say you run into your manager's manager in the hallway and she asks you what you're working on. Heck, let's make it the CEO. What do you say? This isn't a rhetorical question—try it out right now, out loud. Go ahead—you have 30 seconds.

Ugh, that didn't sound great. You obviously haven't practiced your elevator pitch. Work on it. Your pitch should explain what you are working on, the technical insight that's driving it, how you are measuring your success (particularly customer benefit), and perhaps how it fits into the big picture. Know this and practice it so you can say it with conviction.

Job seekers should also have an elevator pitch. This shouldn't be a condensed version of your résumé, but should rather highlight its most interesting parts along with what you want to do and the impact you know you will have—the benefit to the customer and the company. What can you say that no one else can?

Go abroad

Business, regardless of size or scope, is forever, permanently global, while humans are naturally provincial. So it doesn't matter where you are or where you came from, get out of there whenever you have the chance. Go live and work somewhere else. If you're at a big company, seek the international assignments. Your managers will love you for it and you'll be a much more valuable employee as a result.

If working overseas isn't an option, then travel, and when you are out and about don't forget to see the world as your customers do. If you're in retail, walk through a store or two. If you're in media, pick up a paper or turn on the radio. It's amazing how often people come back from business trips to foreign lands with insights gleaned solely from their conversation with the taxi driver who took them from the airport to the hotel. If those drivers only knew how much power they have in shaping global business strategy!

Combine passion with contribution

This from our estimable former colleague Sheryl Sandberg: "It is the ultimate luxury to combine passion and contribution. It's also a very clear path to happiness."[115] She couldn't be more right. You will not be as successful as you could be if you only *like* what you do and don't love it. Trite, perhaps, but true. Sheryl is also right in saying that combining passion and contribution is a luxury: not that it's expensive, but just rare. It's something that many people either can't figure out (how many people truly know their passion at the outset of their careers?) or can't afford (you may love whittling garden gnomes, but the world loves engineers and your spouse and children love a regular paycheck).

That's why we make this our last career point and not our first. Finding your passion isn't always simple. Perhaps when you were starting out you were just happy to find a job, regardless of your passion. Then as your career progresses you find that it's not the rocket ship you expected it to be. Perhaps you haven't nailed both sides of the passion/contribution equation.

You could drop everything and start over. "Hi, honey.... Fine....Oh, by the way, I quit my job and bought a cattle ranch in Montana....Honey?"

Or you could take a more deliberate approach. Adjust your course. Make your five-years-out *ideal* job closer to your if-only-I-could *dream* job, yet attainable from your current path. We've seen even this simple act of setting the right goal turn around people's careers.

---

115. Sheryl Sandberg, Barnard College Commencement, May 17, 2011.

Decisions—The True Meaning of Consensus

In December 2009, we learned that Google was under attack from hackers. That we were under some form of attack wasn't unusual, in fact it happened practically every day. But this time was different. The sophistication of the attack was something we hadn't experienced before, and so was its objective. A criminal (or, more likely, team of criminals) had somehow found a way to access Google's corporate servers. Up until then, most bad guys who attacked us were intent on disrupting Google's services, to shut us down or make it harder for users to access us. This time the bad guys wanted our confidential information.

Sergey immediately started working on stopping the attack and figuring out who was perpetrating it and how. In a matter of hours he formed a team of the smartest computer security experts he could find, and gathered them in a nondescript building near our Mountain View headquarters. Over the next couple of weeks, the team set up systems that ultimately allowed them to watch the attacks as they were in progress, and what they found was chilling. The hackers weren't just stealing intellectual property, but were also trying to access Gmail accounts, including those of human rights activists. And the attacks originated from within the nation with the fastest-growing major economy in the world: China.

It was about five and a half years earlier, in mid-2004, that we began to get involved in the Chinese market. From a business standpoint, entering China was not a controversial decision. China was (and is) a huge market, with more people than any other country, tens (now hundreds) of millions of Internet users, and an economy that was growing very quickly. There was a local competitor, Baidu, who had already developed a formidable presence in search, and Yahoo was also gaining momentum. Larry and Sergey visited the country and came away very impressed by all the innovation and energy they witnessed. They had always wanted to hire all the best engineers in the world, and a lot of those engineers were in China.[116]

But while the business indicators all pointed to a slam dunk decision to get involved, the *don't-be-evil* indicators were much more mixed. Information did not flow freely across the Chinese Internet. We knew this from direct experience: On most days, Chinese citizens were allowed to access our US site, Google.com, and get its unfettered (albeit English) results. But occasionally, Chinese traffic would drop to zero, and people from China trying to get to Google.com would instead be routed to Baidu (and its filtered results). Would opening up a localized site in China be better for the Chinese people, even if we would have to abide by local regulations, or would it make us complicit in the government's censorship, something that ran counter to the essence of our company's culture and values? Would establishing ourselves as a local business give us a chance to improve access to information and shed light on the questionable (and nontransparent) practices of the other search providers in China?

From the get-go, Sergey Brin was squarely in the "stay out" camp. His family had immigrated to the United States from the

---

116. We opened our first engineering center in China in 2005.

Soviet Union when he was a child, so he had firsthand experience with Communist regimes and he didn't want to support the one in China in any way. But many others on Eric's staff disagreed, and the business factors—plus the hope of being able to change the information climate in China—tipped the scale in favor of entering. Sukhinder Singh Cassidy, who was running our Asia operations at the time, moved quickly, and within a few months established a Google China subsidiary. We set up a business office in Beijing, and we grudgingly decided to comply with local censorship regulations, but with a twist: We would inform users when results were being blocked. They couldn't access the censored information, but at least they would be informed that censorship was occurring.[117]

One thing that surprised us was that many of the censorship requests we received were intended to suppress links to content that didn't violate any clear, written law. Sometimes these requests were an attempt to mitigate spats between various government departments (one agency censoring the public statements of another agency) or to suppress scandals that had been planted online. For example, rumors started circulating that the sparkling new Beijing headquarters of CCTV (China Central Television) had a design based on rather salacious images. So we received, and complied with, a request to censor searches related to, among other things, CCTV, genitalia, and porn jokes. (And for all of you who just Googled those terms, (1) shame on you, and (2) we hope you're not at work!)

---

117. There was a precedent to this approach: Under the Digital Millennium Copyright Act, a US law enacted in 1998, copyright owners can notify websites (in our case, You-Tube, Blogger, or other Google-owned sites) of content that allegedly infringes on their copyright. If Google removes content in response to a take-down notice, we try to indicate that to users.

In January 2006, we launched our localized Chinese site, Google.cn, with in-country servers, and a few months later Eric visited Beijing to promote the site. During one of his press interviews he somehow ended up sitting directly below a framed picture of Mao Zedong and Ho Chi Minh. The US press, which was already ambivalent about Google entering China, had a field day with that one. But things went well after that inauspicious beginning: Our local engineers helped the product get much better, and traffic and revenue grew steadily between 2006 and the end of 2009.

With the hacking attacks, all that progress was suddenly in danger. Eric had always believed that engaging in China was not only the right business decision, but the right moral decision as well. While Sergey had always disagreed, Larry had sided with Eric. In light of the attacks, though, Larry was changing his mind. The behavior we were seeing was evil, he told Eric, and wasn't going to stop; in fact, the harassment would likely get worse. Eric agreed with this assessment, but was surprised that self-eviction was our answer. Both founders were now firmly against censoring our results on Google.cn.

For leaders, decisions are when the hard work begins; there's a reason why the word "tough" is so often followed by "decision." (In recent decades it's also often followed by "love," but the implementation of *that* policy is beyond the sphere of this book.) Google's decision to leave China was emblematic of how we reach decisions, how our process works. Formulating a strategy, hiring the right people, and creating a unique culture are all preliminaries to the fundamental activity of all businesses and business leaders: decision-making.

Different institutions take different approaches to decision-making based on their hierarchical structure. The Marines (top-down) keep it simple: One guy gives the orders to take the hill; everyone else takes the hill. "Dammit, there's only one guy in charge here so put on your helmet and get going." Most big corporations (bureaucratic) have far more analyses to perform before they can decide the best course of action. Do they have all the data they need? Have the analysts crunched it? Did they calculate pro forma revenues and EBITDA?[118] Weeks go by, the seasons change, and the hill stays before them, untaken. "Maybe next quarter; the hill is definitely one of our stretch goals." And in the hip start-up (enlightened), the CEO proclaims that she works for the employees so decisions are made by consensus. Everyone gets a say and the arguments are collegial, considerate, and last forever. "Let's everyone go chillax, grab a cappuccino, and meet back here in a half hour to see where we stand, hill-wise."

So who's right—top-down Marines, bureaucratic corporations, or enlightened start-ups? The pace of business change in the Internet Century dictates that decisions be made quickly; the Marines win in that regard. More demanding and informed customers and increased competition dictate that they be as well informed as possible; the corporations may have an edge there. And having a team of smart creatives dictates that everyone gets a say; hello, start-ups. So all of them are right, of course. And they are all wrong too.

The answer lies in understanding that when it comes to making decisions, you can't just focus on making the right one. The process by which you reach the decision, the timing of when you reach it, and the way it is implemented are just as important as the decision itself. Blow

---

118. We have nothing against accountants, who have good reasons for calculating pro forma revenues and EBITDA (earnings before interest, taxes, depreciation, and amortization).

any of these, and the outcome will likely be negative. And since there's always another decision to be made, the impact of a poorly executed decision-making process can reverberate past that one issue.

As Sergey and his team continued their investigation throughout the latter part of December 2009, Eric knew that one of the most important decisions in the company's history was at hand. Although he believed that staying in the China market was the best thing for the company, he also knew that both of the founders now disagreed with him. They no longer felt that our presence in the market was helping change government censorship practices, and didn't want to participate in any way in that censorship. It would be an uphill battle to change their minds, so Eric's focus shifted. It wasn't just about making the best decision for the company, but about orchestrating the process so the company reached that decision in the best possible way. There would be other crises and other important decisions, and the smart creatives who populated his staff and ran the company would be paying attention to and learning from how this one was handled. It was especially challenging, given that he was reasonably confident he would disagree with the outcome.

Sergey and his investigative team conclusively confirmed the origin and scale of the attack in early January, and the news was bad. Not only were the hackers trying to steal source code, they had also attempted to compromise the Gmail accounts of several Chinese political dissidents. Sergey felt it was important to announce the attack, and how Google would react, very quickly. There was little disagreement on that point. In Eric's staff meeting that first week of January, Sergey forcefully made the argument that, as a response to the hacker attacks, we should stop complying with government censorship policies. He wanted us to stop filtering search results on Google.cn, even if it meant that the government would likely shut down the site, reversing much of our hard-won progress in the market. He stood up in the meeting to deliver his point; usually Sergey stands in meetings only when he's wearing his Rollerblades. Eric was traveling that day and attending the meeting via video conference, so he counseled his team to consider all the data and come to the next meeting prepared to express and defend a position on what the company should do.

Because of the urgency of the situation, Eric convened the next team meeting for the following Sunday afternoon—January 10, 2010—at four p.m. It started with Sergey conducting a detailed technical review of the situation for well over an hour. He then reiterated the position he had expressed earlier in the week: We should stop filtering our results. Eric knew that Larry was on Sergey's side, which meant that the decision was effectively made. But it was critically important that all of the members of his team be heard and have a vote. Everyone would have to pull together and rally behind the decision, regardless of where they stood on the matter. So the meeting continued for several hours. We reviewed the facts and had a lengthy, sometimes heated discussion. Finally, Eric called for a vote. The sentiment in the room was clearly favoring Sergey's position, and the vote wasn't really necessary, but Eric felt it was important that each person get a chance to record his or her position. Some agreed with Eric that leaving China was tantamount to disengaging from that market for the next hundred years. The majority sided with Sergey, who believed that the Chinese government would eventually change their behavior because their current model would not be sustainable, leaving the door open at some point in the future for Google to reenter the market.

The ultimate decision, which the weary team reached around nine p.m. that evening, wasn't to pull out immediately. Rather, we would disclose the hacking attack with as much transparency as possible; to the best of our knowledge, of the numerous companies that were affected, we were the only one to go public with the details. And we would announce our plans to stop censoring results on Google.cn. We would not make this change immediately, instead giving ourselves time to—as our lead attorney, David Drummond, put it in the blog post announcing the decision—"[discuss] with the Chinese government the basis on which we could operate an unfiltered search engine within the law, if at all." On Monday, Eric discussed the decision with the board, and on Tuesday, January 12, 2010, we announced it publicly.

The morning we made the announcement, we got several calls from government officials to our Beijing office wondering if it was some sort of joke. No one does this, one of them told us. Everyone just leaves quietly.

We were not leaving quietly. It was a public ultimatum, and Eric had complete clarity on what was going to happen. We would continue to talk with Chinese officials, to see if we could find a solution that was consistent with both our new public position and Chinese law, but that would fail. Google wouldn't back down from its public stance, and China wouldn't repeal its laws. So, as expected, in March we took the preordained step of shutting down search on Google.cn. Users visiting that page who tried to perform searches were directed to our site in Hong Kong, Google.com.hk. From that point on, Google search results would be subject to being blocked by the Great Firewall of China. Our traffic dropped precipitously.

The TGIF of January 15, 2010, was dominated by discussion of the Chinese issue. Sergey and the security team presented in great detail what had happened, and reviewed the process by which the management team had made its decision. But before he could even get started, Googlers gave the entire senior team a long and thunderous standing

ovation. The response from employees in China was of course very different. They feared for their jobs and even their security. Head of Engineering Alan Eustace, along with several dedicated team members in China, was instrumental in steering morale back on track, ensuring that the China team remained safe, engaged, and successful throughout that turbulent time. As a result, the legacy of the China decision was a giant dose of goodwill from Googlers around the world, and the legacy of the thoughtful process by which it was made was the reaffirmation of a set of principles governing how all tough decisions should be made.

Decide with data

One of the most transformative developments of the Internet Century is the ability to quantify almost any aspect of business. Decisions once based on subjective opinion and anecdotal evidence now rely primarily on data. Companies like ours aggregate anonymous signals from mobile phones to provide accurate traffic data in real time. London's water pipes are monitored by thousands of sensors, reducing leakage by 25 percent.[119] Ranchers embed sensors into their cattle that transmit information about the animals' health and location; each cow transmits about 200 megabytes of data per year,[120] allowing ranchers to fine-tune what, when, and how much they feed their cattle. That's a cattle list for change!

John Dewey, an American philosopher and writer, said that "a problem well put is half solved."[121] In Dewey's time, which spanned

---

119. Roman Friedrich, Matthew Le Merle, Alex Koster, and Michael Peterson, "The Next Wave of Digitization: Setting Your Direction, Building Your Capabilities" (Booz and Company, June 28, 2011).

120. See Dave Evans, "The Internet of Things" (Cisco Internet Business Solutions Group, April 2011).

121. Apparently, this was already a familiar saying in Dewey's day. See Larry A. Hickman, *The Essential Dewey, Volume 2: Ethics, Logic, Psychology* (Indiana University Press, 1998), page 173.

the latter half of the nineteenth century and first half of the twentieth, putting a problem well would usually entail an opinion and an anecdote. But as Berkeley political science professor Raymond Wolfinger once observed, "the plural of anecdote is data,"[122] which means, by our interpretation, that if you don't have data, you can't decide. (Wolfinger went on to note that the singular of data is datum, then dismissed class early because he had a date.)

This is why most conference rooms at Google have two projectors. One of them is for videoconferencing with other offices or for projecting meeting notes. The other is for data. When discussing options and opinions, we start the meetings with data. We don't seek to convince by saying "I think." We convince by saying "Let me show you."

A bias toward data is a great way to kill the death-by-PowerPoint syndrome. How many meetings have you been in where the first dozen or so slides are full of words, and the person stands up there and repeats the words? People who are presenting a point of view in a meeting shouldn't need the crutch of slides to present that argument, only to support it. Slides should not be used to run a meeting or argue a point. They should just contain the data, so that everyone has the same facts. If the data is wrong or not relevant, you can't fix it with fancy slides. Edward Tufte, the uber-guru of data presentation and visualization, advocates putting more data on fewer slides: "Visual reasoning usually works more effectively when relevant information is shown side by side. Often, the more intense the detail, the greater the clarity and understanding."[123]

It should go without saying—but it usually doesn't, so we'll say it—that data is best understood by those closest to the issue, which is often not management. As a leader, it is best not to get lost in details

---

122. Wolfinger made this comment during a seminar he was teaching at Stanford in 1969 or 1970. It was a rejoinder to a student who had dismissed a factual, data-based statement as being mere anecdote. See Nelson W. Polsby, "Where Do You Get Your Ideas?" (*PS: Political Science and Politics*, Volume 26, Number 1, March 1993).

123. Edward Tufte, "PowerPoint Is Evil" (*Wired*, September 2003).

you don't understand, but rather trust the smart people who work for you to understand them. When making financial decisions, for example, don't worry about the ABCs of the MBAs' and CPAs' EBIT-DAs, ADRs, and RPMs; focus on what matters, which is usually cash and revenue. (A frequent Eric aphorism during financial discussions: "Revenue solves all known problems.") This applies to technical and product decisions as well. Eric was once in a meeting with the CEO of one of Google's partners. The executives were debating some technical issues, and doing a rather poor job of it. So a young Googler who had been listening from the corner stepped up and presented several data points to clarify Google's position. In a meeting crowded with impressive titles, this young woman with the least seniority was obviously the best-informed person in the room. She ultimately carried the day simply by having the best grasp of the facts.

Beware the bobblehead yes

You may be familiar with the bobblehead dolls baseball teams often give away at games—Jonathan has a bobblehead of San Francisco Giants catcher Buster Posey[124] in his office. But you may not know that bobbleheads are also prevalent in conference rooms, where they sit around a table nodding their heads in almost rhythmic unison. Tim Armstrong, AOL CEO and former Googler, dubbed this phenomenon the "bobblehead yes." (When Eric was CEO at Novell, he gave it his own name: the "Novell nod.") Bobblehead yessers are different from your classic "yes-men" because, unlike them, bobbleheads have a nasty tendency to complain and whine and not do or support the very thing to which they just agreed as soon as they walk out of the meeting. This is something bobblehead Buster Posey would never do.

Getting everyone to say yes in a meeting doesn't mean you have

---

124. Buster plays catcher for the San Francisco Giants baseball team and was the National League Most Valuable Player in 2012.

agreement, it means you have a bunch of bobbleheads. Many leaders strive for "consensus-driven" decisions, but they fundamentally misunderstand the meaning of consensus. For those of you who skipped Latin, it stems from the Latin *cum*, meaning "together with," and *sentire*, meaning "to think or feel," so it literally means "to think or feel together." Note that this implies nothing about unanimity; consensus is not about getting everyone to agree. Instead, it's about coming to the best idea for the company and rallying around it.

Reaching this best idea requires conflict. People need to disagree and debate their points in an open environment, because you won't get buy-in until *all* the choices are debated openly. They'll bobblehead nod, then leave the room and do what they want to do. So to achieve true consensus, you need dissent. If you are in charge, do not state your position at the outset of the process. The job is to make sure everyone's voice is heard, regardless of their functional role, which is harder to achieve when the top dog puts a stake in the ground.

As General Patton famously said, "If everyone is thinking alike, then somebody isn't thinking."[125] If you've hired well, there's good news: There is dissension in the ranks. Lots of people are thinking. Smart creatives, especially at the most senior leadership level, should and usually do think of themselves as owners of the business, rather than leaders of just their particular area. Therefore they should have opinions, and quite possibly valuable insights, even about decisions that fall outside their realm. Encourage this, since it helps build a stronger bond among the team and stronger support for the ultimate decision.

Using data can be helpful to get everyone to weigh in, since it's not personal.[126] Be especially aware of the quiet people; call on the ones

---

125. Although this quote is commonly attributed to Patton, we couldn't find any direct proof of his actually saying it, at least not from his memoir *War As I Knew It* or from his famous speech to the Third Army. But the Internet says he did, so it must be true (that's a joke).

126. See Kathleen M. Eisenhardt, Jean L. Kahwajy, and L. J. Bourgeois III, "How Management Teams Can Have a Good Fight" (*Harvard Business Review*, July–August 1997).

who haven't spoken up yet. They may be dissenters who are afraid to disagree with you in public (but need to get over that fear), or they may be of the shy but brilliant type. Or perhaps they truly have nothing to say, in which case maybe they shouldn't be at the meeting in the first place. One technique is to throw out a few "stupid softballs" that let people dip their toe in the water of disagreeing with the boss. ("I think we should all pour hydrochloric acid on ourselves. Thoughts?") Do your best to surface all potential dissent early in the process; there is a natural (and valid) bias toward rejecting dissent the later it surfaces in the decision-making process.[127]

Once everyone weighs in with an opinion, then the argument will be on, and everyone can participate in the decision-making process and have their voice be heard. A proper consensus-driven process has elements of inclusion (involving all the stakeholders in a participatory manner); cooperation (aiming for the best decision for the group, sometimes at the expense of a minority or individual); and equality (everyone on the team counts and can at least temporarily engage in blocking behavior). Above all it is solution-oriented: The right decision is the best decision, not the lowest common denominator decision upon which everyone agrees. And it's not always *your* solution. As Coach Wooden once said, "Be interested in finding the best way, not in having your own way."[128]

These researchers, who studied executives making group decisions, write: "Some managers believe that working with too much data will increase interpersonal conflict by expanding the range of issues for debate. We found that more information is better—if the data are objective and up-to-date—because it encourages people to focus on issues, not personalities.... There is a direct link between reliance on facts and low levels of interpersonal conflict."

127. See Arie W. Kruglanski and Donna M. Webster, "Group Members' Reactions to Opinion Deviates and Conformists at Varying Degrees of Proximity to Decision Deadline and of Environmental Noise" (*Journal of Personality and Social Psychology*, Volume 61, Number 2, August 1991).

128. John Wooden and Steve Jamison, *Wooden on Leadership* (McGraw-Hill, 2005), page 2.

Know when to ring the bell

This conflict-based approach works only if it is managed by a single decision-maker who owns the deadline and will break a tie. Often there is too much data, or the data is inconclusive. When that happens, people can debate for hours, a time sink that often ends in mediocre compromise and always incurs a hefty opportunity cost, since there are *always* better things for smart creatives to be doing than rehashing a decision for the umpteenth time. There is a point at which more analysis won't lead to a better decision. This is the most important duty of the decision-maker: Set a deadline, run the process, and then enforce the deadline. It's like the kids on the playground at recess; they will play forever, but when the bell rings they know they have to wrap it up and head back to class. (Hopefully employees are better behaved and less prone to hogging the monkey bars.) The decision-maker gets to decide how long recess lasts, then ring the bell.[129]

Our coach and mentor Bill Campbell told us a story of how he had just joined Intuit as its CEO when he heard of an important product decision that had stalled. The executive in charge of the product had gathered plenty of data, but the numbers were inconclusive. So he ordered up more research. Then, when the new set of data was still not helpful, he ponied up for yet another feeding at the data trough. Bill got wind of this and ordered a stop to the dillydallying. "Do *something*," he told the executive, "even if it's wrong."

Tom Peters would call Bill's attitude in this situation a "bias for action," and his book *In Search of Excellence* lists it as a top common

---

129. Just the act of setting a deadline can help a team pace itself and reach a decision in a timely manner. See Connie J. G. Gersick, "Marking Time: Predictable Transitions in Task Groups" (*Academy of Management Journal*, June 1989). And Kathleen Eisenhardt, who has long studied decision-making in technology companies, finds that executive teams that make fast decisions actually consider more, not fewer, options. See Kathleen M. Eisenhardt, "Making Fast Strategic Decisions in High-Velocity Environments" (*Academy of Management Journal*, Volume 32, Number 3, September 1989).

attribute of the companies he studied.[130] Many designers also believe a bias for action is a positive force, nothing short of "a core . . . mindset of design thinking," according to the Stanford design school (aka the d.school, because "design school" isn't designy enough).[131] It promotes a hands-on, trial-and-error approach: If you're not sure if a course of action is right, the best thing you can do is try it out and then correct course.[132]

But some behavioral economists believe that a bias for action can be deleterious, since it can favor hasty, poorly thought-out decisions, and in some situations we agree. In a negotiation, for example, Eric's "PIA" rule can help get the best outcome: Have patience, information, and alternatives. P is especially important. You want to wait as long as possible before committing to a course of action. This is true in fields beyond business too (or should we say "pitches"): Soccer goalies who are facing penalty kicks can double their save rate by simply doing nothing at the moment the shooter kicks the ball, rather than following the common bias-for-action practice of guessing in advance to which side the kick will go and diving in that direction.[133] In that way, goalies could learn from pilots, who are trained not to act instantly in emergencies but to take a moment to assess the situation before deciding what to do.

---

130. See Thomas J. Peters and Robert H. Waterman Jr., *In Search of Excellence: Lessons from America's Best-Run Companies* (Harper & Row, 1982).

131. The school is officially called the Institute of Design at Stanford.

132. See Ingo Rauth, Eva Köppen, Birgit Jobst, and Christoph Meinel, "Design Thinking: An Educational Model Towards Creative Confidence" (*Proceedings of the 1st International Conference on Design Creativity*, 2010).

133. If a penalty kicker assumes that the bias-for-action goalie is going to leap in one direction or another at the moment the ball is kicked, she can just kick it in the middle, which is an easy shot to make. See Michael Bar-Eli, Ofer H. Azar, Ilana Ritov, Yael Keidar-Levin, and Galit Schein, "Action Bias Among Elite Soccer Goalkeepers: The Case of Penalty Kicks" (*Journal of Economic Psychology*, October 2007). For a discussion of the similarity between this case of action bias and action bias in investment decisions, see Carl Richards, "In Soccer and Investing, Bias Is Toward Action" (*Bucks* blog, *New York Times*, May 13, 2013).

The job of the decision-maker, then, is to get the timing just right. Exhibit a bias for action, to cut off debate and analysis that is no longer valuable, and start moving the team to rally around the decision. But don't be a slave to a sense of urgency. Maintain flexibility until the last possible moment.

Make fewer decisions

When Eric joined Google, he was well aware of the not-so-good history of CEOs being hired by founders into their companies. Typically, the founder hires the CEO, eventually they disagree on something fundamental, the board backs one of them, and the other leaves. Steve Jobs's hiring of John Sculley, a Pepsi executive, to succeed him as CEO at Apple in 1983 is the classic example. The two clashed and Sculley (backed by the board) fired Steve in 1985.[134]

To avoid a similar fate when he joined Google, Eric decided he would let Larry and Sergey do what they did best and he would focus more on the stuff needed to build the company at such an incredible pace, so it could continue to operate effectively and efficiently. The scenario of having a ruling triumvirate was so unique that Larry and Sergey described it in some detail in the letter that accompanied Google's IPO in 2004. In fact, codifying the who-does-what working process of the trio was very helpful. The letter stated that Eric "focuses on management of our vice presidents and the sales organization. Sergey focuses on engineering and business deals. [Larry focuses] on engineering and product management," and that the three leaders were meeting daily (which continued throughout most of Eric's stint

---

134. Speaking at a conference in 2013, Sculley reflected on the decision to fire Jobs: "I did not have the breadth of experience at that time to really appreciate just how different leadership is when you are shaping an industry, as Bill Gates did or Steve Jobs did, versus when you're a competitor in an industry, in a public company, where you don't make mistakes because if you lose, you're out...My sense is that there could have been a different outcome." See Daniel Terdiman, "John Sculley Spills the Beans on Firing Steve Jobs" (CNET, September 9, 2013).

as CEO). Most important, it said that the arrangement "works because we have tremendous trust and respect for each other and we generally think alike."

This all worked very well as long as the three agreed on key issues, which was most of the time. But it did occasionally lead to some difficult situations; when you have three strong-willed leaders, they will sometimes disagree. When that occurred, Eric's process to get to a good resolution was similar to his general decision-making process: Identify the issue, have the argument (alone, just the three of them), and set a deadline. And he often added a corollary: Let the founders decide.

The tendency of a CEO, and particularly (speaking from experience) of a new CEO trying to make an impact in a founder-led company, is to try to make too big an impact. It is hard to check that CEO ego at the door and let others make decisions, but that is precisely what needs to be done. In general, when you are CEO you should actually make very few decisions. Product launches, acquisitions, public policy issues—these are all decisions that CEOs should make or heavily influence. But there are many other issues where it is OK to let other leaders in the company decide, and intervene only when you know they are making a very bad call. So a key skill to develop as the CEO or senior leader in a company is to know which decisions to make and which to let run their course without you.

This skill is even more important when you find yourself in the situation Eric did, running a company in the presence of two very active, respected, smart founders. For example, there was one product review meeting where Eric, Sergey, and Larry ended up disagreeing about a key feature of a new product. There were about twenty people in the meeting, and after a few minutes Eric suspended the argument and then resumed it later that afternoon with just the three of them. It was there he discovered that the two founders not only disagreed with him, but with each other as well. So Eric said fine, he would let the two of them decide, but they had to decide by the next day. When he dropped by the office they shared in building 43 the next day at noon, he asked them, "Which one of you won?" And the response was typical: "Actually, we came up with a new idea." It turned out to be the best solution, and the decision was made.

Meet every day

One of the frustrating aspects of being a leader of smart creatives is how little power you actually have. Look at this chapter so far. Even if you are the CEO of a company, it says, you can't just pound your fist on a table and dictate decisions (well, you can, but if that's your modus operandi you will quickly lose most of your smart creatives), and in fact you shouldn't even make many decisions. Instead, you have to analyze data and orchestrate consensus by encouraging debate and then knowing, through some divine skill, exactly the right time to cut off that debate and make the decision. Sort of makes you yearn for those days a long time ago, when Darth Vader could unilaterally crush someone's throat with the power of the Force and then destroy a planet.

But there is one thing that leaders can still control, and that is the company's calendar. When faced with a critical decision, there is real signaling value in using your convening power as a leader to hold regular meetings. If the decision is important enough, the meetings should be daily. Scheduling meetings with this frequency lets everyone know the importance of the decision at hand. And there is another simple benefit: When you have daily meetings, you spend less time in each meeting rehashing things that were discussed at the previous meeting, since everyone's memory is still fresh. That leaves more time to consider new data or opinions.

Eric used this approach to good effect in 2002, when Google was negotiating a deal with AOL to be the popular portal's search and ads engine. It was a difficult negotiation, and Eric was particularly concerned about the financial commitment Google was potentially taking on. AOL had a number of advertisers on their platform that were not as yet advertising with Google, so the deal had tremendous strategic value: It would bring those advertisers to our platform. Nevertheless, Eric felt the commitment was too big for a small company like ours to take.

Omid Kordestani, our head of sales, led the negotiations with AOL, which had merged with Time Warner in early 2001 and was eager for the revenue this deal would bring it. Omid agreed with Eric that we shouldn't accept AOL's terms. But Larry and Sergey wanted to take the risk; they had always felt that being aggressively generous with partners on revenue share would ultimately benefit the company ("If it doesn't bankrupt us first," Eric thought when they expressed this point). David Drummond, the company's lead attorney, agreed with them, as did the board of directors, who felt we could always borrow to cover any cash shortfalls. There was an honest disagreement, and the team wasn't making a lot of progress in its meetings. So Eric acted. He set up even more meetings, and he set a deadline. For the next six weeks, the team would get together every day at four p.m. to review the AOL deal. By the end of that time period, they would come to a decision and conclude the negotiations with AOL, one way or another.

At first they didn't make much progress. But the sheer drudgery of repeating the same argument every day helped spur the team to delve even deeper into the data we had on how our ads engine was performing, and over the weeks we performed analyses that demonstrated that the deal wasn't as risky as we had originally thought. We started to realize that we could afford it, and we were right. We did the deal, basically on AOL's terms, and our performance exceeded all of the guarantees. But no one knew this at the time we were in negotiations; we got to the right answer through a rigorous, time-intensive process of considering all the details. It was a critical decision, and when you are considering something that is fundamental to the existence of the company, you should meet every day.

"You're both right"

There is a mistake technical and scientific people make. We think that if we have made a clever and thoughtful argument, based on data and smart analysis, then people will change their minds. This isn't true. If you want to change people's behavior, you need to touch their hearts, not just win the argument. We call this the Oprah Winfrey rule. (It's also the way that good politicians operate, but Oprah does it better than anyone.)[135] When companies are run by smart creatives and product people, they need to learn the Oprah rule. Otherwise they are apt to make smart decisions, but to fail to execute them well.

There is a simple trick to getting this right. When ending a debate and making a decision that doesn't have 100 percent support, remember these three words: "You're both right." To emotionally commit to a decision with which they don't agree, people have to know that their opinion was not only heard, but valued. "You're both right" accomplishes this. It tells the person whose argument lost that there are elements of truth amidst the rubble of their failed position. It provides an emotional boost—people like hearing that they are right. And fortunately, it is often true, since in a group of smart creatives there are usually elements of truth in everyone's position. It's rare for a good person to be completely, 100 percent wrong.

Then, after reassuring the argument's losers and articulating what needs to be done, the decision-maker must ensure that everyone who was involved does one of two things: disagree but commit, or escalate *publicly*. If it's the latter, then the escalator must let the decision-maker know the reasons for her objections, and how and to

---

135. Credit for this rule really belongs to Aristotle, whose discussion of appeals to logos (argument), ethos (character), and pathos (emotion) influenced countless politicians, trial lawyers, and salespeople. See translation by George A. Kennedy, *On Rhetoric: A Theory of Civic Discourse* (Oxford University Press, 1991), pages 37–38. It is Oprah, though, who models this truth in every TV appearance she makes and each commencement address she delivers. "You have to tell the story so that people feel something," she's said. "They only want to do something after they feel something." See "Oprah Winfrey Talks to Dan Pink, Part 2" (YouTube.com/watch?v=kRfT8ujRfOA).

which higher-up she plans to escalate. ("I'm sorry, I still don't think this is the right decision because of. . . . How about we see what Barack thinks?") Public escalation is a valid option and should be encouraged, because if you don't it will just happen anyway, only with a lot more rancor.

Every meeting needs an owner

The forum for decision-making is almost always a meeting, which may be the most hated of all business practices, except for Secret Santa. People complain about meetings and how they are a great waste of time, but in fact a *well-run* meeting is a great thing. It's the most efficient way to present data and opinions, to debate issues, and yes, to actually make decisions. Note the italics on well-run though, since most meetings are anything but. A badly run meeting—we probably don't need to tell you this—is a giant, demoralizing time waster.

Computer scientists hate inefficiency, so over the years Eric's team developed a series of rules for meetings that we found to be quite effective:

Meetings should have a single decision-maker/owner. There must be a clear decision-maker at every point in the process, someone whose butt is on the line. A meeting between two groups of equals often doesn't result in a good outcome, because you end up compromising rather than making the best tough decisions. Include someone more senior as the decision-maker.

The decision-maker should be hands on. He or she should call the meeting, ensure that the content is good, set the objectives, determine the participants, and share the agenda (if possible) at least twenty-four hours in advance. After the meeting, the decision-maker (and no one else) should summarize decisions taken and action items by email to at least every participant—as well as any others who need to know—within forty-eight hours.

Even if a meeting is not a decision-making meeting—for example it's designed to share information or brainstorm solutions—it should have a clear owner. Again, that owner should ensure that the right people are invited to the meeting, that there's a clear agenda, that the necessary prep work has been done in advance, and that action items are circulated promptly.

Meetings are not like government agencies—they should be easy to kill. Any meeting should have a purpose, and if that purpose isn't well defined or if the meeting fails to achieve that purpose, maybe the meeting should go away. The decision-maker needs to ask the hard questions: Is the meeting still useful? Is it too frequent / not frequent enough? Do people get the information they need?

Meetings should be manageable in size. No more then eight people, ten at a stretch (but we would seriously discourage this). Everyone in the room should be able to give their input. If more people need to know the result of the meeting, make sure you have a process for communicating it rather than bringing them in as observers, which lowers the quality of the meeting and people's ability to talk openly.

Attendance at meetings is not a badge of importance. If you aren't needed, leave, or better yet, excuse yourself ahead of time. This is especially true of meetings with customers or partners. Many times we have walked into an "intimate" meeting with a senior executive from one of our customers or partners, only to find the room full of people. We can't help it if customers feel the need to bring their entire org chart to the meeting, but we try to control our side. Fewer people is almost always better.

Timekeeping matters. Begin meetings on time. End them on time. Leave enough time at the end to summarize findings and action items. If the meeting has accomplished its goal before its allotted time runs out, then end it early. Remember, we are human: Schedule time for lunch and bio breaks, and be respectful of employees working in different time zones. They like to spend time with their families too. These common courtesies get forgotten too often. Paying attention to them will earn the respect of employees and colleagues.

If you attend a meeting, attend the meeting. Multitasking doesn't work. If you are in a meeting and using your laptop or phone for something not related to the meeting, it's obvious your time is better spent elsewhere. Everyone attending a meeting should focus on the meeting, not other work. And if people have so many meetings that they can't get work done, then there is a simple solution: Prioritize and go to fewer meetings.

Among all of these rules, this last one has been the most challenging for us to implement. In our own team meetings, people so often ignored our edicts to close their laptops that we had to give up. But it's still a good rule!

Horseback law

Lawyers are, by training, backward looking. This makes sense, since so much of the law is determined by precedent: What happened before dictates what is OK going forward. They are also highly risk-averse. This also makes sense, because so many business lawyers practice in law firms and the job of a corporate law firm is to keep its clients out of trouble. So when you ask most lawyers to assess a situation, and if that situation is 99 percent good and 1 percent questionable, they will spend most of their time with you reviewing the questionable.

This sign is a good example. Jonathan snapped a picture of it one day when he walked across the street to check out the athletic fields that Google had just opened. The sign includes a nice map of the fields, but a quarter of its space is taken up by a legal disclaimer that basically says if you get hurt using these fields, don't sue us. (Some lawyer reading this is about to correct our interpretation of the carefully worded legal phrasing. Please stop.) A well-meaning, backward-looking, risk-averse lawyer decided that even though the Googlers using the fields are intelligent grown-ups, there was still an infinitesimal chance that one of them would step on the field, twist an ankle, and sue Google. Hence, yet more brain-dead obvious legalese clouding our landscape.

Lawyers can be smart creatives too, which is why we were so surprised to see this sign at Google. The backward-looking, risk-averse approach to the law, which is so common in corporate America, doesn't work in the Internet Century, when business evolves at a pace that is several orders of magnitude faster than the pace of legal change. A smart creative–fueled business that is trying to innovate will be lucky to be right 50 percent of the time, which can be a problem for a lawyer whose risk tolerance is in the single digits.

This is why, when they were building Google's legal department, David Drummond and his colleagues Kulpreet Rana and Miriam Rivera set out to create an environment where lawyers approached their jobs differently. Our current general counsel, Kent Walker, likes to call this approach "horseback law." Take a look at any old Western movie (we like *Butch Cassidy and the Sundance Kid*; Eric is Butch because thinkin' is what he's good at, and Jonathan is Sundance because he's fast on the draw—but unfortunately not as accurate as the Redford-played bank robber). There is always the scene where a cowboy rides up on his horse and comes to a stop, surveying the situation and deciding what to do next. Kent advises his lawyers to do something similar: In certain situations, it's often enough to ride up on a horse (figuratively speaking, usually), make a quick assessment, then mosey on. While many decisions (e.g., a major acquisition, a legal compliance question) may call for detailed analysis, don't feel that you always have to dismount and spend weeks writing a fifty-page legal brief (ha!) of all the things that could possibly go wrong and what would happen if they did. In the early stages of a new project, the analysis won't be 100 percent correct anyway. In those situations, it isn't the lawyer's job to cover every possible angle in detail; it's his job to look into an unforeseeable future and provide educated, quick guidance to the business leaders making the decisions. Then saddle back up, pardner.

Horseback law works only if the lawyer is an integral part of the business and product teams, rather than just summoned occasionally. It works only with the right mixture of lawyers, which is why, in our early days, we tried to hire more generalists than specialists and spread our recruiting efforts across firms, businesses, and even nonprofits (but we rarely hired lawyers straight out of school). And since legal issues are bound to crop up when you are moving quickly and changing industries, it always helps to be doing the right thing by consumers and customers.

Spend 80 percent of your time on 80 percent of your revenue

One of the most important decisions any business leader makes is how to spend his or her time. When Eric became CEO of Novell in 1997, he got some great advice from Bill Gates: Spend 80 percent of your time on 80 percent of your revenue. But this rule can be deceptively hard to actually follow. At Novell, the company's core business was the NetWare software suite, which enabled local area networking between PCs and workstations. Eric and his staff, though, were excited about growing a new product (NetWare Directory Services, or NDS) that provided a central point of management and access to network resources ranging from people and groups to printers and workstations. NDS clearly had big growth potential as networks proliferated, and it was hard for Eric and the team to resist spending more time on it.

Leadership teams often underestimate how long it takes for revenue from a new product area to ramp up. That shiny new stuff can be much more interesting than the boring old core business stuff, but it's the core stuff that pays the bills, and if you make a mistake there, you probably won't be able to recover. Even though Eric thought he was heeding Bill's advice, in retrospect he should have been spending more time on NetWare.

You have to focus on your core business. You have to love it.

Have a succession plan

Loving a business means having a plan for leaving it, but leaders often neglect to think about who will succeed them. In most companies, your successor is already there, you just haven't figured out who it is. (Eric's experience, where his successor was the person who hired him, is rare!) Many companies get the idea right, but their timing is off:

They identify the brother, someone ready to take over in the next few years, whereas they should be looking for the son, someone who could take over in a decade. Or they try to lock in the hundred most senior people in the company, not the hundred with the highest potential. The right approach is to look for the outstanding smart creatives who are already progressing rapidly through the ranks. Ask the question, Could one of these people be running the company in ten years? When the answer is yes, give them a lot of compensation and make sure their career doesn't bog down. Losing these high-potential employees (especially to competitors) is very costly to the company, so be proactive and aggressive in your efforts to keep them happy. It may not always work out, but the benefits of the successes far outweigh the misses.

Then there's the interesting experience of actually executing the succession plan. Those rising superstars tend to get smarter with the passage of time, but the generation at the top still looks at them as brash and inexperienced, and certainly not wise enough to take over. The solution for this is for the leader to remember what he was like back in the day.

When Google was preparing for its IPO, Eric, Larry, and Sergey made a commitment to each other that the three of them would work together for at least the next twenty years. Eric had always assumed that either Larry or Sergey would end up running the company—probably Larry, as he had previously been CEO. It was just a question of when. That time came in early 2011, when Eric, Larry, and Sergey decided that Larry would resume as Google's CEO. It was the right decision for the company and the trio, but still, Eric was a little uncertain. After all, he was so much older and wiser! But then Eric mapped his age onto Larry's: At the time, Larry was nearly thirty-eight years old, and when Eric was that age he felt he was ready to run a company (he was forty-one when he took over the reins at Novell). It was a bit of a surprise, but by following this thought process Eric realized that Larry was quite ready, and would be very successful as Google's CEO.

The World's Best Athletes Need Coaches,
and You Don't?

In the summer of 2002, when Eric had been on the job as Google CEO for about a year, he wrote a self-review of his performance and shared it with his team. The document included highlights ("developed proper business processes"), objectives for the next year ("run the clock faster without compromising the future"), and areas where he could have performed better. The last category included several points, but one self-critique stands out as the most important:

Bill Campbell has been very helpful in coaching all of us. In hindsight, his role was needed from the beginning. I should have encouraged this structure sooner, ideally the moment I started at Google.

This was a 180-degree turnaround from a year earlier: When Eric started at Google, board member John Doerr suggested that he work with Bill as his coach. Eric's reply? "I don't need a coach. I know what I'm doing."

Whenever you watch a world-class athlete perform, you can be sure that there is a great coach behind her success. It's not that the coach is better at playing the sport than the player, in fact that is almost never the case. But the coaches have a different skill: They can observe players in action and tell them how to be better. So why is it that in the business world coaches are so unusual? Are we all like Eric when he started at Google, so confident of ourselves that we can't imagine someone helping us to be better? If so, this is a fallacy. As a business leader, you need a coach.

The first ingredient of a successful coaching relationship is a student who is willing to listen and learn. Just like there are hard-to-coach athletes, there are hard-to-coach executives. But once they get past that initial reticence, they find there are always things to learn. Business coaches, like all coaches, are at heart teachers, and Bill Campbell, the best coach around, tells us he believes that management is a skill that is completely learnable.

For Jonathan, class began right around the time when Larry Page was calling the regimented product plan that he created "stupid." The following week, Jonathan was sitting in Coach Campbell's office, wondering why he had ever joined this chaotic start-up and contemplating quitting. Don't quit, Bill implored him. Stick it out. Maybe you'll even learn something.

For that, and everything else you have done for us, thank you, Coach.

Communications—Be a Damn Good Router

At one point early in his career at Google, Jonathan was in a conversation with one of our engineers, who wondered about Jonathan's propensity to respond to emails immediately and route his replies to so many Googlers. The engineer was frustrated with what he saw as Jonathan's misplaced priorities—obviously someone so responsive to email and so prolific at spreading information must not be busy enough. So he told Jonathan, in a fit of pique, "You're just an expensive router!" This was meant as an insult, since a router is a fairly basic networking device whose main job is to move packets of data from one point to another. Jonathan took the barb as a compliment.

Here's a way to think about corporate communications: Picture a twenty-story building. You are on a middle floor, say the tenth, standing on a balcony. The number of people on each floor decreases as you go up. The top floor is occupied by just one person, while the bottom floor, aka the "entry level," has hordes of people. Now imagine you are standing out on a balcony when the person above you—let's call her your "boss"—yells something and drops a few documents. You catch them, being careful not to let them flutter away in the wind, and take them back inside to read. There's some good stuff in there, and you carefully parse out a few bits that you think the people on the ninth floor should see, given the carefully pre-scripted boundaries of their jobs. So you go back out to the balcony and drop a sheet here and a paragraph there to your team below, who consume them as if they were the proverbial cold waters to a thirsty soul.[136] When they're done, they turn around and perform their own parsing ritual for the benefit of the thirsty people on eight. Meanwhile, up on eleven, your boss is starting the process all over again. And up on twenty...well, who knows what that guy's doing.

This is the traditional model of information flow in most companies. The upper echelons of management gather information and carefully decide which bits to distribute to those that toil beneath them. In this world, information is hoarded as a means of control and power. As the leadership scholars James O'Toole and Warren Bennis note, many businesspeople who rise to positions of power often get there "not for their demonstrated teamwork but for their ability to compete successfully against their colleagues in the executive suite, which only encourages the hoarding of information."[137] We are reminded of the Communist apparatchiks of the Soviet Union, who kept all office copiers behind double-locked, steel-plated doors lest someone use the wonders of xerography to create an unauthorized copy of the five-year plan for grain production.[138] Most managers still think like those Soviet-era bureaucrats: Their job is to parse information and distribute it sparingly, because obviously you can't trust those young rabble-rousers on the lower floors with the information keys to the company's kingdom.

But the Soviet Union collapsed, and while such a parsimonious approach to spreading information may have been successful when people were hired to *work*, in the Internet Century you hire people to

---

136. Literally proverbial, as in Proverbs 25:25: "As cold waters to a thirstie soule: so is good newes from a farre countrey." See *The Holy Bible: King James Version*, Quatercentenary edition (Oxford University Press, 2010), page 38.

137. James O'Toole and Warren Bennis, "What's Needed Next: A Culture of Candor" (*Harvard Business Review*, June 2009).

138. Michael Parks, "Soviets Free the Dreaded Photocopier" (*Los Angeles Times*, October 5, 1989).

think. When Jonathan was in business school, one of his finance professors used to say that "money is the lifeblood of any company." This is only partially true. In the Internet Century money is obviously critical, but information is the true lifeblood of the business. Attracting smart creatives and leading them to do amazing things is the key to building a twenty-first-century business, but none of that happens if they aren't flush with information.

The most effective leaders today don't hoard information, they share it. (Bill Gates in 1999: "Power comes not from knowledge kept but from knowledge shared. A company's values and reward system should reflect that idea.")[139] Leadership's purpose is to optimize the flow of information throughout the company, all the time, every day. This is an entirely different skill set.

As Jonathan told that engineer on that day several years ago, "If all I am is a very expensive router, I intend to be a damn good one." What does that entail? Default to open, set challenging public goals and regularly fail to achieve them, and when in doubt, talk about your travels.

Default to open

Your default mode should be to share everything. Case in point: the Google board report. When Eric was CEO, he started a process that continues today. Every quarter the team creates an in-depth report on the state of the business, to be presented to the board. There is a written section—the board letter—which is crammed with data and insights on the business and the products, and slides with data and charts that the product leads (the senior executives in charge of the various product areas, including Search, Ads, YouTube, Android, and so on) use to guide the board meeting. Not surprisingly, much of this information is not for public consumption. But after the board meeting we do something that *is* surprising. We take the material that we presented to our

---

139. Bill Gates, "Bill Gates' New Rules" (*TIME*, April 19, 1999).

board and share it with all of our employees. Eric presents the slides—the exact same slides that were presented to the board—to a company-wide meeting, and the entire board letter goes out in a Google-wide email.

Fine, Mr. Technicality, not the *entire* letter. Since it contains some data that shouldn't be shared with everyone for legal reasons, we need to send the lawyers, along with a few communications folks, traipsing through the text to find and redact the legal landmines. This is where the "share everything" rubber hits the "but you can't possibly mean *everything*, can you?" road. Every quarter, well-meaning and other-wise Googley Googlers highlight sentences and paragraphs with the red marker of death (digitally, of course—no paper was inked in the evisceration of this letter). "We can't put that in the letter," they say. "What if it leaks? It would cause problems." Or "We can't tell employees this, even though it's true and it's what we told the board. It might hurt morale."

Fortunately, the people running this process understand that "share everything" doesn't mean "share everything that wouldn't look bad if it leaked and that doesn't hurt anyone's feelings," it means "share everything except for the very few things that are prohibited by law or regulation." Big difference! This is why we make everyone who wants something to be removed justify exactly why it needs to come out, and the reason better be very good. We have shared our board letter every quarter since the company went public in 2004, and leaks have not been a problem. Meanwhile, nobody complains that they don't know what's going on across the company. Or if they do, we tell them to read the board letter and watch Eric's presentation. And there is an ancillary benefit to sharing the board materials: quality. While people will do a good job in preparing something for the board's consumption, they will do a *great* job if they know that material will be shared with the entire company.

Defaulting to open doesn't just cover board communications. We try to share virtually everything. The company's intranet, Moma, includes information on just about every upcoming product, for example, and the weekly TGIF meeting usually features presentations by product teams of coming attractions, complete with demos and screenshots of cool things that are under development. Attending TGIF would be like scoring a Willy Wonka golden ticket for those legions of bloggers who love to speculate on what Google will be up to next, because we put it all out there, sharing stuff that in most companies would stay carefully hidden. Again, no grainy photos of screenshots or herky-jerky videos of demos are leaked, furtively captured from the back row. We trust our employees with all sorts of vital information, and they honor that trust.[140]

OKRs are another great example of transparency. These are an individual's Objectives (the strategic goals to accomplish) and Key Results (the way in which progress toward that goal is measured). Every employee updates and posts his OKRs company-wide every quarter, making it easy for anyone to quickly find anyone else's priorities. When you meet someone at Google and want to learn more about what they do, you go on Moma and read their OKRs. This isn't just a job title and description of the role, it's their first-person account of the stuff they are working on and care about. It's the fastest way to figure out what motivates them.

Of course, this starts at the top. Every quarter at Google, Larry—like Eric before him—posts his OKRs and hosts a company-wide meeting to discuss them. All the various product and business leads join him onstage to talk through each OKR and what it means for their teams, and to grade themselves on how they performed against the previous quarter's OKRs. This isn't for show—the OKRs are real objectives, hammered out between the various product leaders at the outset of each quarter, and the grades of the previous quarter's OKRs

---

140. We have experienced leaks, but never, to the best of our knowledge, from TGIF. We do our best to track down the source of leaks and have a very high success rate. Frequently leaks come from partners, but when they do come from Googlers, those Googlers get fired.

are usually full of red and yellow marks. The top leaders of the company candidly discuss where they failed and why. (At your company, does the top brass stand up each quarter and talk about the ambitious goals that they *didn't* achieve?) After this meeting, when people go off to create their own OKRs, they have no doubt what the company priorities are for the quarter. This helps maintain alignment across teams even as the organization scales tremendously.

Know the details

John Seely Brown, the former director of Xerox's Palo Alto Research Center, once said, "The essence of being human involves asking questions, not answering them."[141] Eric likes to put this concept to the test when he walks the halls of Google or of the other companies with which he's involved. When he runs into an exec he hasn't seen in a while, the pleasantries don't last long. After a cordial hello he'll get to the point: "What's going on in your job? What issues do you have? Tell me about that deliverable you owe me." This has a couple of results: It helps Eric keep on top of the details of his business, and it helps him know which of his executives are on top of the details of *their* business. If someone is in charge of a business and can't rattle off the key issues she faces in a matter of ten seconds, then she's not up to the job. A hands-off approach to leadership doesn't cut it anymore. You need to know the details.

Eric tends to remember everything and knows the deliverables people owe him, so the approach works well for him. Jonathan's not quite in Eric's league memory-wise, so he keeps the things that people owe him in the notes field of their contact on his phone. Then, if he

141. Quoted in John Markoff, "A Fight to Win the Future: Computers vs. Humans" (*New York Times*, February 14, 2011). Brown made this comment to downplay the significance of IBM's artificially intelligent Watson computer taking on human competitors in the game of *Jeopardy!*, the object of which *is* to ask questions. What is ironic?

runs into that person, he takes a moment and brings up the list, so he can query them on their progress.

Even when you ask the right questions, the true details can be hard to get. One day early in Eric's tenure at Google, Larry and Sergey were upset about some problems in engineering and how some of the leaders were handling them. Eric listened to them talk about it for a while, then interjected, "Well, I've talked to them, and I'll tell you what they are doing." He then went on to describe what he believed was happening with that particular team.

Larry listened for a few sentences and then interrupted. "That's not what they're doing. Here's what they're doing." Larry listed some things and Eric quickly realized that Larry was right. Eric had details, but Larry had the truth. The forest always trumps the trees.

How had this happened? Eric was listening to the managers, who were doing their old-school best to control the flow of information upward (the regurgitation and parsing technique works both ways, as any red-blooded middle manager worth his weight in plausible deniability knows full well). But Larry was listening to the engineers—not directly but via a smart little tool he had implemented called "snippets." Snippets are like weekly status reports that cover a person's most important activities for a week, but in a short, pithy format, so they can be written in just a few minutes or compiled (in a doc or draft email) as the week goes on. There is no set format, but a good set of snippets includes the most important activities and achievements of the week and quickly conveys what the person is working on right now, from cryptic ("SMB Framework," "10% list") to mundane ("completed quarterly performance reviews," "started family vacation"). Like OKRs, they are shared with everyone. Snippets are posted on Moma, where anyone can see anyone else's, and for years Larry received a weekly compendium of the snippets from engineering and product leads. That way he always could get at the truth.

Speaking of which...

It must be safe to tell the truth

Jonathan once took a history class in college that he knew was a favorite of the school's football players. When the time came to present his research project for the semester, he remembered that the kids in the class, most of whom actually knew something about history, had been challenged by the instructor to ask difficult questions of their peers, not out of spite but to boost the class-participation portion of their grade. Jonathan did not relish the idea of standing before a bunch of grade-hungry history majors intent on skewering a wayward econ geek, so he devised a plan. He wrote his own questions and distributed them to the football players, who were also eager to improve their class-participation score. The quarterbacks and safeties lobbed their softballs, Jonathan knocked them out of the park, and everyone went home happy (except for you English majors cringing at our mixed sports metaphor).

Sometimes it seems like Jonathan's questionable techniques have found their way to the business world. People are afraid to ask their leaders the tough questions, so they serve up softballs instead. This doesn't just apply to questions. It is one of the most universal of human truths: No one wants to be the bearer of bad news. Yet as a leader it is precisely the bad news that you most need to hear. Good news will be just as good tomorrow, but bad news will be worse. That's why you must make it safe to ask the tough questions and to tell the truth at all times, even when the truth hurts. When you learn of something going off the rails, and the news is delivered in a timely, forthright fashion, this means—in its own, screwed-up way—that the process is working. Canaries are dying in the coal mine, but at least you are aware of the avian carnage and the poor guy who brought their sad yellow corpses up into the light knows he won't be thrown back down the shaft.

There are a few things we can recommend to make it easier to speak bad truth to power. After a product or key feature launches, we ask teams to conduct "postmortem" sessions where everyone gets together to discuss what went right and what went wrong. We then post the findings for everyone to see. The most important result of all these postmortems is the process itself. Never skip a chance to promote open, transparent, honest communications.

Another example is TGIF. The weekly company-wide meeting that Larry and Sergey host has always featured a no-holds-barred Q&A session, but as the company grew, this got harder and harder to manage. So we developed a system called Dory. People who can't (or don't want to) ask a question in person can submit it to Dory (named after the memory-challenged fish in *Finding Nemo*, though, like Dory herself, we can't recall why), and when they do, others get to vote on whether it's a good question or not. The more thumbs-up votes a question receives, the higher it goes in the queue, and the tougher questions tend to get a lot of thumbs-up. At TGIF the Dory queue is put on the screen, so as Larry and Sergey go through the questions they can't cherry-pick which ones they want to answer. They just go down the list, top to bottom, tough questions and easy. Dory lets anyone directly ask the CEO and his team the toughest questions, while the crowdsourcing aspect of it keeps the lame questions to a minimum. Lame answers, on the other hand, are judged in a much lower-tech fashion: TGIF attendees are equipped with red and green paddles and encouraged to wave the red paddles if they don't feel the questions are fully addressed.[142]

Eric calls our approach to transparency a "climb, confess, comply" model. Pilots learn that when they get in trouble, the first step is to climb: Get yourself out of danger. Then, confess: Talk to the tower and explain that you screwed up and how. Finally, comply: When traffic controllers tell you how to do it better next time, do it! So in your venture, when someone comes to you with bad news or a problem, they are in climb, confess, and comply mode. They have spent a lot of time considering the situation, and

---

142. The red and green paddles were originally featured in the movie *The Internship*. After the movie came out we started using them at the real TGIF, and they were so popular that they stayed around for about a year. Then we upgraded to a digital version so folks watching remotely could register their red and green opinions, too.

you need to reward their transparency by listening, helping, and having the confidence that next time around they will nail the landing.

Start the conversation

When the Michael Jackson concert movie, *This Is It*, was first released in October 2009, Jonathan got an idea. Google's main campus in Mountain View is right next to a multiscreen movie theater, so Jonathan bought a bunch of tickets for the day of the premiere and invited the product team to select a viewing time and go. Hundreds of colleagues took him up on the offer. Teams organized outings to see the "King of Pop" at work on what was to be his comeback concert series, before his tragic death wrecked those plans.

Jonathan got some criticism from friends and coworkers—was it really worth the cost and lost productivity just so a bunch of Googlers could go see a movie? The answer was a resounding yes. The movie showed a world-class smart creative pushing his team and himself to be great by paying attention to every detail and always taking the concert audience's point of view. But the more subtle objective of the Michael Jackson outing was that it was a way to start conversations. For months afterward, members of Jonathan's team, from senior leaders to associates right out of college, would stop him by the espresso machine or in the café to thank him for the movie. Jonathan usually asked what they liked about it, and the conversation always took off from there.

Conversation is still the most important and valuable form of communication, but technology and the pace of work often conspire to make it one of the rarest. We are all connected 24/7, anywhere in the world, which is awesome but also tempting: How often have you emailed, chatted, or texted someone who was sitting only a few feet away? Yeah, too often; us too. Sociologists have a name for this phenomenon (as do anthropologists and mixologists): laziness. But in all fairness to tech-happy smart creatives, there is another factor at work, especially at big companies and especially for people who are newer to the company. As much as top executives and other company bigwigs may profess to be willing to talk, the open door works only when people walk through it. It can be hard for people who don't know the organization to start that conversation. As a leader, you need to help them.

Some of our best leaders have taken unusual steps to facilitate. Urs Hölzle wrote and published a "user manual"...about himself. Anyone on his team (which numbers a few thousand) can read the manual and understand the best way to approach him, and how to fix him if he breaks.[143] Marissa Mayer held regular office hours—another cultural characteristic of early Google inspired by academia. Like a university professor, she set aside a few hours per week where anyone could come and talk to her. People signed up on a whiteboard outside her office (which she shared with a couple of other Googlers who usually decamped to other locations during her office hours), and on Wednesday afternoons the nearby couches were full of young product managers with some question or other to discuss.

Most every company has "tribal elders" who possess unique expertise in their field and a deep knowledge of the organization. Some of them are well known within the company, but others may not be, and one of the biggest favors a leader can do for a new smart creative is to connect her with them. At Bell Labs, these savants were often called "the guys who wrote the book," because they had written a definitive book or article on the topic, and new employees were often directed by their supervisors to seek them out.[144] At many companies (universities too), the incorrect, knee-jerk management reaction is to *discourage* employees from connecting with company rock stars. After all, they

---

143. Some of our favorite Urs quotes from the user manual: "I didn't grow up in the US, and I tend to be more direct than others when I talk about something....I tend to overstate points for clarity of argument—it's easier to summarize something in black and white vs in shades of gray....If you think I am wrong, you need to tell me. I'll never blame anyone for speaking up....If you feel I'm beating you up all the time and all you're getting is negative feedback, then it's very likely that this wasn't intentional."

144. Jon Gertner, "True Innovation" (*New York Times*, February 25, 2012). Gertner himself wrote the book on innovation at Bell Labs. See Jon Gertner, *The Idea Factory: Bell Labs and the Great Age of American Innovation* (Penguin, 2012).

might waste their time with stupid questions, right? Yes, that does happen, but it turns out that most rock stars have very little patience for people wasting their time and they make doing so a very unpleasant experience. The inexperienced smart creative who does it once quickly learns not to do it again.

Repetition doesn't spoil the prayer

In most aspects of life, you need to say something about twenty times before it truly starts to sink in.[145] Say it a few times, people are too busy to even notice. A few more times, they start to become aware of a vague buzzing in their ear. By the time you've repeated it fifteen to twenty times *you* may be completely sick of it, but that's about the time people are starting to get it. So as a leader you want to habitually overcommunicate. As Eric likes to say, "Repetition doesn't spoil the prayer," an axiom any Hail Mary–dispensing priest would second (or third, or fiftieth).

But there's a right way to overcommunicate and a wrong way. In the Internet Century, the typical method, especially given the ease of the technology, is to share more stuff with more people. See an interesting article? Cut and paste the link into an email and send it to anyone who may be remotely interested. Yay! You've overcommunicated! You've also wasted hours of people's time. Overcommunication done wrong leads to a careless proliferation of useless information, an avalanche of drivel piling into already overwhelmed inboxes.

Here are a few of our basic guidelines for overcommunicating well:

1. Does the communication reinforce core themes that you want everyone to get?

To get this right, you first need to know what the core themes are. When we say repetition doesn't spoil the prayer, *these* are the prayers we are talking about. They are the things you want everyone to grasp; they

---

145. Jonathan kept telling his wife this, but she shut him up after the fourth time.

should be sacred; and there should be only a few of them, all related to your mission, values, strategy, and industry. At Google, our themes include putting users first, thinking big, and not being afraid to fail. Also, we are all technology optimists: We believe technology and the Internet have the power to change the world for the better.

By the way, if you repeat something twenty times and people don't get it, then the problem is with the theme, not the communications. If you stand up at your company's all-hands meeting every week and reiterate your strategy and plan, and people still don't understand or believe in it, then it's the plan that's flawed, not the method of delivering it.

2. Is the communication effective?

To get this right, you need to have something fresh to say. When we say repetition doesn't spoil the prayer, we don't quite mean it literally. This isn't the Pledge of Allegiance, to be pounded verbatim into schoolchildren's heads until the words are branded on the brain and the meaning has evaporated. Sometimes the presentation of the idea has to be varied to grab (or re-grab) attention. For example, Eric's periodic memos to Googlers almost always made the point to focus on the user. To make it fresh, in one of his notes Eric pointed out that users are getting more sophisticated, as proven by the fact that search query length was increasing nearly 5 percent annually. This was a new and interesting stat that most Googlers didn't know. It took a venerable theme and made it relevant.

3. Is the communication interesting, fun, or inspirational?

Most management teams are not curious—they are focused on doing the job at hand and tend to keep their communications equally businesslike. Smart creatives, though, have a wide array of interests. So if you come across an article that is insightful or interesting, and somehow relates to a core theme you have been communicating, go ahead and share it. Make it relevant to the team by picking a highlight or arguing a point. People will like it when you take off the blinders and talk about a wider variety of things. They want to be curious.

A few years ago Jonathan spotted an article by journalist and founding *Wired* editor Kevin Kelly called *Was Moore's Law Inevitable?*,[146] which explored the history of Moore's Law and predicted that its next iteration was inevitable. He sent a link to the article to his team with a short summary and a couple of simple questions: Do *you* think the next iteration of Moore's Law is inevitable? How much longer before the current one runs its course? Given Kelly's conclusions, is there anything Google should do differently? The email kicked off a spirited debate—a conversation!—that lasted a week. The subject of the future of Moore's Law had no direct bearing on our business or on the jobs of the people who got involved in the discussion, but it was consistent with Google's broader strategy to bet on the future of technology.

4. Is the communication authentic?

If it has your name on it, it should have your thoughts in it. Effective communication cannot be 100 percent outsourced. Yes, you can have people help you make the words pretty, but the thoughts, ideas, and experiences need to be yours. The more authentic the better.

When Eric toured Iraq in late 2009, he wrote a short, thoughtful analysis of his trip, with his observations about what was and wasn't working there. His note had nothing to do with our employees as Googlers, but it had everything to do with them as citizens of the world, and it quickly circulated throughout the company. On a much lighter note, Jonathan often entertained his team with video clips of his daughter's stellar exploits on the soccer field. Whether you are traveling to war zones or bursting with parental pride, don't be afraid to tell your story!

5. Is the communication going to the right people?

The problem with email is that it's too easy to add recipients. Not sure if someone should get something? What the hell, add them! Or better

---

146. "Was Moore's Law Inevitable?" (*The Technium*, July 2009), retrieved from http://www.kk.org/thetechnium/archives/2009/07/was_moores_law.php.

yet, just send it to the team distribution list. But a good communication goes only to the people who will find it useful. Choosing this list takes time, but the investment of a few seconds can have a big payoff. When you avoid distribution lists and instead actually pick the right people for the note, they are more likely to read it. Think about it from the other end: Which email are you more likely to read, the note to a distribution list or the one to you? It's like the difference between junk mail and a hand-addressed card.

6. Are you using the right media?

Say yes to all forms of communication. People assimilate information in all sorts of ways, so what works for some people won't work for others. If the message is important, use all the tools at your disposal to get it across: email, video, social networks, meetings and video conferences, even flyers or posters taped to the wall in the kitchen or café. Learn which methods work to connect with your colleagues, and then use them.

7. Tell the truth, be humble, and bank goodwill for a rainy day.

Smart creatives don't have to work for you; they have plenty of options. Setting a constant tone of truth and humility creates a store of goodwill and loyalty among the team. Then, when you screw up, communicate that story with truth and humility too. You may draw down that balance of goodwill, but not completely.

How was London?

Most businesspeople go to staff meetings. You have probably lived through hundreds of them, so you already know what their agenda is: Receive status updates, conduct administrivia, nap with eyes open, check email surreptitiously under the table, wonder what mistakes in life were made to warrant this torture. The problem with the typical staff meeting is that it is organized around functional updates, rather than around the key issues facing the team, so you may end up spending too much time on things that don't matter (do you really need a weekly update on everything?) and not enough on things that do. This structure also reinforces the organizational boxes around people—Pam is in quality control, Jason is the sales guy—rather than creating a forum where everyone has a stake in the key issues of the day.

One simple tactic to break the staff meeting monotony is the humble trip report. When people travel, ask them to put together a "What I Did on My Summer Vacation"–style report on what they did and what they learned. Then start all staff meetings with trip reports. (If no one traveled that week, then ask someone to do a weekend report instead.) The trip report makes the staff meeting more interesting. It inspires conversation, and when a person knows he is expected to present the trip report at the staff meeting, he'll do a better job of it. Also because the well-done trip report gets people out of their functional rut, which is exactly what helps make a staff meeting successful. No matter what a person's job is, they should be encouraged to have opinions about the business, industry, customers and partners, and different cultures.

Not long after he joined Google in 2008, CFO Patrick Pichette visited our office in London. When he returned, Eric opened his staff meeting by asking Patrick to talk about his trip. After saying how great the office was and whom he met with and blah blah blah, Patrick veered onto a completely different tangent. While in London, he had walked into every mobile phone store he saw and talked to the salespeople about the different phones and plans. So in his trip report he gave the executive team at Google an impromptu update on how our new mobile operating system, Android, and our slew of mobile apps were doing at the ground level. This had nothing to do with finance—Patrick didn't assume he could offer observations only within his own jurisdiction—and it set the expectation that anyone could and should have insights across the entire business.

Review yourself

One of Eric's most basic rules is sort of a golden rule for management: Make sure you would work for yourself. If you are so bad as a manager that you as a worker would hate working for you, then you have some work to do. The best tool we have found for this is the self-review: At least once per year, write a review of your own performance, then read it and see if you would work for you. And then, share it with the people who do in fact work for you. This will elicit greater insights than the standard 360-degree review process, because when you are initiating criticism of yourself it gives others the freedom to be more honest.

We mentioned Eric's self-review from 2002 earlier in the book, when we were talking about Bill Campbell and how Eric initially (and incorrectly) believed he didn't need a coach. There are other passages from that review where Eric candidly admitted his failings to his staff. For example: "I should have empowered the team earlier and forced more decisions down into the organization." And: "I should have been more forceful to force closure on certain decisions and be impatient. I have tended to value the development of consensus more than I should in some situations." These critiques were very well received by Eric's team, because they showed a CEO who was as interested in improving as they were.

Email wisdom

Communication in the Internet Century usually means using email, and email, despite being remarkably useful and powerful, often inspires momentous dread in otherwise optimistic, happy humans. Here are our personal rules for mitigating that sense of foreboding:

1. Respond quickly. There are people who can be relied upon to respond promptly to emails, and those who can't. Strive to be one of the former. Most of the best—and busiest—people we know act quickly on their emails, not just to us or to a select few senders, but to everyone. Being responsive sets up a positive communications feedback loop

whereby your team and colleagues will be more likely to include you in important discussions and decisions, and being responsive to everyone reinforces the flat, meritocratic culture you are trying to establish. These responses can be quite short—"got it" is a favorite of ours. And when you are confident in your ability to respond quickly, you can tell people exactly what a non-response means. In our case it's usually "got it and proceed." Which is better than what a non-response means from most people: "I'm overwhelmed and don't know when or if I'll get to your note, so if you needed my feedback you'll just have to wait in limbo a while longer. Plus I don't like you."

2. When writing an email, every word matters, and useless prose doesn't. Be crisp in your delivery. If you are describing a problem, define it clearly. Doing this well requires more time, not less. You have to write a draft then go through it and eliminate any words that aren't necessary. Think about the late novelist Elmore Leonard's response to a question about his success as a writer: "I leave out the parts that people skip."[147] Most emails are full of stuff that people can skip.

3. Clean out your inbox constantly. How much time do you spend looking at your inbox, just trying to decide which email to answer next? How much time do you spend opening and reading emails that you have already read? Any time you spend thinking about which items in your inbox you should attack next is a waste of time. Same with any time you spend rereading a message that you have already read (and failed to act upon).

When you open a new message, you have a few options: Read enough of it to realize that you don't need to read it, read it and act right away, read it and act later, or read it later (worth reading but not urgent and too long to read at the moment). Choose among these options right away, with a strong bias toward the first two. Remember the old OHIO acronym: Only Hold It Once. If you read the note and

---

147. Quoted many times, including in Dennis McLellan, "Elmore Leonard, Master of the Hard-Boiled Crime Novel, Dies at 87" (*Los Angeles Times*, August 20, 2013).

know what needs doing, do it right away. Otherwise you are dooming yourself to rereading it, which is 100 percent wasted time.

If you do this well, then your inbox becomes a to-do list of only the complex issues, things that require deeper thought (label these emails "take action," or in Gmail mark them as starred), with a few "to read" items that you can take care of later.

To make sure that the bloat doesn't simply transfer from your inbox to your "take action" folder, you must clean out the action items *every day*. This is a good evening activity. Zero items is the goal, but anything less than five is reasonable. Otherwise you will waste time later trying to figure out which of the long list of things to look at.

4. Handle email in LIFO order (Last In First Out). Sometimes the older stuff gets taken care of by someone else.

5. Remember, you're a router. When you get a note with useful information, consider who else would find it useful. At the end of the day, make a mental pass through the mail you received and ask yourself, "What should I have forwarded but didn't?"

6. When you use the bcc (blind copy) feature, ask yourself why. The answer is almost always that you are trying to hide something, which is counterproductive and potentially knavish in a transparent culture. When that is your answer, copy the person openly or don't copy them at all.

The only time we recommend using the bcc feature is when you are removing someone from an email thread. When you "reply all" to a lengthy series of emails, move the people who are no longer relevant to the thread to the bcc field, and state in the text of the note that you are doing this. They will be relieved to have one less irrelevant note cluttering up their inbox.

7. Don't yell. If you need to yell, do it in person. It is FAR TOO EASY to do it electronically.

8. Make it easy to follow up on requests. When you send a note to someone with an action item that you want to track, copy yourself,

then label the note "follow up." That makes it easy to find and follow up on the things that haven't been done; just resend the original note with a new intro asking "Is this done?"

9. Help your future self search for stuff. If you get something you think you may want to recall later, forward it to yourself along with a few keywords that describe its content. Think to yourself, How will I search for this later? Then, when you search for it later, you'll probably use those same search terms.

This isn't just handy for emails, but important documents too. Jonathan scans his family's passports, licenses, and health insurance cards and emails them to himself along with descriptive keywords. Should any of those things go missing during a trip, the copies are easy to retrieve from any browser.

Have a playbook

As a business leader, you have several constituencies: employees, bosses, boards of directors and advisors, customers, partners, investors, and so on. It helps to have a playbook with notes on how to communicate most effectively in each of these scenarios. Here are ours:

1:1s—match the lists

Bill Campbell once suggested to us an interesting approach to organizing 1:1s (aka one-on-ones, the periodic meetings between manager and employee). The manager should write down the top five things she wants to cover in the meeting, and the employee should do the same. When the separate lists are revealed, chances are that at least some of the items overlap. The mutual objective of any 1:1 meeting should be to solve problems, and if a manager and employee can't independently identify the same top problems that they should solve together, there are even bigger problems afoot.

Bill also suggests a nice format for 1:1s, which we have adopted with good results:

1. Performance on job requirements
   a. Could be sales figures
   b. Could be product delivery or product milestones
   c. Could be customer feedback or product quality
   d. Could be budget numbers
2. Relationship with peer groups (critical for company integration and cohesiveness)
   a. Product and Engineering
   b. Marketing and Product
   c. Sales and Engineering
3. Management/Leadership
   a. Are you guiding/coaching your people?
   b. Are you weeding out the bad ones?
   c. Are you working hard at hiring?
   d. Are you able to get your people to do heroic things?
4. Innovation (Best Practices)
   a. Are you constantly moving ahead . . . thinking about how to continually get better?
   b. Are you constantly evaluating new technologies, new products, new practices?
   c. Do you measure yourself vs. the best in the industry/world?

Board Meetings—noses in, fingers out

The goals of a board meeting are harmony, transparency, and advice. You want to exit the meeting with the board's support of your strategy and tactics. You need to be completely transparent in everything you communicate. And you want to hear their advice, even if you plan to ignore it—they are usually trying to be helpful, and cannot have all the context that you have. Another way to put this: You want their noses in, but fingers out.[148]

---

148. The phrase, often abbreviated NIFO, was coined by the founder and former president of the National Association of Corporate Directors, John M. Nash. It means that a board should take an active oversight role, but not get involved in micromanaging the

As CEO, Eric started his board meetings with a concise review of the highlights and lowlights of the previous quarter. The lowlights were especially important, and Eric always spent more preparation time on them than anything else. This is because it is always harder for people to present bad news to a board than good. The highlights are easy, but when you ask a team for a list of lowlights, you often get a sugarcoated version of the truth: "Here's the problem but it's not all that bad and we already have a solution in the works." This can't possibly be true for all the problems the company faces, and the board knows it. So the best approach is also the honest one: We have difficult problems and we don't have all the answers. Eric's lowlights brought up issues ranging from revenue to competition to products, honestly and frankly, which always set the stage for an engaged board discussion. For example, at one board meeting we wanted to discuss our concern that bureaucracy was slowing us down. The lowlight read: "Google constipated: key challenges we need to address."

Eric followed the highlights and lowlights with a detailed review of each of the company's product and functional areas, with an emphasis on succinct, data-driven discussions. The process of constructing this presentation wasn't run by a communications or legal team, but by product managers on Jonathan's team who were embedded in the business. Jonathan picked his brightest smart creatives for the task. He knew they would do a great job, despite the big time commitment the task required. He also knew that the experience of constructing detailed board presentations (and the accompanying letter) would give these talented people incredible insights into the art and skill of executive communications and a solid purview over what was going on across the company. To delegate this task to communications people

business. See "A Leader Ahead of His Time: NACD Founder John Nash" (*NACD Directorship*, May 15, 2013).

would have been a huge lost opportunity to give the company's future leaders hands-on training.[149]

Board members want to talk about strategy and products, not governance and lawsuits. (If this isn't true, get new board members.) Remember this when you establish the rules and agenda of the board, and stick to it even when the going gets tough. When Eric was on the board of Siebel Systems, a software company acquired by Oracle in 2005, the company became embroiled in a series of SEC violations in the early 2000s. The board meetings became dominated by legal conversations and the board spent much more time thinking about lawyers and liabilities than it did about the business, which was slowly eroding.

Administrivia, even important board stuff, can become a nice refuge when the alternative is to have difficult conversations about the decay of the core business. The board should be of strategic value, but you won't get these interesting conversations and valuable insights if you are constantly distracted by governance issues. Of course the board needs to understand what's going on with critical legal stuff and other tactical issues, but these can generally be handled in subcommittees and summarized at the board level in fifteen-minute segments. When he came to Google, Eric made a commitment to the board that it would get to focus on issues relevant to the scale and strategy of the business. The Apple board also did this well during the time Eric served on it, as the meetings were full of great conversations about products, leadership, and strategy. And there was no question who was in charge!

In between meetings, call board members periodically. But hope you get voice mail. ;-)

---

149. It's not a coincidence that many of the product managers who worked on the board preparation team have been very successful at Google. For example, Sundar Pichai ran the team for Jonathan for several years and now heads up the company's Android, Chrome, and Apps product areas. Caesar Sengupta partnered with Sundar on the board slides, and now runs the Chromebooks team for him.

Partners—act like diplomats

To build platforms and successful product ecosystems, companies must work with partners. This often creates interesting situations (and bastardized words: "coopetition," "frenemy") where the two companies may be competing in some realms but collaborating in others. The key to success in these situations lies in one of the oldest of the communications arts: diplomacy.

In many ways, complex business partnerships are similar to the realpolitik style of diplomacy between countries, which holds that relations should be managed based on pragmatic, not ideological principles. Countries can have a long list of grievances with each other, but it is in their mutual best interests to figure out a way to work together. The alternative—a lack of a relationship, or war—is destructive for everyone. For example, China and the United States have lots of issues, but there is so much trade between the two countries that we must find ways to maintain and build our relationship in spite of our differences.

Countries, like business partners, have their own belief systems, and everyone is aware when they have moved from one system to the other. An important first step in managing a successful partnership is to acknowledge those differences and assume that they are here to stay. The other country/company has a right to its own system and believes in it just as fervently as you do, so to work effectively with it as a partner, you need to put aside moral judgment. As Henry Kissinger said in 1969, when he was the US National Security Adviser, "We have always made it clear that we have no permanent enemies and that we will judge other countries, including Communist countries, and specifically countries like Communist China, on the basis of their actions and not on the basis of their domestic ideology."[150] Less than two years later he traveled to China, in secrecy, which led to the reopening of

---

150. See Henry Kissinger, *White House Years* (Little, Brown, 1979), page 192.

diplomatic relations between the two countries for the first time since World War II.

If managing partnerships is like diplomacy, then it stands to reason that it needs to be conducted by diplomats. For the most important partnerships, companies should create a role with the objective of serving dual constituencies: To keep the external partner happy, while also pursuing the interests of their own company.[151] This is different from a traditional sales role, which is often weighted toward the company's interests, not the partner's.

Press Interviews—have a conversation, not a message

When you are doing a press interview, do you have people to help prepare you? If so, do they give you a document of "frequently asked questions" (FAQs) that includes all the questions that the pesky journalist might ask and a carefully scripted set of sanitized responses that are designed to stick as closely as possible to the messaging themes of the launch? When said helpful person gives you said FAQs, do you ever look at them and say to yourself, "That's exactly what I would say?" Because if you do, you are probably made out of a silicon-titanium alloy.

Many believe that a press interview is a marketing speech, to be scripted word for word. Jonathan, who can be a rather difficult client for a communications person, used to suggest rather loudly upon seeing his scripted messages that if they wanted a trained monkey to give the interview, he'd be happy to arrange it. But if they wanted him, a person who usually bears no resemblance to a monkey, to do the interview, they better start over and come back with something intelligent to say. Because a successful interview shouldn't be an exercise in regurgitating bland marketing messages, it should be a conversation with insight.

---

151. In diplomatic circles this is called "two-level game theory." See Robert D. Putnam, "Diplomacy and Domestic Politics: The Logic of Two-Level Games" (*International Organization*, Volume 42, Number 3, Summer 1988).

A good communications person will understand the difference between messaging and conversation. Messages don't answer the question. In a conversation you listen to the questions and try to figure out a way to answer intelligently, with insights and stories, while reinforcing the message but not parroting it. Too many people try to manage the downside of communications, which messaging certainly accomplishes, but it also uniformly fails to accomplish anything else. The world can spot messaging a mile away.

Having an insightful conversation with a journalist is challenging—much more challenging than memorizing a script—and not because [insert witty barb about journalists here]. A back-and-forth conversation with a journalist often results in tension, which is something that journalists often try to create but most people try to avoid. So, if you want to engage in actual conversations with a reporter, you have to have a tough skin when the resulting article has negative elements. If you aren't being criticized, then you probably didn't have a good conversation.

Mostly, though, people don't have smart conversations with the press because it is much easier to draft messages than it is to discover insights. But the insights are there, you just have to push the team to find them. Remind them, as our communications colleague Ellen West always tells her team, "To be a thought leader, you have to have a thought."

Relationships, not hierarchy

One advantage of hierarchical, process-laden organizations is that it's easy to figure out with whom you need to talk: Just look for the right box on the right chart, and you've got your person. But the steady state of a successful Internet Century venture is chaos. When things are running perfectly smoothly, with people and boxes on charts enjoying a one-to-one relationship, then the processes and infrastructure have caught up to the business. This is a bad thing. When Eric was

CEO at Novell, the company was running like a well-oiled machine. The only problem was that the new-great-product cupboard was bare. (Champion racecar driver Mario Andretti: "If everything seems under control, you're just not going fast enough.")[152]

The business should always be outrunning the processes, so chaos is right where you want to be. And when you're there, the only way to get things done is through relationships. Take the time to know and care about people. Note the little things—partner's and kids' names, important family issues (these can be easily recorded in your contacts). Eric believes in the three-week rule: When you start a new position, for the first three weeks don't do anything. Listen to people, understand their issues and priorities, get to know and care about them, and earn their trust. So in fact, you are doing something: You are establishing a healthy relationship.

And don't forget to make people smile. Praise is underused and underappreciated as a management tool. When it is deserved, don't hold back.

---

152. Quoted in "The 25 Coolest Athletes of All Time" (*GQ*, February 2011).

Innovation—Create the Primordial Ooze

On a sunny spring day in March 2010, Eric sat in his car at the intersection of Embarcadero Avenue and El Camino Real in Palo Alto, looking at the trees surrounding Stanford's football stadium and reflecting on the past couple of hours and waiting for the light to change. He had just come from having coffee with Apple CEO Steve Jobs at a restaurant called Calafia.[153] The two had sat outside at the California cuisine–oriented café, discussing Google's growing mobile operating system, Android. Steve was convinced that the open-source operating system was built on intellectual property created by Apple. Eric responded that we hadn't used Apple's IP and had in fact built Android on our own. But his argument was to no avail. "They are going to fight us," he thought.

Eric first met and started working with Steve Jobs in 1993, when Eric was at Sun and Steve was at NeXT Computer. NeXT was built using a computer language called Objective-C, and Eric and a few others traveled to NeXT's offices to hear Steve give them an update. Steve started extolling the virtues of Objective-C and tried to convince the computer scientists from Sun that they needed to use it in

153. Calafia is owned by chef Charlie Ayers, who was Google's first chef (the café on our main campus is named after him). But the reason Steve and Eric chose to meet there was that it was close to Steve's home.

the next-generation programming framework they were developing. Eric knew that Steve was wrong on some of his technical points, but Steve's arguments were so persuasive that Eric and his Sun colleagues couldn't figure out exactly *how* he was wrong. They stood by their car in the NeXT parking lot after the meeting, dissecting the discussion and trying to escape what was often called the Jobs "reality distortion field." No such luck. Steve saw them in the parking lot and rushed out to continue the conversation. For another hour.

Steve and Eric built a friendship over the years, and in the summer of 2006 Eric was invited to join the Apple board. Before he accepted the job, he and Steve had a conversation about the potential conflicts of interest between Apple and Google. Apple was working on the iPhone, and Google had been working on a mobile operating system for about a year, having purchased Andy Rubin's company, Android, in August 2005. The definition of what Android would produce was still in flux, but at the time it looked like it would be an open-source operating system without a user interface (other companies would build the UI). Our hope was that Android could become the software guts for phones built by companies like Motorola, Nokia, or Samsung, who would build their own designs and applications. Both Android and the iPhone were in their early stages, and Eric joined the Apple board in August.

The Apple iPhone launched in June 2007, and it was nearly perfect. It was designed and optimized to be connected to the Internet, and it worked with a level of seamless convenience that was just great. Later that year, the Android team posted a YouTube video that unveiled what they had been working on. Steve scrutinized the video and concluded that the user experience it portrayed was too much like the iPhone's and its underlying operating system, iOS. Eric ultimately stepped down from the Apple board in August 2009, and the legal skirmishes between the companies and their partners continue today.

Eventually, everyone who wants to will have some sort of smartphone, and most of those phones (at least for the next decade) will run on either iOS or Android. More engineers are developing apps for these platforms than for any other computing platform in history (it helps to have a potential user base of just about everyone on the planet). Dozens of manufacturers are competing, and their ups and downs aren't just chronicled in trade magazines, but in mainstream media too. This is obvious to us now, but it was only a few years ago that personal computing meant a PC running Microsoft Windows. Regardless of whose side you are on in the patent arguments (to be clear: We are on our side), there is no disputing the fact that these two platforms have spurred enormous economic development and innovation and have changed people's lives for the better around the globe.

Steve Jobs saw this future with great clarity. There is no better example of the impact a smart creative can have on the world than him. He embodied a combination of technical depth, artistic and creative talent, and business savvy that allowed him to create computing products with which people actually fell in love. He merged beauty and science in a tech community that had a lot of nerds and business people, but very few artists. The two of us learned a lot about smart creatives from working with and observing Steve, about how much personal style can influence company culture and about how that culture is directly tied to success.

Yet the most important aspect of the Android/iOS saga is how it demonstrates two *different* ways to achieve innovation. Both platforms—and companies—are tremendously innovative, and there are a few key similarities in our approaches. Apple and Google both operate in industries with extraordinarily fast product life cycles. In both the Internet and mobile computing businesses, the next big thing becomes old hat pretty quickly, so we both need to innovate constantly or fall behind. Both companies tend to eschew traditional market research and rely on our own abilities to figure out what consumers will want. We trust our vision. And both companies place the highest priority on creating the best experience for our consumers.

But beyond these similarities, our approaches to innovation are quite different, primarily when it comes to control. With Android,

Google bet on the superior economics of an open platform and on our ability to navigate the fragmentation that results from such openness. Android is—and we mean this in the most positive way—out of control. The software source code is available to anyone to use for free, under the Apache license agreement.[154] This "open source" model means that anyone can take the operating system and do what they want with it; Android is the sand in the sandbox.

We also let anyone create and sell applications that run on Android-based devices; they don't require Google's approval. We encourage makers of Android devices (such as Samsung, HTC, and Motorola) to build those devices so that they are compatible at the application level, so that all Android apps run well on all Android devices. We are highly, but not 100 percent, effective in achieving that goal, which is to be expected in an environment where there is no cost to entry and no controlling power. Android is growing and expanding in ways that we could have never predicted. It is used to power electronic readers (including Amazon's), tablets, game players, and phones. It also can be found in refrigerators, treadmills, TVs, and toys. Many pundits talk about the coming "Internet of things," when all sorts of devices—not just tablets and phones—will be connected to the Internet. We hope that many of those things will run on Android.

Apple represents the opposite approach. iOS code is closed, and applications that want to be on the App Store must receive Apple's formal approval. Steve always believed that the best experience for the consumer comes from maintaining complete control of everything. He paid tremendous attention to the details in everything he and his company did, with a singular purpose of creating the best possible products. This showed in his extraordinary product presentations to his board, which were always highly orchestrated and produced as if they were Broadway shows. New products weren't just demonstrated

---

154. Written by the Apache Software Foundation, the Apache license allows the user of the software to use, distribute, or modify the software under the license terms, without having to pay royalties.

at board meetings, they were unveiled. At Google we regularly had APMs demo new products to our board, not just because they did it so well (though not as well as Steve!) but also for the sheer theatricality of having kids a year or two out of college (sometimes wearing their alma mater's sweatshirt) show board members our newest innovations. We learned the value of that type of showmanship from Steve.

Apple's control model works not just because of Steve Jobs's excellence, but also because of how he organized the company. At Apple—just like Google—the leaders are product people with technical backgrounds. When you build a team of great smart creatives, and put the world's uber-smart creative in charge, then you have a good chance of being right most of the time. And when you are right most of the time, then a highly controlled model can yield tremendous innovation.

As we were writing this chapter on innovation and sharing it with friends and family, whenever someone took issue with our principles they would often use Steve Jobs as the counterexample. "Yes, but Steve Jobs didn't do it that way, and look how many great things he created." They were right of course, so we generally responded by saying that if they were the equal of Steve Jobs, with instinct and insights matched by few people, then they should go ahead and try it his way. But if you are like most of the rest of us, then when it comes to innovation we have some other ideas you might want to try out.

What is innovation?

Innovation: It's the next big thing. Or at least the next big word. According to the *Wall Street Journal*, some form of that word appeared in the annual and quarterly reports of US companies over 33,000 times in 2011 alone.[155] Everyone wants to be "innovative" (the *Journal* didn't supply a figure for the number of times "Luddite" appeared in those

---

155. The exact number tallied was 33,528. See Leslie Kwoh, "You Call That Innovation?" (*Wall Street Journal*, May 23, 2012).

reports, but we bet it was quite low), but before we embark on how to do that, let's be clear on what it means.

To us, innovation entails both the production and implementation of novel and useful ideas. Since "novel" is often just a fancy synonym for "new," we should also clarify that for something to be innovative it needs to offer new functionality, but it also has to be surprising. If your customers are asking for it, you aren't being innovative when you give them what they want; you are just being responsive. That's a good thing, but it's not innovative. Finally, "useful" is a rather underwhelming adjective to describe that innovation hottie, so let's add an adverb and make it *radically* useful. Voilà: For something to be innovative, it needs to be new, surprising, and radically useful.

Google's project to create cars that can drive themselves clearly fits our definition: It is new, surprising (except to *Knight Rider* fans), and radically useful. But Google also releases over five hundred improvements to its search engine every year. Is that innovative? Or incremental? They are new and surprising, for sure, but while each one of them, by itself, is useful, it may be a stretch to call it radically useful. Put them all together, though, and they are: The Google search engine radically improves from year to year because of the power of all these improvements. Like five hundred tiny steps forward, collectively they get you somewhere.

This more inclusive definition—innovation isn't just about the really new, really big things—matters because it affords everyone the opportunity to innovate, rather than keeping it the exclusive realm of those few people in that off-campus building whose job it is to innovate. Google's search team, working on a product that is fifteen years old, is just as much in the innovation business as Google[x], the team working on the self-driving car. And this inclusive spirit gives most everyone the chance to come up with those really new, really big things.

Understand your context

Google[x] has a simple Venn diagram that it uses to determine if it will pursue an idea. First, the idea has to be something that addresses a big challenge or opportunity, something that affects hundreds of millions or billions of people. Second, they have to have an idea for a solution that is radically different from anything currently in the market. We aren't trying to improve on an existing way of doing something, rather we want to start over. And third, the breakthrough technologies that could bring that radical solution to life have to be at least feasible, and achievable in the not-too-distant future. For example, Project Loon, which hopes to offer broadband Internet access to the billions of people who don't have it yet by using helium balloons, checks all three boxes: It addresses a huge problem with a radical solution enabled by technologies that either already exist or are within reach. (Imagine something the size of a hot-air balloon floating about twenty kilometers high and delivering wireless broadband service to the homes on the ground below it. That's Loon.) On the other hand, time travel would probably solve a lot of problems (and make some sports gamblers quite rich), but the technology is infeasible (or so we want you to believe—cue evil laugh). Before the [x] team starts pursuing any idea, it first checks to see if the idea fits into this three-part paradigm. If it doesn't, it is rejected.

Before there can be innovation, there needs to be the proper context for innovation. This is usually found in markets that are growing quickly and full of competition (lots of companies are working on automated cars; most of them are actually car companies!). Don't look for empty space and then be lonely; it is much better to use an innovative approach to become a player in a space that is or will be large. This may seem counterintuitive, since many entrepreneurs dream of entering "greenfield" markets that are brand new and have no competition. But usually there's a reason the market is empty: It's not big enough to sustain a growing venture. It still may be a good business

opportunity—someone must make money off of all those niche products we see in the SkyMall catalog—but if you want to create an environment of innovation, it's better to look for big markets with huge
growth potential. Remember, Google was late to the search-engine
party, not early.

Another element to consider is technology: How do you think the
technology in the space will evolve? What is different now, and what
further change do you expect? Do you have the talent to create sustainable differentiation within that evolving world? When Google engineer
Paul Buchheit developed Gmail, he was innovating into a large and
growing space (email) by betting that he could create a browser-based
email system with as rich a set of features and user interface as a client-
based one.[156] Since Google was full of engineers who could build great
web-based applications, we had the talent to execute successfully on his
insight. Therefore, the context for innovation was perfect.

The CEO needs to be the CIO

Many years ago, one of our colleagues, Udi Manber, was an engineer
at Yahoo when the company decided it wasn't innovative enough. So
its executives did what any well-trained MBA types would do when
faced with a problem: They put someone in charge of fixing it. They
offered the job of head of innovation to Udi and he accepted, but three
weeks into his stint he realized he had made a mistake. His bosses
wanted him to set up an innovation council, with forms that employees
could use to submit ideas and a process for the council to review and
approve those ideas. In other words, Udi's job was to set up an innovation bureaucracy. That's pretty much an oxymoron. So instead, he
left the company. (He may have been motivated by his twelve-year-old
daughter, who, when seeing him working on a presentation to give at

---

156. Client-based applications use software programs that reside on the computer or
device on which they run. Browser-based applications reside entirely on the Internet and
are accessed via a browser such as Internet Explorer, Firefox, Safari, or Chrome.

an engineering all-hands, said: "You are going to waste hundreds of engineers' time to tell them that they have to be innovative. How innovative is that?") Udi eventually came to Google. He has been very successful here and has led some of our most innovative product teams... just not as head of innovation.

The idea of imbuing one top executive with responsibility for all things innovative isn't unique to this one company. A few years ago, a major consulting firm published a report advising *all* companies to appoint such a "Chief Innovation Officer."[157] Why? Allegedly, to establish a "uniformity of command" over all the innovation programs. We're not sure what that means, but we're pretty sure that "uniformity of command" and "innovation" don't belong in the same sentence (unless it's the one you're reading right now).

As business managers, we like to manage things. Want something done? Then put someone in charge of it. But innovation stubbornly resists traditional, MBA-style management tactics. Unlike most other things in business, it cannot be owned, mandated, or scheduled. As Udi told us when recounting his Yahoo experience, "Innovative people do not need to be told to do it, they need to be *allowed* to do it." In other words, innovation has to evolve organically. It is the final destination of a path that starts when ideas spawn like mutations from a primordial ooze and traverse a long, perilous route from inception to fruition. Along the way, stronger ideas accumulate believers and momentum, and weaker ones fall to the wayside. There is no process by which to implement this evolution; its defining characteristic is its *lack* of process. Think of it as natural selection for ideas.[158] To paraphrase Darwin from *The Origin of Species:*

---

157. Adi Alon, North American managing director of Accenture's Innovation Performance group, wrote this report. For a summary, see Adi Alon, "10 Ways to Achieve Growth Through Innovation" (*TMC News*, March 9, 2010). See also Wouter Koetzier and Adi Alon, "You Need a Chief Innovation Officer" (Forbes.com, December 16, 2009).

158. The general idea of natural selection for ideas goes back at least as far as 1976, when Richard Dawkins introduced the concept of a "meme" in *The Selfish Gene*. But what we're talking about is more akin to what Jim Collins and Jerry Porras described, in *Built to*

As many more [ideas] are born than can possibly survive; and as, consequently, there is a frequently recurring struggle for existence, it follows that any [idea], if it vary however slightly in any manner profitable to itself, under the complex and sometimes varying conditions of life, will have a better chance of surviving, and thus be naturally selected.[159]

(PS: Although we are evolutionists, we are not above trying to create some pretty amazing stuff in six days.)

All companies that want to be innovative, which is to say all companies, need to start by creating an environment where the different components of creation are given free rein to collide in new and interesting ways, and then give these new creations the time and freedom to evolve and live, or—much more often—stagnate and die. The Chief Innovation Officer position is doomed to fail because it will never have enough power to create a primordial ooze (and only the ooze will lead to "ahhhs"). To put it another way, the CEO needs to be the CIO. God created Earth's primordial ooze; He didn't delegate the task.[160]

Creating a culture of ooze isn't a new idea. Thomas Edison became famous for the unique, throw-it-against-the-wall-and-see-if-it-sticks environment at his Menlo Park lab in the nineteenth century. In the twentieth century, AT&T's Bell Labs and Xerox's Palo Alto Research Center (PARC) were renowned incubators of innovation. The difference now, though, is the speed and scale at which the Darwinian struggle plays out. The Internet provides everyone with the tools of creation;

Last, as "branching and pruning"—trying a lot of different stuff and keeping what works. See Jim Collins and Jerry I. Porras, *Built to Last: Successful Habits of Visionary Companies* (HarperBusiness, 1994), pages 148–54. For more information about how variation and selection characterize creativity, see Dean Keith Simonton, *Origins of Genius: Darwinian Perspectives on Creativity* (Oxford University Press, 1999).

159. Charles Darwin, *The Origin of Species* (Digireads.com edition, 2007), page 17.

160. For you atheists out there, this is a metaphor. You may not believe in God, but even God believes in CEOs.

moreover, it is an ideal testing ground, allowing for prototypes to be rolled out and meaningful data to be collected in a fraction of the time needed before. Species evolution takes eons, but in the hands of smart creatives, today's process of idea evolution can—and needs to—work at Internet speed.

Innovative ooze forms easily in a start-up environment, when the culture is still fresh and the entire company has an us-against-the-world mentality. People who join start-ups crave risk; it's part of what attracts them to the venture. But once a company gets past about five hundred people it begins to attract more risk-averse employees. These can still be very talented smart creatives, they just aren't going to be the first to jump. The fact is, not everyone is innovative. So the ooze doesn't just allow the innovators to innovate, it needs to let everyone else participate and thrive too.

A few years ago we were both captivated by a TED talk by entrepreneur and musician Derek Sivers.[161] He showed a video of a seemingly crazy man dancing all by himself at an outdoor concert. The man stands on the side of a hill, shirtless and barefoot, gesticulating wildly and having the time of his life. At first, no one goes within twenty feet of him. But then, one venturesome person joins him, and then another and another, and then the floodgates open. Dozens of people rush, creating a mosh pit of dancing fools where once there had been only one. Derek calls this the "first follower" principle: When creating a movement, attracting the first follower is the most crucial step. "The first follower is what transforms a lone nut into a leader." The primordial ooze of innovation needs to encourage the people who want to be innovative—the lone dancing fool on the side of the hill— to do their thing. But just as important, it also needs to encourage the people who want to join something that is innovative—dancing fools two through two hundred—to do their thing as well. This is

---

161. Derek Sivers, "Derek Sivers: How to Start a Movement" (*TED*, February 2010), retrieved from http://www.ted.com/talks/derek_sivers_how_to_start_a_movement .html.

why innovation needs to be integrated into the fabric of the company, across every function and region. When you isolate it under a particular group, you may attract innovators to that group, but you won't have enough first followers.

Robert Noyce, cofounder of Fairchild Semiconductor and Intel, said, "Optimism is an essential ingredient for innovation. How else can the individual welcome change over security, adventure over staying in a safe place?"[162] Hire people who are smart enough to come up with new ideas and crazy enough to think they just might work. You need to find and attract those optimistic people, then give them the place to create change and adventure.

Focus on the user…

In late 2009, a team of search engineers showed us a prototype of a feature that had been percolating for a while. It was based on a simple idea: What if we started to populate search results while the user was typing the query, rather than waiting for her to hit the return key? We had always believed that speed was one of the core factors in determining the quality of search and were proud that we answered the vast majority of searches in under a tenth of a second. But that clock didn't start ticking until the user actually entered the query. Typing the query could still take several seconds. What if we didn't have to wait? What if we showed results as the user typed? Once we saw the prototype, the go decision was a no-brainer. Both the organic and paid search teams got to work, and several months later the feature launched to the world as Google Instant.

A few weeks before the launch Jonathan was in his staff meeting when a basic question occurred to him: Would Instant affect revenue at all? Perhaps, when results populated as the user typed, the user might

162. Leslie Berlin, *The Man Behind the Microchip: Robert Noyce and the Invention of Silicon Valley* (Oxford University Press, 2005), page 264.

be less likely to click on ads, so he asked his team if we had enough good data about potential revenue impact. No, was the answer, and everyone agreed that someone should investigate it. Then they all proceeded with planning the launch. In every other company where Jonathan had worked, a financial analysis was one of the most important hoops that a product needed to jump through before getting approved. How much revenue will the product make? What will the return on investment (ROI) be? The payback period? Yet here we were, a few weeks away from launching a major change to our core product, and no one had performed a detailed financial analysis. The product was obviously great for the user, so we all knew that launching it was the best business decision.

When Instant launched, it had only a modest effect on revenue, but Google has launched plenty of other features with a more significant financial impact. Knowledge Graph, which launched in 2012, populates the right-hand side of the web results page for queries about people, places, and things with a concisely formatted panel of algorithmically curated information about that entity. It pulls all the most relevant facts together into one, easy-to-read box. For most queries, the panel replaces the ads that previously appeared on that part of the page. That one hurt revenue a little bit. In early 2011, we made a series of changes to our search algorithms that reduced the quality scores of certain types of websites. We didn't want users clicking on links only to find themselves on crummy sites. That release, called "panda," affected nearly 12 percent of queries, and because many of the affected sites were part of our ad network, the change hurt Google's revenue.

Google knows that in the Internet Century user trust is just as important as dollars, euros, pounds, yen, or any other currency. Product excellence is the only way for a company to be consistently successful, so our prime directive when it comes to product strategy is to focus on the user (while not interfering with the internal development of alien civilizations). As Larry and Sergey put it in their IPO letter,

"Serving our end users is at the heart of what we do and remains our number one priority."

But focus on the user is only half the story. The full sentence should read "focus on the user and all else will follow." This means that we will always do what's right for the user, and we trust that our smart creatives will figure out how to make money from it. It could take a while, so sticking it out requires a lot of confidence.[163] But it is usually worth it.

In 2004, Jonathan and fellow Googler Jeff Huber took Sergey on a field trip to meet with a small start-up called Keyhole. Jeff, who had been the first product manager Jonathan hired at Excite@Home, was one of the lead engineers on the ads team.[164] One of Keyhole's cofounders was Brian McClendon, with whom Jonathan and Jeff had worked at Excite@Home. Keyhole had developed some extremely cool ways to visualize and interact with maps, and Sergey immediately decided that Google should buy the company.

A few weeks later Sergey brought the acquisition to the board for its approval, and when they asked him how we would ever make money from the technology, his response was simple: "I'll let Jonathan answer that question; he's the business guy." Jonathan had been leaning back, enjoying Sergey's presentation, and had given exactly zero thought to how buying Keyhole might make Google money (clear evidence that after two years, Jonathan was now guzzling from the Google Kool-Aid dispenser). Jonathan plowed forward with some muddled answer that was memorable only in how forgettable it was. The truth was that we had no idea how buying Keyhole would benefit Google's bottom line.

The board decided to trust Sergey's judgment and let him proceed

---

163. Not just confidence, you might say, but capital as well. What about companies, such as most small and medium businesses, that can't afford to ship products that may have great user benefits but no associated revenue or profit? You should still focus on the user, but be as scrappy as possible and invest as little as possible until the idea is proven. At that point profits may still be well down the road, but if you have proven the user value, this becomes a financing decision based on sound data.

164. For years, Jeff's bio on the Google website said that he had a master's degree from Harvard. It's actually an MBA, but Jeff neglected to mention that fact lest it harm his engineering street cred.

with the deal. About eight months later, Google Earth, which was based on Keyhole technology, launched. It was an immediate hit with users, and also generated millions of dollars. How could that be, since there were no ads on the app and it was free? Not long after we launched it, one of our smart creatives, Sundar Pichai, realized that all those people who were downloading and installing Google Earth might be interested in Google Toolbar as well. Toolbar was a simple utility that integrated with the browser. It had a lot of interesting features for users, one of which was a little Google search box that constantly resided in the browser's interface. People with Toolbar could initiate a Google search without going to Google.com, so they tended to conduct more searches, click on more ads, and generate more revenue. Sundar's idea met some resistance, but, with a push from Urs Hölzle, it was quickly implemented.

This simple insight—that people downloading Earth might be interested in getting Toolbar as well—increased Toolbar's user base significantly and generated lots of revenue, but there's practically no way Jonathan could have anticipated it when he stood before the board that day. Looking back, we realize the correct answer would have been, "I have no idea . . . but I'm sure we'll figure it out."

Focus on the user . . . and the money will follow. This can be particularly challenging in environments where the user and customer are different, and when your customer doesn't share your focus-on-the-user ethos. When Google acquired Motorola in 2012, one of the first Motorola meetings Jonathan attended was a three-hour product review, where the company's managers presented the features and specifications for all of Motorola's phones. They kept referring to the customer requirements, most of which made little sense to Jonathan since they were so out of tune with what he knew mobile users wanted. Then, over lunch, one of the execs explained to him that when Motorola said "customers," they weren't talking about the people who use the phones but about the company's real customers, the mobile carriers such as Verizon and AT&T, who perhaps weren't always as focused on the user as they should have been. Motorola wasn't focusing on its users at all, but on its partners.

At Google, our users are the people who use our products, while our customers are the companies that buy our advertising and license our technology. There are rarely conflicts between the two, but when there are, our bias is toward the user. It has to be this way, regardless of your industry. Users are more empowered than ever, and won't tolerate crummy products.

Think big

Our colleague Vint Cerf has been working on a new suite of network protocols that will work in the harsh and very, very large environment of space. According to Vint, he started this project after asking himself what he could work on that would be needed twenty-five years later.[165] His answer: the interplanetary Internet. No one can accuse Vint of not thinking big enough.

For the rest of us humans, though, it can be a different story. Perhaps it's human nature, or just corporate nature, but most people tend to think incrementally rather than transformationally or galactically.[166]

---

165. See Adam Mann, "Google's Chief Internet Evangelist on Creating the Interplanetary Internet" (*Wired.com*, May 6, 2013).

166. It's not that people suffer from a failure of the imagination: Lots of folks have lofty visions, but their pragmatism prevents them from *trying* to turn these into reality. This is explained by what psychologists have termed the expectancy-value theory. In deciding which goals to pursue, people consider both the expected payoff and the odds of success. This calculation often steers them away from trying the most ambitious stuff, which of course jacks their failure rate even higher. As hockey Hall of Famer Wayne Gretzky noted, you miss 100 percent of the shots you don't take. See Allan Wigfield and Jacquelynne S. Eccles, "Expectancy-Value Theory of Achievement Motivation" (*Contemporary*

Our colleague Regina Dugan, who was the director of the Defense Advanced Research Projects Agency (DARPA)[167] before coming to Motorola and then Google, talks about how innovation often happens when people are working in "Pasteur's Quadrant,"[168] which is where they try to advance basic science while solving real-world problems. But most companies end up in the opposite quadrant, "where the science is not interesting and no one cares about the goals being pursued. Talent exits, and projects fail more often, not less."[169]

That's why one of Eric and Larry's challenges to engineers and product managers in Google product reviews was always "you aren't thinking big enough." In the Internet Century, with infinite information, reach, and computing power, global scale is available to just about everyone. But too many people are stuck in the old, limited mindset. "You aren't thinking big enough"—later replaced by the Larry Page directive to "think 10X"—helps fix that. It encompasses the art of the possible...and the impossible.

The obvious benefit of thinking big is that it gives smart creatives much more freedom. It removes constraints and spurs creativity. Astro Teller, the head of Google[x], notes that if you want to create a car that gets 10 percent better mileage, you just have to tweak the current design, but if you want to get one that gets five hundred miles per gallon, you need to start over. Just the thought process—How would I start over?—can spur ideas that were previously not considered.

There are other, more subtle benefits to thinking big. Big bets

---

Educational Psychology, January 2000) and Jacquelynne Eccles and Allan Wigfield, "Motivational Beliefs, Values, and Goals" (*Annual Review of Psychology*, 2002).

167. DARPA is part of the US Department of Defense.

168. The idea of Pasteur's Quadrant comes from the late political scientist Donald Stokes, who saw Louis Pasteur as the exemplar of simultaneously pursuing basic and applied research. The quadrant represents the best combination on a 2 × 2 matrix of whether or not research advances basic understanding and whether or not it solves real-world problems. See Donald E. Stokes, *Pasteur's Quadrant: Basic Science and Technological Innovation* (Brookings Institution, 1997).

169. Regina E. Dugan and Kaigham J. Gabriel, "'Special Forces' Innovation: How DARPA Attacks Problems" (*Harvard Business Review*, October 2013).

often have a greater chance for success by virtue of their size: The company can't afford to fail. On the other hand, when you make a bunch of smaller bets, none of which are life threatening, you can end up with mediocrity. We see this all the time in business: the company with a large line of not-great products. When Google bought Motorola and Jonathan started helping new CEO Dennis Woodside, he discovered that the company had dozens of different phones, with each device targeted at a particular, market-research-defined segment, such as millennials, Gen X, boomers, and soccer moms. There was some logic behind this—different carriers wanted their own unique models—but it led to a sprawl of mediocrity. Each phone had its own set of product people who would work hard to make their product great, but they also knew that if their product was only good, the company would survive. (Dennis largely fixed these problems and created a much more user-focused Motorola before Google sold the company to Lenovo in 2014.)

On the other hand, the iPhone is a popular product precisely because it is the only phone Apple makes. If there's a problem in the development of the next-generation iPhone, no one on that team goes home until there's a plan to fix it. It's no coincidence that Apple has only a few product lines. None of them can afford to fail.

It can also be easier to take on big problems because bigger challenges attract big talent. There is a symbiotic relationship between big challenges and highly smart, skilled people: The challenges get solved and the people get happy. Give the wrong people a big challenge, and you'll induce anxiety. But give it to the right people, and you'll induce joy.[170] They enjoy rising to the challenge for the sake of it, but also, as sociologist and management guru Rosabeth Moss Kanter has pointed

---

170. This idea comes from psychologist Mihaly Csikszentmihalyi and his notion of "flow," that joyous state of mind when you are so deeply, single-mindedly absorbed in your work that time seems to stand still. "Your whole being is involved, and you're using your skills to the utmost," Csikszentmihalyi has said. Flow is rare and precious because it requires the ideal match between a highly challenging task and your ability to meet that challenge: If the task is extremely challenging and your skill level is low, you'll be anxious; and if the task is no match for your abilities, you'll be bored. Creating opportunities for more-frequent flow states is one of the jobs of managing smart creatives. See John

out, for the very real benefits it can bring: new skills, new connections with colleagues in the field, enhanced reputation—what economists would describe as investing in their human capital.[171] For these reasons, thinking big is actually a very powerful tool for attracting and retaining smart creatives. Put it this way: Let's assume you are a brilliant smart creative just graduating from college. You have two competing job offers, which are virtually identical except for one difference. One of the companies tells you that they like to try to make things 10X better, while the other settles for 10 percent improvement. Which one will you choose?

Our friend Mike Cassidy is a great example of the power of 10X thinking in retaining smart creatives. A cofounder of a company called Ruba, Mike joined Google in 2010 after we acquired Ruba's intellectual property and hired its team. Mike is a serial entrepreneur—Ruba was his fourth company; his second one was a search engine called Direct Hit that briefly competed with Google before it was sold to Ask Jeeves. So we figured that it was only a matter of time before Mike would leave the Google mother ship to start something new. Over time we lost track of what Mike was working on, but we would occasionally see him around campus so we knew he was still a Googler. Then, in June 2013, Google announced Project Loon, the aforementioned Google[x] project that aims to use helium balloons to bring broadband Internet access to the five billion people who don't yet have it. We soon learned that Mike, who has a degree in aerospace engineering, was one of the Loon project leads and had been working on it for over a year.

Geirland, "Go with the Flow" (*Wired*, September 1996), and Mihaly Csikszentmihalyi, *Flow: The Psychology of Optimal Experience* (Harper & Row, 1990).

171. Rosabeth Moss Kanter, drawing on her research on what creates commitment to communities and organizations, writes that knowledge workers "are attracted by the chance to take on big responsibility and stretch their skills even further. The 'stickiest' work settings (the ones people leave less frequently and more reluctantly) involve opportunity and empowerment. Cutting-edge work with the best tools for the best customers is important in the present because it promises even greater responsibility and rewards in the future. Knowledge workers want to build their human capital—their individual package of skills and accomplishments—as much as their financial capital." See Rosabeth Moss Kanter, *Evolve!: Succeeding in the Digital Culture of Tomorrow* (Harvard Business School Press, 2001).

If it weren't for that opportunity to do something audacious, he likely would have left Google, so by continuing to think big and push the boundaries of technology we got to hang on to at least one great smart creative.

And doing big things that matter, as Larry often puts it, inspires people even if they aren't the Mike Cassidys who get to be directly involved in them. We often hear people around Google talk about "10Xing" their job, even though most of their jobs are far removed from the audacious projects the company has become famous for. These are salespeople, lawyers, financial folks, all of whom are inspired by the company's prevalent attitude to shoot for the moon. Thinking big is not only a very powerful recruiting and retention tool, it's contagious.

Set (almost) unattainable goals

The well-worn corporate manager has mastered many skills, and high on that list is the setting of annual and quarterly goals. This requires a certain finesse. Set the objectives too low and you are obviously trying to make yourself look good by "miraculously" exceeding them at the end of the quarter.[172] But set them too high and you run the risk of failure. The trick is to find the sweet spot by creating objectives that look difficult but are actually easily doable. The perfect scorecard at the end of the quarter and year is one that is full of 100 percent marks.

In late 1999, John Doerr gave a presentation at Google that changed the company, because it created a simple tool that let the founders institutionalize their "think big" ethos. John sat on our board, and his firm, Kleiner Perkins, had recently invested in the company. The topic was a form of management by objectives called OKRs (to which we referred in the previous chapter), which John had learned

---

172. In sales the practice of setting artificially low goals and then exceeding them by a lot is called sandbagging. Our first head of sales, Omid Kordestani, acquired such a reputation of being a sandbagger that he regularly delivered quarterly sales updates to the company from a small stage constructed out of…sandbags.

from former Intel CEO Andy Grove.[173] There are several characteristics that set OKRs apart from their typical underpromise-and-overdeliver corporate-objective brethren.

First, a good OKR marries the big-picture objective with a highly measurable key result. It's easy to set some amorphous strategic goal (make usability better…improve team morale…get in better shape) as an objective and then, at quarter end, declare victory. But when the strategic goal is measured against a concrete goal (increase usage of features by X percent…raise employee satisfaction scores by Y percent…run a half marathon in under two hours), then things get interesting. For example, one of our platform team's recent OKRs was to have "new WW systems serving significant traffic for XX large services with latency < YY microseconds @ ZZ% on Jupiter."[174] (Jupiter is a code name, not the location of Google's newest data center.) There is no ambiguity with this OKR; it is very easy to measure whether or not it is accomplished. Other OKRs will call for rolling out a product across a specific number of countries, or set objectives for usage (e.g., one of the Google+ team's recent OKRs was about the daily number of messages users would post in hangouts) or performance (e.g., median watch latency on YouTube videos).

Second—and here is where thinking big comes in—a good OKR should be a stretch to achieve, and hitting 100 percent on all OKRs should be practically unattainable. If your OKRs are all green, you aren't setting them high enough. The best OKRs are aggressive, but realistic. Under this strange arithmetic, a score of 70 percent on a well-constructed OKR is often better than 100 percent on a lesser one.

Third, most everyone does them. Remember, you need everyone thinking in your venture, regardless of their position.

Fourth, they are scored, but this scoring isn't used for anything and isn't even tracked. This lets people judge their performance honestly.

---

173. Grove discusses OKRs in his book *High Output Management* (Random House, 1983).

174. We have substituted WW, XX, YY, and ZZ for the actual numbers in the OKR that was shared internally.

Fifth, OKRs are not comprehensive; they are reserved for areas that need special focus and objectives that won't be reached without some extra oomph. Business-as-usual stuff doesn't need OKRs.

As your venture grows, the most important OKRs shift from individuals to teams. In a small company, an individual can achieve incredible things on her own, but as the company grows it becomes harder to accomplish stretch goals without teammates. This doesn't mean that individuals should stop doing OKRs, but rather that team OKRs become the more important means to maintain focus on the big tasks.

And there's one final benefit of an OKR-driven culture: It helps keep people from chasing competitors. Competitors are everywhere in the Internet Century, and chasing them (as we noted earlier) is the fastest path to mediocrity. If employees are focused on a well-conceived set of OKRs, then this isn't a problem. They know where they need to go and don't have time to worry about the competition.

70/20/10

When someone pitches you a new idea, are you inclined to say yes or no? If you have spent too much time in the wrong organization, your knee-jerk reaction is likely to say no. Or "NO!" Organizations have a way of breeding antibodies whose sole purpose is to preach from the gospel of "Thou shalt not." Saying no lets managers avoid risk and reserve their resources (by "resources," we mean headcount, or for those of you who speak human, "people") for projects that are more likely to succeed. Do I really want to dedicate precious smart creatives to that crazy project? What if it fails? They might pull my headcount next year! I think I'll just say no and let my team keep working on streamlining the widgets.

As much as people might preach about creating a culture of yes (including some very smart, handsome people who like to write books), it is very difficult to do without a structural framework to enable it. And when your most precious resource is your people—which is almost always the case—then developing a smart system to allocate those resources is a critical element to success.

In 2002, we still managed resource allocation and our project portfolio by maintaining the top-100 list, but as the company grew we all became concerned that this simple system would not scale well enough. We worried that a creeping culture of no might take hold. So one afternoon, Sergey examined the top-100 list and put the projects in three different buckets. About 70 percent of the projects were related to the core businesses of search and search advertising, about 20 percent were related to emerging products that had achieved some early success, and about 10 percent involved completely new things that had a high risk of failure but a big payoff if successful. That started a lengthy discussion, the end result of which was that 70/20/10 became our rule for resource allocation: 70 percent of resources dedicated to the core business, 20 percent on emerging, and 10 percent on new.

While the 70/20/10 rule ensured that our core business would always get the bulk of the resources and that the promising, up-and-coming areas would also get investment, it also ensured that the crazy ideas got some support too, and were protected from the inevitable budget cuts. And 10 percent isn't a lot of resources, which is fine, because overinvesting in a new concept is just as problematic as under-investing, since it can make it much harder to admit failure later on. Million-dollar ideas are a lot harder to kill than thousand-dollar ones, so overinvestment can create a situation wherein willful confirmation bias—the tendency to see only the good things in projects in which a lot has been invested—obscures sound decision-making.

Jonathan saw this happen when he was at Apple and worked on the infamous Newton. (For those of you too young to remember, or who worked at Apple and suppressed the memory, the Newton was a digital notebook that was a precursor to today's tablets, except for the fact that it was an #epicfail. A fact that may be interesting only to us: The Newton was manufactured in part by Motorola.) The company had poured a lot of resources into the product and therefore chose to overlook a major shortcoming. One of the Newton's major features was handwriting recognition—you could write whatever you wanted on the screen and it would recognize what you were saying...theoretically. The problem was that, for most people, it didn't work. In fact, about the only people whose handwriting it could read well were the people who had developed and tested the product, and even they had to adjust their handwriting to achieve their results. Nevertheless, a lot of money had been invested in the project, and the success of the handwriting recognition feature with this small, pliant sample group provided Apple with the answer it wanted to hear. The company plowed ahead with launch plans, and the rest, as the Newton itself might transcribe, is *hamstery*.

Ten percent also works because creativity loves constraints.[175] It's why pictures have frames and sonnets have fourteen lines. It's why Henry Ford set pricing for his cars so low, because he knew that "We make more discoveries concerning manufacturing and selling under this forced method than by any method of leisurely investigation".[176] A lack of resources forces ingenuity.

In 2002, Larry Page began wondering if it was possible to make every book ever published searchable online—not just the most popular titles or some other subset, but every single book. (We later calculated there were precisely 129,864,880 different book titles in the world.)[177] When every book ever published was available online, he reasoned, *and* when universal translation became available, then all of the world's knowledge would be accessible to every person.

As the cofounder, Larry could have assigned a team of engineers to the problem and given them a nice budget. Instead he got a digital

---

175. The phrase "creativity loves constraints" is a favorite of Marissa Mayer's. The counter-intuitive idea that constraints can often foster creativity has been explored by a number of researchers. See, for example, Patricia D. Stokes, "Variability, Constraints, and Creativity: Shedding Light on Claude Monet" (*American Psychologist*, Volume 56, Number 4, April 2001).

176. See Henry Ford, *My Life and Work* (Doubleday, 1922), page 147.

177. As of August 5, 2010, anyway. See "You can count the number of books in the world on 25,972,976 hands" (Google's official blog, August 5, 2010).

camera, rigged it to a tripod, and set the contraption up on a table in his office. He pointed the camera down at the table, turned on a metronome to pace his movements, and started snapping pictures while Marissa Mayer turned the pages. Based on this crude prototype, they were able to estimate what it took to digitize a book, and made some calculations that the audacious project was indeed feasible. Google Books was born. (Sergey later employed a similar approach to see if Google's Street View project was feasible. He took a drive around town with a camera and snapped a photo every few seconds. He showed off the pictures in Eric's next staff meeting to rally support for what is now called Street View. Today Street View covers over five million miles of roads.)

It's possible that Google Books would have happened if Google had funded it with a coterie of engineers and a healthy budget. But it's also possible that being well funded might have hobbled the project before it could get started. Larry's scrappy digitizing system, built from parts purchased at Fry's,[178] proved to be a lot more cost efficient than the more advanced systems he might have purchased if he had allotted the time and budget. When you want to spur innovation, the worst thing you can do is overfund it. As Frank Lloyd Wright once observed, "The human race built most nobly when limitations were greatest."[179]

20 percent time

In the summer of 2004, a Google engineer named Kevin Gibbs came up with an idea. He described it as a system to "perform real-time completion against all URLs in our repository and all historical Google search queries, with results sorted by their overall popularity." In English, this means that Google would try to anticipate what your query was and suggest ways to complete it. Working in his spare time, Kevin developed

---

178. Fry's is an electronics store near Mountain View.

179. The quote continues: "... and, therefore, when most was required of imagination in order to build at all. Limitations seem to have always been the best friend of architecture." See Frank Lloyd Wright, *The Future of Architecture* (Horizon Press, 1953), page 55.

a prototype and sent a description of his incipient project to an email list for people who wanted to share new ideas.[180] The note included a link to his prototype, where people could enter queries into Google search and watch the system perform the real-time completion.

The prototype drew the interest of several other engineers, who joined Kevin's project. (Derek Sivers would call these engineers Kevin's first followers.) This feature, now called Google Suggest, is why, when you type "we", Google suggests that you are looking for the weather forecast and provides you with a drop-down menu to click on the full query without needing to type the whole thing out yourself. Google Suggest shaves seconds off search times and helps users get exactly what they need even more quickly. One guy, from idea to launch to global availability to "how did we ever live without it?" for billions of people, in just a few years.

This is the power of 20 percent time,[181] the Google program whereby engineers can spend 20 percent of their time working on whatever they choose. Twenty percent time has spawned a host of great products—Google Now, Google News, transit information on Google Maps, and many more—but it is generally misunderstood. It's not about time, it's about freedom.[182] The program doesn't mean that the campus turns into summer camp every Friday, with all the engineers goofing off in

---

180. The list allows its members to vote on ideas and it automatically tabulates the votes, so that good ideas rise up the leaderboard. Kevin's proposal was called "URL and Query Autocompletion (with Demos)." It was the 917th submission to the list, which at last count numbers over fifteen thousand.

181. The 20 in "20 percent time" is not to be confused with the 20 in 70/20/10. Twenty percent time is about individual freedom, while 70/20/10 is about resource management. Although perhaps it would have been less confusing if we had adopted 70/19/11 as our resource management guideline.

182. This is the sense of freedom that comes from doing what you want to do, not doing what you're told. According to self-determination theory (SDT), a prevailing theory of human motivation originated by psychologists Edward Deci and Richard Ryan, all human beings have powerful needs to be autonomous (free to behave of their own volition rather than in response to external pressure), competent, and related to others. SDT posits that people find their work motivating and fulfilling to the extent that the work satisfies these needs. See Richard M. Ryan and Edward L. Deci, "Self-Determination Theory and the Facilitation of Intrinsic Motivation, Social Development, and Well-Being" (*American Psychologist*, Volume 55, Number 2, January 2000).

(hopefully) creative ways. In fact, 20 percent time is more like 120 percent time, since it often occurs on nights and weekends. But it can also be stored up and used all at once—Jonathan had one product manager take a summer to work on a 20 percent project. Regardless of when you take your 20 percent time, assuming it doesn't get in the way of doing your regular job, no one can stop you from doing it. Twenty percent time is a check and balance on imperial managers, a way to give people permission to work on stuff they aren't supposed to work on. It helps bring to life the Steve Jobs maxim that "you have to be run by ideas, not hierarchy."[183] And we have found that when you trust people with freedom, they generally do not waste it on extravagant pies in the sky. You don't get software engineers writing operas—they write code.[184]

The Street View trike, which lets us capture ground-level photos along streets and paths too narrow for cars, got its start when Street View cars engineer Dan Ratner went on a trip to Spain. When Dan had to walk the last stretch to his Barcelona hotel through narrow alleyways where his cab couldn't drive, he realized there was a lot of great stuff that the Street View cars couldn't access. When he returned home, he initiated a 20 percent project building a tricycle that could navigate these places, and the Street View trike was born. It has since been adapted to snowmobiles (to chronicle the ski runs at the Vancouver Olympics, for example) and pushcarts (to walk the halls of some of the world's great museums). Up next: Street View skateboards?

---

183. The full comment was: "If you want to hire great people and have them stay working for you, you have to let them make a lot of decisions, and you have to be run by ideas, not hierarchy. The best ideas have to win, otherwise good people don't stay." Quoted in Mark Milian, "Why Apple Is More Than Just Steve Jobs" (*CNN Digital Biz* blog, August 25, 2011).

184. Google wasn't the first company to use this strategy: Back in 1948, 3M started a program letting employees spend 15 percent of their time on projects outside their core responsibilities. Perhaps the best-known product to come out of 3M's 15 percent time is Post-it notes, but the program also yielded Scotch tape, Scotchgard fabric protector, and innovative materials such as multilayer optical films that are used in many of the company's products. William McKnight, 3M's president and chairman for decades, said his approach was to "hire good people, and leave them alone." See "A Culture of Innovation" (3M corporate brochure) and Paul D. Kretkowski, "The 15 Percent Solution" (*Wired*, January 1998).

There's no doubt that when you give people a lot of freedom, they can be very difficult to rein in. A stubborn smart creative sometimes won't take no for an answer. When is this OK? There is no absolute answer to this question—like all aspects of leadership, judgment matters—but it sure does help if the employee turns out to be right.

When Paul Buchheit decided that email could be a lot better, he started a 20 percent project he called Caribou. At some point, he decided that his new product, which is now called Gmail and has hundreds of millions of users, should generate revenue, so he suggested placing ads next to emails based on the content of the note. We didn't initially agree, and told him to just concentrate on making Gmail great. We'd worry about revenue later.

But Gmail was Paul's baby, and he ignored us. He hacked the internal system to talk to the AdWords ad server (Gmail + AdWords = combinatorial innovation), and one morning we came in to work to see ads alongside our emails. At first people were angry, but then we started noticing that the ads were actually pretty useful. At the time, Jonathan happened to be trading emails with his siblings about what to get their parents for their fiftieth wedding anniversary, and a Gmail ad for Williams-Sonoma appeared in Jonathan's browser next to the note. His sister had brought up their mom's love of gardening, and the ad helpfully suggested a garden bench. Jonathan proposed the idea to his brothers and sister, and not only did his parents end up with a nice gift, but Jonathan got credit for being sensitive and thoughtful. (This is atypical.)

Gmail launched a few months later. Its ads did not generate much revenue, but the technology that Paul developed to match ads with emails was later refined to improve our AdSense product, which is now a multibillion-dollar business. Needless to say, Paul was not punished for his insubordination.

That example notwithstanding, this doesn't mean that if you work for us and you have an idea we hate, you can just plow ahead with it unhindered by our boorish, wrongheaded, unenlightened managerial opinions. The first step toward bringing a good idea to fruition is to build a team of people who are committed to it, and while *we* may be clueless, your peers probably are not. Our constant advice to anyone who wants to launch a 20 percent project is to start by building a prototype, because that's how you get people excited about the project. Coming up with an idea is pretty easy. Getting a few of your colleagues to join your project and add their 20 percent time to your 20 percent time is a lot harder. This is where the Darwinian process begins.

Finding collaborators can be difficult in a nonhierarchical organization, especially for newcomers, because it's much harder to figure out where to go to get things done. Relationships become highly critical, and since they take time to build (and this isn't everyone's natural skill set), you can end up with a lot of great ideas dying on the vine.

One of our search teams tries to circumvent this through a program called "demo days." The concept is pretty simple: A team spends a week building prototypes of new ideas that they will be expected to demo by the end of the week. Before the week starts, the engineers clear their calendars of all meetings and launches, no exceptions. This not only makes the demo days logistically possible, it serves as a forcing function to get everyone to commit. Since some people may be expected to work in unfamiliar areas, they can get training in the systems they may want to use. All systems are set up and ready to go, so there's no time wasted. They need to recruit at least one other person to their project—no teams of one are allowed—and are encouraged to collaborate with people they don't normally work with on a daily basis. Then the week starts and they get on it.

The result at the end of the week is a set of prototypes, generally shared in a sort of science-fair open house on a Friday afternoon. Most of those prototypes won't progress any further—"I have a lot of ideas and throw away the bad ones," said Linus Pauling[185]—so the teams also learn that it's OK to fail.

Steve Jobs once told Eric that he did something similar when he

---

185. Quoted in Tom Hager, *Linus Pauling and the Chemistry of Life* (Oxford University Press, 1998), page 87.

was running NeXT. Every six months or so, the engineering team would stop what they were doing and dedicate themselves to creating applications for the NeXT platform. This was a critical tactic to building their ecosystem, but it also gave everyone fresh insights into the work they were doing in their "day jobs."

The most valuable result of 20 percent time isn't the products and features that get created, it's the things that people learn when they try something new. Most 20 percent projects require people to practice or develop skills outside of those they use on a day-to-day basis, often collaborating with colleagues they don't regularly work with. Even if these projects rarely yield some new, wow innovation, they always yield smarter smart creatives. As Urs Hölzle likes to point out, 20 percent time may be the best educational program a company can have.

Jonathan's Favorite 20 Percent Project

Jonathan's favorite 20 percent project is the one that digitized and published online the artifacts of Yad Vashem, the Jerusalem-based center for remembering the Holocaust's victims and survivors. The project got its start when Jonathan visited the museum with his family in 2007. During their visit, the guide told them how he had recently learned something about a photo in the exhibit from another visitor. This got Jonathan thinking about how the youngest survivors of the Holocaust, those who can remember the people and places in these photos, were in their seventies and eighties. Their firsthand knowledge was literally dying out.

The next day, Jonathan visited our Israeli office and talked about the museum. Team Israel took it from there, using their 20 percent time to create a partnership with the museum to build its online presence. Today there are over 140,000 images and documents digitized and online, searchable from anywhere in the world. And the real beauty of it is the survivors who have added their own knowledge and stories to these photos, via comments or videos, to form a more complete picture of this important part of history.

When project leader Yossi Matias demoed the Yad Vashem project for Larry and Sergey, their response was typical: Why only this museum? Why not all museums? Why not create a product that helps all the archives in the world digitize their content? So they did. Google's Open Gallery product, which lets any museum (or owner of cultural content) create online exhibitions, launched in 2013. And the Google Cultural Institute site has hundreds of online collections, with high-definition images of art and artifacts belonging to museums ranging from the Acropolis Museum to the Museo de Zaragoza.

Ideas come from anywhere

The last time you saw a suggestion box, what did you think? Maybe you were at an amusement park or ski area, or maybe you were at work, sipping a coffee in the breakroom. You spied the box and the sign next to it that said WE'RE LISTENING! or WE CARE WHAT YOU THINK! The sign probably inspired just the opposite feeling: You're not listening, you don't care what I think, and the slit in that box transports the paper dropped therein to a wormhole in space, emerging somewhere in the Andromeda galaxy.

How jaded we've become. When the concept of the suggestion box was first introduced to business, it was quite revolutionary. As chronicled in Alan Robinson and Sam Stern's *Corporate Creativity*, the father of the modern-day suggestion box was Scottish shipbuilder William

Denny, who in 1880 distributed a pamphlet to all his employees entitled "Rules for the Awards Committee to Guide Them in Rewarding the Workmen for Inventions and Improvements." Denny offered two to fifteen pounds for employee-submitted ideas that were accepted; his workforce responded with hundreds of them over the next decade. Denny's program soon crossed the Atlantic to land at John Patterson's National Cash Register Company, where suggestions from employees peaked at over seven thousand in 1904—roughly two per employee—with a hit rate of roughly one-third.[186] That's over two thousand ideas from rank-and-file employees in one year that were deemed good enough to implement, which is a pretty good hit rate for a suggestion box.

A century later, Marissa Mayer ran meetings at Google that were like *The Gong Show*[187] for geeks. People got up to present their ideas and could keep talking until they were gonged. The better the demo, the longer the person was allowed to go on. Then Craig Nevill-Manning, who founded our New York engineering office, morphed that idea into weekly "Beer and Demos" meetings, where people would gather to sip beer and watch demos, voting with marbles for the ones they liked best. (The demos, that is. The beers they voted on by continuing to drink them.) Patterson and Denny (and Marissa and Craig) were smart enough to realize that good ideas could come from anywhere. They knew that workers could not only work, but think too. This is more true than ever today, when everyone in the organization is armed with abundant information and great tools. In fact, the biggest danger is not the conceit that only managers have good ideas, it's the conceit that only the company's employees have them. When we say good ideas come from anywhere, we mean *anywhere*. They are just as likely to come from outside the company as from inside.

When Google started to expand internationally, we quickly figured

---

186. Recounted in Alan G. Robinson and Sam Stern, *Corporate Creativity: How Innovation and Improvement Actually Happen* (Berrett-Koehler, 1997), pages 66–70.

187. *The Gong Show* was a 1970s TV talent show where most of the acts were terrible and any performance could be cut short by one of the judges striking a loud gong.

out that most California-based engineers lack the skills necessary to translate web pages into other languages. The traditional way to solve this problem would have been to hire professionals to do the translation work, which would have been both expensive and time-consuming. Instead, we let our users do the job. We published all of our text and asked for volunteers to translate it into their local languages. They did, and did a fantastic job. Similarly, when our Geo team set out to chart the world's geography, they discovered that for many areas good maps simply didn't exist. They created a product called Map Maker, which lets anyone contribute to Google Maps. Live on a street that doesn't show up on the Map? No problem: Just draw it in and we'll add it (after we check to make sure it's actually there). Thus was built a new community of grassroots citizen cartographers, who made it so that maps of entire cities were just a mouse-click away for our users. For example, they mapped over twenty-five thousand kilometers of roads in Pakistan in just two months.

Not long after we joined Google, the executive team had an offsite where we discussed opening more engineering offices around the world. When Eric asked Larry how many engineers he thought the company should have, Larry's response was: "A million." He wasn't joking, but he also didn't mean the company should have a million employees (at least, we don't think he meant that). Today, developers around the world regularly work with Android, Google App Engine, Google APIs, Google Web Toolkit, and open-source tools to which Google contributes. These are not Google employees, but if we add them all up it's likely that the total number of people using Google tools or creating cool stuff on top of Google platforms is in the millions. So it could be that we have met Larry's goal, in which case he will probably 10X it to 10 million.

Ship and iterate

So we have just the right amount of resources set aside for new ideas, we've muzzled the imperial managers, freed our geniuses to do their

thing, and opened our minds to pull ideas from the masses. The innovation is flowing; good ideas are a-bubblin'. Most of them die before
they see the light of day, but a precious few are good enough to reach
the promised land. You cue the blog post, push the green button, and
pop a cork to celebrate with the team.

Then you get back to work, because if you did the job well, the
product is not yet done. Voltaire wrote, "The perfect is the enemy of
the good."[188] Steve Jobs told the Macintosh team that "real artists
ship."[189] New ideas are never perfect right out of the chute, and you
don't have time to wait until they get there. Create a product, ship it,
see how it does, design and implement improvements, and push it back
out. *Ship and iterate.* The companies that are the fastest at this process
will win.

When we launched our flagship product, AdWords, there was
a debate about whether new ads should go live without an internal
review. There was a strong internal contingent who believed that
allowing ads to go live instantly would lead to a lot of bad, spammy
ads. But there was another contingent who believed that if advertisers could see their ad in action right away, they could gather performance data and improve the ads much more quickly. They argued that
a faster cycle time would lead to higher quality, not lower. We opted for
minimal internal reviews, and the ship-and-iterate approach worked.

Ship and iterate applies in many realms. It is easiest to practice
in our world of software, where our product is bits and bytes that are
distributed digitally, and not physical goods. But with new technologies like 3-D printing and the ability to model many types of things
online, the cost of experimentation has dropped in many industries,

---

188. Although Voltaire did write that line in one of his poems ("*Le mieux est l'ennemi du
bien,*" literally "The best is the enemy of the good"), he actually credited it to an Italian
sage (*Il meglio è l'inimico del bene*).

189. For those outside the industry a more wordy explanation might be in order: "Ship"
means sending a product to customers. Steve's point was that while it can be tempting to
polish your work to a fine gloss, you haven't accomplished anything until your work gets
into the hands of actual customers.

sometimes precipitously, making a ship-and-iterate process feasible in many more places.

The hardest part of ship and iterate is to iterate. It's easy to rally a team to ship a new product, but much harder to get them to stick around and do the hard work to make that product better. One form of motivation we found to work well was negative feedback. From Larry scrawling "These ads suck" to Marissa posting negative product reviews on the wall outside her office and scrutinizing them with the product managers and engineers, we often used criticism to inspire teams to iterate their products. There is a fine line to walk here, and we haven't always gotten it right. The right criticism is motivating, but too much has the opposite effect.

Ship and iterate doesn't always work. After launching, some products will get better and gather momentum while others will wither. The problem is, by the time a product has gone to market there has been a significant amount of resources and emotion invested in it, which can get in the way of good decisions. Forgetting sunk costs is a tough lesson to heed, so in a ship-and-iterate model, leadership's job must be to feed the winners and starve the losers, *regardless of prior investment*. Products that get better and gather momentum should be rewarded with more resources; products that stagnate should not.

To decide which efforts are winners and which are losers, use data. This has always been the case, but the difference in the Internet Century is how quickly data is available and how much of it there is. A key factor in picking the winners is to decide which data to use and to set up the systems so that it can be retrieved and analyzed quickly. Using data will muffle the sunk-costs fallacy—that irrational tendency most humans have to count the amount of resources that have already been invested in a project as one of the reasons to continue to invest in the project ("We have already invested millions, we can't stop now").[190]

---

190. The desire to recoup sunk costs often leads people not only to stick with a bad course of action but to double down on it, in a pattern scholars call "escalation of commitment." In fact, from an individual's perspective, investing based on sunk costs can be a rational

Too often, the tendency is to feed the losers in hopes of making them winners. When Jonathan ran products at Excite@Home, the company's portal, Excite.com, had various sections, such as news, real estate, sports, finance, and so on. Each of those sections competed for clicks on the front page, and when a section's traffic dropped, Excite's management would try to rectify the situation by moving that section to a *better* spot on the page. Hey, finance, your traffic is dropping this quarter and you're behind on your objectives. No problem, we'll pop you to the top of the page! Excite used data to determine which of the content areas were losers, but rather than starving those sections and forcing them to improve, they fed them by giving them better real estate. In retrospect, Excite's mantra wasn't so much to focus on its users as it was to focus its users on its worst products so it could meet its artificial objectives. Which, as it turned out, didn't Excite anyone.

In practice, ship and iterate means that marketing programs and PR pushes should be minimal at launch. If you are in the restaurant business, you call this a soft opening. When you push the babies out of the nest, don't give them a jetpack or even a parachute—let them fly on their own. (Note: *This is a metaphor.*) Invest only when they get some lift. Google's Chrome is a great example of this—it launched in 2008 with minimal fanfare and practically no marketing budget and gained terrific momentum on its own, based solely on its excellence. Later, around the time the browser pushed past seventy million users, the team decided to pour fuel on the fire and approved a marketing push (and even a TV advertising campaign). But not until the product had proven itself a winner did it get fed.

To be clear, ship and iterate doesn't mean you have license to push crummy products out the door and then hope to make them better.

---

decision, since sticking with a losing project (and concealing that the project is doomed) protects the decision-maker's own reputation within the organization. See Barry M. Staw, "The Escalation of Commitment to a Course of Action" (*Academy of Management Review*, Volume 6, Number 4, October 1981), and R. Preston McAfee, Hugo M. Mialon, and Sue H. Mialon, "Do Sunk Costs Matter?" (*Economic Inquiry*, Volume 48, Issue 2, April 2010).

In fact, Jonathan often warned his team not to launch crummy products and depend on the Google brand name to get early user traction. The products should be great at what they do, but it's OK to limit functionality at launch. Withholding significant marketing and PR resources at launch helps with this, as customers are much more likely to feel disappointed by a highly hyped product than one that is quietly launched. Then you can expand functionality with new features (and tweak the existing ones) later. As Eric wrote to Googlers in February 2006: "There should be a plan for a 'wow' feature reasonably soon after launch."[191] With this approach, users get accustomed to seeing products launch with a high-quality, if somewhat limited, set of functions that they know will expand rapidly after launch.

Ship and iterate is easy when your product is entirely digital—software, media—and the costs of physical production are minimal. It's easy for us to ship a new feature in Google search and tweak it based on usage data; it's much harder for an automobile or chip manufacturer to do the same thing. But there are often other ways to use the reach and power of the Internet to gather valuable user data. For example, ship designs or prototypes or create software that lets people virtually use the product. Figure out some way to let people experience the product, and use the data to make the product better.

Fail well

On the flip side of the Chrome ship-and-iterate story is Google Wave, which launched with fanfare in 2009. Wave was a poster child of innovation. It was the creation of a small team of engineers in our Sydney office who took their 20 percent time to explore the question, "What would email be like if it were invented today?" They eventually produced a very compelling prototype that wowed the executive team. We

---

191. This is in line with the concept of "Underpromise, Overdeliver," popularized by Tom Peters. See Tom Peters, *Thriving on Chaos: Handbook for a Management Revolution* (HarperCollins, 1988), pages 118–20.

gave them the OK to proceed (although they probably would have even if we hadn't), and they produced a platform and protocols to support a new way for people to communicate in the Internet Age.

Wave was a technological marvel, but a major flop. We launched it in 2009, and usage never took off. The Wave team shipped and iterated like crazy, but its user base never came close to critical mass. A year after consumer launch, we announced that we would be canceling Wave. The press excoriated us, calling Wave an overhyped bust and a tremendous failure.

They were right, Wave was a tremendous failure. It failed quickly: We did not pour good money after bad. It failed without anyone being stigmatized: No one on the Wave team lost their jobs, and in fact most of them were highly recruited within Google after the project shut down, precisely because they had worked on something that had pushed the boundaries. And it failed after having created a lot of valuable technology: Pieces of the Wave platform migrated to Google+ and Gmail. As a failure, Wave failed well.

To innovate, you must learn to fail well. Learn from your mistakes: Any failed project should yield valuable technical, user, and market insights that can help inform the next effort. Morph ideas, don't kill them: Most of the world's great innovations started out with entirely different applications, so when you end a project, look carefully at its components to see how they might be reapplied elsewhere. As Larry says, if you are thinking big enough it is very hard to fail completely. There is usually something very valuable left over. And don't stigmatize the team that failed: Make sure they land good internal jobs. The next innovators will be watching to see if the failed team is punished. Their failure shouldn't be celebrated, but it is a badge of honor of sorts. At least they tried.

Management's job is not to mitigate risks or prevent failures, but to create an environment resilient enough to take on those risks and tolerate the inevitable missteps. Author and professor Nassim Taleb writes about making systems that are "antifragile": They don't just survive failures and external shocks, they get stronger as a result.[192] Don't get us wrong: Failure is not the objective. But, if you are measuring the health of your innovation environment, you need to count the failures as well as the successes, to become more "antifragile." As Dilbert cartoonist Scott Adams says, "It helps to see failure as a road and not a wall."[193] Mulla Nasrudin, the thirteenth-century wise fool of Sufi lore, seconds the notion: "Good judgment comes from experience; experience comes from bad judgment."[194]

The timing of failure is perhaps the trickiest element to get right. A good failure is a fast one: Once you see that the project will not succeed, you want to pull the plug as quickly as possible, to avoid further wasting resources and incurring opportunity costs (those smart creatives working on a doomed project could be better deployed working on one that is a potential success). But one of the hallmarks of an innovative company is that it gives good ideas plenty of time to gestate. Projects like self-driving cars or Google Fiber, which will deliver up to 1 gigabit bandwidth to homes (about a hundred times more than the average US

---

192. More from Taleb: "Some things benefit from shocks; they thrive and grow when exposed to volatility, randomness, disorder, and stressors and love adventure, risk, and uncertainty. Yet, in spite of the ubiquity of the phenomenon, there is no word for the exact opposite of fragile. Let us call it antifragile. Antifragility is beyond resilience or robustness. The resilient resists shocks and stays the same; the antifragile gets better." See Nassim Nicholas Taleb, *Antifragile: Things That Gain from Disorder* (Random House, 2012), page 3.

193. See Scott Adams, "Scott Adams' Secret of Success: Failure" (*Wall Street Journal*, October 12, 2013).

194. This quote is usually attributed to the late computer scientist Jim Horning, but he said that is incorrect, and when we dug into it we found that it actually comes from Nasrudin. Once we learned that, we decided that all we wish for our legacy is to be recalled, centuries from now, as wise fools, because that's just cool. The story is retold in Joel ben Izzy, *The Beggar King and the Secret of Happiness* (Algonquin Books, 2003), pages 206–7.

household has today), have the potential to be highly profitable, but it will take a very long time. As Jeff Bezos points out, "Just by lengthening the time horizon, you can engage in endeavors that you could never otherwise pursue. At Amazon we like things to work in five to seven years. We're willing to plant seeds, let them grow—and we're very stubborn. We say we're stubborn on vision and flexible on details."[195]

So fail quickly, but with a very long time horizon? Huh? How does that work? (See, we told you this was the tricky part.) The key is to iterate very quickly and to establish metrics that help you judge if, with each iteration, you are getting closer to success. Small failures should be expected and allowed, since they often can shed light on the right way to proceed. But when the failures mount and there is no apparent path to success (or, as Regina Dugan and Kaigham Gabriel put it, when achieving success requires "multiple miracles in a row"),[196] it is probably time to call it a day.

It's not about money

While we believe in paying extraordinary people extraordinarily well for extraordinary success, we *don't* pay people for successful 20 percent projects. Dan Ratner may have received very generous compensation for being part of the transformational Street View product team, but he didn't get anything directly tied to his work on trikes.[197] We don't provide any monetary incentive for 20 percent projects for the simple reason that we don't need to: It may sound corny, but the reward comes from the work itself. Several studies have shown that extrinsic rewards don't encourage creativity, and in fact hinder it, by turning an inherently rewarding endeavor into a money-earning chore.[198]

---

195. Steven Levy, "Jeff Bezos Owns the Web in More Ways Than You Think" (*Wired*, November 13, 2011).

196.Regina E. Dugan and Kaigham J. Gabriel, " 'Special Forces' Innovation: How DARPA Attacks Problems" (*Harvard Business Review*, October 2013).

197. In this way, Dan has a lot in common with toddlers.

198. See, for example, Teresa M. Amabile, "How to Kill Creativity" (*Harvard Business Review*, September–October 1998).

Our favorite example of the inherent rewards 20 percent projects can yield comes from August 2005, when Hurricane Katrina ravaged the US Gulf Coast. Google Earth had been in the market for only about eight weeks, and the team that developed our "geo" products—Maps and Earth—was small and overworked. But when the hurricane hit it sprang into action, launching over eight thousand up-to-the-minute satellite images (from the National Oceanic and Atmospheric Administration—NOAA) that accurately showed the scope of the disaster and provided high-resolution images of streets and neighborhoods. This helped rescue workers, who were having a hard time navigating when so many signs and signal lights had been wiped out. It also helped agencies distribute relief supplies, and later aided survivors in deciding whether or not to return to their homes.

This was a classic 20 percent project. The idea was born from within a team. No hippo told them to do it. No one suggested they camp out at the office for several nights in a row, no one asked them to reach out to the growing Google Earth community to solicit the help of volunteers, and no one told them to work with NOAA to get the images. In fact, the only executive involvement was when Eric visited their war room, looked around, and issued the wise edict to keep doing what they were doing.

Since Hurricane Katrina, that 20 percent project has turned into a full-time Crisis Response team in Google.org, the organization that leads philanthropic initiatives across Google. Aided by that team, Googlers have used our platforms to help people suffering from natural disasters ranging from the 2008 Chinese New Year snowstorms that stranded thousands of travelers to the 2011 Japan earthquake and tsunami that killed thousands and left hundreds of thousands more homeless. With each disaster, they come up with new ways to use our products to help people, building on previous experiences. Most of them don't get paid a dime for their efforts. They are motivated by the work itself.

Conclusion—Imagine the Unimaginable

Eric spent the holidays at the end of 2013 vacationing with his family. Amidst the usual family activities, the kids got to spend some time watching videos. What struck Eric was that none of that time was spent in front of an actual television; in fact the TV remained dark for the duration of the vacation, and all videos were watched on a tablet. None of what they watched were shows in the traditional sense of the word—they were not originally shown on broadcast or cable networks. Rather, they were all created from the outset to be streamed from websites and mobile applications. The TV, and its surrounding ecosystem, is simply not a part of these kids' lives. This, we suspect, is not an isolated anecdote, which bodes well if you are a manufacturer of mobile devices or a maker of web-based video content, but not so much if you make the network sitcoms and dramas that today's kids won't watch when they grow up.

We live in a moment of great optimism but also a time of great anxiety, and not just for TV execs. During the three years we've been writing this book, the disruptive impact of technology has been felt across numerous industries. The economic issues that came to a fore during the latest recession persist even as economies around the world rebound. The rate of technology-driven change outpaces our ability to train people in new skills, putting tremendous pressure on entire classes of workers and the economic structure of many nations. The stable, middle-class jobs that historically are the bedrock of healthy economies are moving to developing nations or online, or disappearing altogether.

There's no doubt that the disruption of once-robust businesses and the resulting economic impact will be painful and confusing in the near term, so it would be irresponsible to end a book on building great twenty-first-century businesses without offering some advice about how to weather the changes ahead, and how to think about them. What's different about today's business landscape? What will happen next? And what can businesses and individual entrepreneurs do to survive and thrive during periods of disruption?

From Downton Abbey to Diapers.com

In order to understand why change threatens traditional corporations, we need to take a quick look back to other moments in history when one form of economic hub passed the baton to another. As we enter the twenty-first century, we're at a hand-off zone not unlike the one where the Western world went from a feudal economy to an industrial one in the nineteenth century. Many of our friends and family members are enamored with a BBC television series called *Downton Abbey*, which chronicles the dramatic ups and downs of the residents of a stately British home and the staff who serve them in the years around World War I. The residents are wealthy British upper crusters who spend a great deal of time dressing up for meals and worrying about the staff, while the staff are working-class people who spend a great deal of time, well, working, and worrying about the residents. All in delightful British accents and wonderful, period-authentic clothes.

In case you didn't notice it because you were too busy weeping at John Bates' imprisonment (he is eventually exonerated) or Matthew's death (barring some sort of Bobby Ewing–like miracle,[199] he stays dead),

---

199. In the hit 1980s TV show *Dallas*, character Bobby Ewing, played by Patrick Duffy, tragically died when his sister-in-law ran him down with a car, but he miraculously

the world of Downton Abbey represents the transition from one economic era to another. The definitive preindustrial nineteenth-century institution was The Household; Downton was a source of economic support for surrounding towns through its demand for people and services.

After the industrial revolution, the definitive twentieth-century institution became The Corporation. Think General Motors, an automobile company where mass production was happening at plants thanks to a confluence of factors, including access to power, water, and a blue-collar labor force. Meanwhile, both union members on factory floors and white-collar workers in headquarters enjoyed safe careers and comfortable middle-class lifestyles.

In the twenty-first century, The Corporation as a hub of economic activity is being challenged by The Platform. We've touched on platforms in the Strategy chapter, but picture Diapers.com (which was subsequently bought by Amazon). A platform is a very different sort of hub than a corporation. A corporation's relationship with consumers is one-way. GM decides how to design, manufacture and market a new product to its consumers, and sells it through a network of dealerships. In contrast, a platform has a back-and-forth relationship with consumers and suppliers. There's a lot more give-and-take. Amazon is a corporation, but it is also a marketplace where buyers and sellers come together. Amazon does not just dictate what it sells to consumers. Consumers tell Amazon what they are looking for, and Amazon sources it for them. Consumers have a voice; they can rate products and services.

Who succeeds and who fails in a world of platforms?

Thanks to the Buggles, we know that video killed the radio star, and thanks to the 2011 bankruptcy of the bookseller Borders, we know that platforms like Amazon can hurt incumbent corporations. Borders was

---

returned to life the following season. It turned out that his death was just a dream. We should all be so lucky.

no lightweight. As late as 2005 it had a market capitalization of over $1.6 billion,[200] and at the time it filed for Chapter 11, it employed more than seventeen thousand people.[201]

So it seems to us that incumbent businesses have a choice to make. They can continue to operate as they always have, existing in a world where technology is something to be used not as a tool of transformation but simply to optimize operational efficiency and maximize profits. In a lot of these incumbent businesses, technology is that interesting thing run by that slightly odd group in the other building; it isn't something that anchors the CEO's agenda every week. And the impending disruption caused by new competitors entering their markets is something to be fought with battalions of lobbyists and lawyers. Although it might take a long time (and cost a lot of money), this dig-a-moat-and-bury-your-head-in-the-sand approach is bound to end tragically. The forces of technology and disruption are too powerful. So the incumbent that follows this strategy will eventually fail, or at the very least become irrelevant. Along the way, it will hamper customer choice and squelch innovation in its industry, because that is exactly its intent. Innovation means change; for incumbents the status quo is a much more comfortable place to be.

Venture capitalist and Sun Microsystems cofounder Vinod Khosla, who sometimes speaks at the class Eric teaches at Stanford, points out a couple of simple reasons for this. First, at the corporate level, most innovative new things look like small opportunities to a large company. They are hardly worth the time and effort, especially since their success is far from certain. And at an individual level, people within big companies aren't rewarded for taking risks, but are penalized for

200. "Examining the Books" (*Wall Street Journal*, August 29, 2005).

201. Joseph Checkler and Jeffrey A. Trachtenberg, "Bookseller Borders Begins a New Chapter...11" (*Wall Street Journal*, February 17, 2011).

failure. The individual payoff is asymmetrical, so the rational person opts for safety.[202]

There is an alternative for incumbents, though: Develop a strategy that takes advantage of platforms to consistently deliver great products. Use that strategy as a foundation to attract a team of smart creatives, then create an environment where they can succeed at scale. Simple, right? Except that of course it isn't; not even close. The very nature of mature companies is to be risk-averse and to attack big change like a body attacks an infection. We know, because we've been there. After all, you are reading a book by a couple of guys who were among the last Googlers to ditch their BlackBerrys and Outlook email boxes. We don't always see change coming, and we don't always handle it that well either. Fortunately, we surround ourselves with people who do, such as our former colleague Vic Gundotra...

The emergence of the social web (and a start-up called Facebook)

The worldwide web has developed in three distinct phases. Web 1.0 started in the '90s with the advent of the browser, HTML, and this thing called websites. During this Web 1.0 phase, users could read text, see small pictures, and complete basic transactions, but beyond that, functionality was pretty limited. Then, in the early 2000s, new technologies came along that led to more powerful websites and a more robust web infrastructure. Broadband proliferated in several countries, online video took off, and it became easier for people not just to consume stuff *from* the web, but also publish stuff *to* it. In this Web 2.0 the web became more than a giant shopping mall and online encyclopedia; it was a place where people could *do* all sorts of things. Billions of

---

202. Vinod Khosla, "The Innovator's Ecosystem," December 1, 2011, http://www .khoslaventures.com.

people from around the world came online, and often one of the first things they did when they got there was search.

Before the summer of 2010, that's where we at Google lived: happily in Web 2.0. Meanwhile, the social web was emerging. Whereas Web 1.0 let you read and buy things and Web 2.0 let you do things, the social web let you talk about and share things. We had been watching this trend build for a while as first Friendster and then Myspace were the hot new things, and we had considered partnerships with a couple of the leading companies in the social space, Twitter and Digg. But those partnership ideas didn't get very far, and perhaps distracted us from a competitor we never expected. Suddenly, the social web wasn't coming, it was here, and it was led by a new platform called Facebook.

Google wasn't really even in the game. The success of Orkut, our first social effort, was mostly limited to the Brazilian and Indian markets. We had launched the aforementioned, much-ballyhooed new form of email called Wave, which was a brilliant piece of technology that thrilled its power users (of which there were few) and confused all other humans (lots). We had also launched Buzz, a product that Googlers loved in our internal "dogfood" trial, but that ultimately raised privacy concerns. By summer 2010, we had stopped working on Wave, and Buzz was also slowing down, making us 0 for 2 in the social web arena.

Vic Gundotra chose to be bothered by this. Vic led mobile; he was the guy helping make all of Google's great services thrive on the small, mobile screens that were rapidly becoming a critical on-ramp to the Internet for hundreds of millions of people. Vic had seen the potential of smartphones early on, and had helped build the team that pushed Google to make "mobile first" a common mantra. Our missteps in social had nothing to do with Vic, except for the fact that he was a Google employee and shareholder and was concerned that we were missing a historic shift in the web. He decided to do something about it. He asked Bradley Horowitz to lunch.

Bradley was in charge of social, and as his lunch with Vic stretched into a meeting and then another meeting, the two of them started to devise a new plan to reinvent Google for the social web and bring a bunch of innovations to consumers. Social wasn't part of Vic's job description, and although we were Vic's ostensible bosses (he reported to Urs Hölzle, who reported to Eric, and attended Jonathan's staff meetings), we certainly didn't tell him to develop a new social platform, or even to offer his ideas on the topic. Rather, he saw we had a problem, felt he could contribute to creating a solution, and decided to make it happen.

Soon, Vic and Bradley's project, code-named "Emerald Sea," gained momentum around the company, and about a year later it launched as the Google+ project, one of the most ambitious bets in the company's history. Google+ is often positioned in the media as a competitive response to Facebook, but this isn't quite right. It's more accurate to say that Google+ is a response to the disruption of Web 2.0 and the emergence of the social web. It is the social fabric that weaves together Google's various platforms, from AdWords to YouTube. And it started because one person saw that a major shift was under way, with the potential to disrupt our business, and decided to do something about it. Even though it wasn't his job.

Ask the hardest questions

Vic got started on his social quest by asking himself questions: What would it mean to Google when the dominant use of the web was as a social platform? Could the social web make search obsolete? Sometimes the most effective way to help change and innovation outrun the antibodies of corporate entropy is a simple one: Ask the hardest question. Understanding what you do about the future, what do you see for the business that others may not, or may see but choose to ignore? (Harvard Business School Professor and business consultant Clayton Christensen: "I keep my attention on the questions I need to ask so I can catch the issues of the future.")[203] When information

---

203. Art Kleiner, "The Discipline of Managing Disruption" (*strategy+business*, March 11, 2013).

truly is ubiquitous, when reach and connectivity are completely global, when computing resources are infinite, and when a whole new set of impossibilities are not only possible, but happening, what will that do to your business? Technology progress follows an inexorable upward trend. Follow that trend to a logical point in the future and ask the question: What does that mean for us?

When Eric worked at Sun in the '90s, the company made computer workstations that offered the best value in the industry. It was a technology-driven company, confident that it could permanently maintain this price-performance advantage, but Sun was also threatened by the improving capabilities of "Wintel" PCs built with Intel processors and running Microsoft Windows operating systems. At that time, the hardest question for Sun was what would happen to Sun's business when the Wintel price-performance finally surpassed Sun's. What would the company do when the advantage to which it owed most of its success and profitability was gone? When Eric posed that question to President Owen Brown and CEO Scott McNealy, their conclusion was that Sun could never lower their costs to be competitive with the PC industry. In other words, they didn't have a good answer (and neither did Eric). That was a problem of course, but the bigger problem is what happened next: Nothing. No one took a substantive action item. In April 2000, Sun's market capitalization was $141 billion. By 2006, Windows-based servers had taken over the market, while the share of Sun's machines languished in the single digits. Sun was sold to Oracle in 2009 for $7.4 billion.

In ongoing companies there are always hard questions, and they often don't get asked because there aren't any good answers and that makes people uncomfortable. But this is precisely why they should be asked—to keep the team uncomfortable. Better for that discomfort to come from friendly fire than from a competitor intent on killing you for real—as Eric learned at Sun. If there aren't good answers to the hardest questions, then there is at least a silver lining. Those hardest questions that have no easy answers can be very effective in mitigating the risk-averse, change-fighting tendencies of big-company culture. They are the imminent hanging that, as Samuel Johnson noted, can concentrate the mind so wonderfully.[204]

Start by asking what could be true in five years. Larry Page often says that the job of a CEO is not only to think about the core business, but also the future; most companies fail because they get too comfortable doing what they have always done, making only incremental changes. And that is especially fatal today, when technology-driven change is rampant. So the question to ask isn't what *will* be true, but what *could* be true. Asking what will be true entails making a prediction, which is folly in a fast-moving world.[205] Asking what could be true entails imagination: What thing that is unimaginable when abiding by conventional wisdom is in fact imaginable?

As Vinod Khosla points out, in 1980 it was hard to imagine that microprocessors would be everywhere, not just in computers but in cars, toothbrushes, and just about everything else.[206] In 1990, when cellular telephones were the size of a sewing machine and cost a fortune, it was hard to imagine they would be smaller than a deck of cards and cost less than a night at the movies. In 1995, it was hard to imagine that the Internet would have over three billion users and over sixty trillion unique addresses. Microprocessors, mobile phones, and the Internet are all ubiquitous today, but virtually no one predicted that when they were in their incipient stages. And yet we all keep

---

204. Originally quoted in James Boswell's biography of the English writer Samuel Johnson: "Depend upon it, sir, when a man knows he is to be hanged in a fortnight, it concentrates his mind wonderfully." See James Boswell, *Life of Johnson* (Oxford World's Classics/Oxford University Press, 2008), page 849.

205. Even experts are poor predictors about highly uncertain events, as the psychologist Philip Tetlock has shown in his twenty-year study of the predictions of hundreds of experts. For example, experts were no better than the average educated person (and no better than random chance) at correctly predicting such outcomes in their field as whether apartheid would end through nonviolent means, whether Quebec would secede from Canada, and the like. See Philip E. Tetlock, *Expert Political Judgment: How Good Is It? How Can We Know?* (Princeton University Press, 2005).

206. See Vinod Khosla, "Maintain the Silicon Valley Vision" (*Bits* blog, *New York Times*, July 13, 2012).

making the mistake: The general reaction when Google's self-driving car was announced was incredulity. Cars that drive themselves couldn't actually happen, could it? We can't imagine it not happening.

So forgo conventional wisdom, crank up that imagination, and ask yourself what *could* happen in your industry in the next five years. What could change most quickly, and what will not change at all? Then once you have an idea of what the future could hold, here are some more hard questions to consider.

How would a very smart, well-capitalized competitor attack the company's core business? How could it take advantage of digital platforms to exploit weaknesses or skim off the most profitable customer segments? What is the company doing to disrupt its own business? Is cannibalization or revenue loss a frequent reason to kill off potential innovation? Is there an opportunity to build a platform that can offer increasing returns and value as usage grows?

Do company leaders use your products regularly? Do they love them? Would they give them to a spouse as a gift? (This obviously isn't applicable in a lot of cases, but it's a powerful thought experiment.) Do your customers love your products? Or are they locked in by other factors that might evaporate in the future? If they weren't locked in at all, what would happen? (Interesting corollary to this question: If you forced your product people to make it easy for customers to ditch your product for a competitor's, how would they react? Could they make your products so great that customers want to stay, even if they don't have to?)

When you go through your pipeline of upcoming new major products and features, what percentage of them are built on unique technical insights? How many product people are on the senior leadership team? Does the company aggressively reward and promote the people who have the biggest impact on creating excellent products?

Is hiring a top priority at the C-suite level? Do top executives actually spend time on it? Among your stronger employees, how many see themselves at the company in three years? How many would leave for a 10 percent raise at another company?

Do your decision-making processes lead to the best decisions, or the most acceptable ones?

How much freedom do employees have? If there is someone who is truly innovative, does that person have the freedom to act on his ideas, regardless of his level? Are decisions on new ideas based on product excellence, or profit?

Who does better in the company, information hoarders or routers? Do silos prevent the free flow of information and people?

These are tough questions, and there are likely no obvious solutions to the problems they spotlight. But there certainly won't be solutions if the questions never get asked. Incumbents usually fail to understand how quickly they can be disrupted, but asking these questions can help them discover the reality. It is also a great way to attract and invigorate the best smart creatives, who are drawn not only to the challenge, but to the honesty of the challenge. "Thank god, someone around here is finally asking the tough questions!" they will say. "Now we can get started on finding the answers."

But this brings up one more hard question: Are you in the right place to attract the best smart creatives? One of the interesting effects of the Internet, mobile, and cloud technologies is that business hubs have grown more powerful and influential. We used to think that the advent of Internet and other communication technologies would lead to more hubs springing up and reduce the importance of existing ones, but in fact the opposite is true. There may indeed be new, small clusters of activity in various industries, but the clusters that already existed have only increased in importance. When it comes to smart creatives, physical location matters more than ever.

This is why, for example, even as countries all over the world try to re-create the technology magic of Silicon Valley, many of their native smart creatives who strive for technology careers leave those countries to go to Silicon Valley. (We are always amazed at the array of languages we hear in Google cafés.) They find that they can have a far greater impact from California than from their home country, and the allure of gathering with other smart creatives of the same ilk often outweighs that of staying close to home. The same goes for hubs in finance (New York, London, Hong Kong, Frankfurt, Singapore), fashion (New York, Paris, Milan), entertainment (Los Angeles, Mumbai), diamonds (Antwerp, Surat), biotech (Boston, Basel), energy (Houston, Dhahran), shipping (Singapore, Shanghai), cars (southern Germany), and most other industries. Any company that wants to build a new venture needs to ask itself the question: Do I go to the smart creatives, or find a way to get them to come to me?

The role of government

Governments also have important decisions to make. They can stand side by side with incumbent businesses, expending their energy to try to stave off the forces of change. This is the natural path of politicians, since incumbents tend to have a lot more money than disrupters and are quite expert in using it to bend the political will of any democratic government. (New challengers usually fail to understand the extent of the legal and regulatory tools that incumbents have in their arsenal.) But, just like businesses, governments have the option to encourage disruption and create environments where smart creatives can thrive. They can choose to have a bias toward innovation.

It starts with education, and not just the traditional K–12, college, and university formats. Education is going to change, and governments should favor disruption over incumbency (currently, they tend to do just the opposite). Technology platforms will help us identify our individual strengths and weaknesses with greater precision, and provide us with educational options customized to what we want to do. As the purveyors of public education, governments can aggressively pursue this model of customized, flexible, lifelong education, particularly for post–high school teens and adults.

A digital infrastructure is a must-have, as is an immigration-friendly policy. Most important, though, is the freedom to innovate. Regulations get created in anticipation of problems, but if you build a system that anticipates everything, there's no room to innovate. Furthermore, incumbents have a big influence on the creation of regulations, and there is often a lot of movement between the public and private sectors, so the people who are making and enforcing innovation-killing regulations today become the executives in the private sector who benefit from them tomorrow. There always needs to be space in the regulatory environment for a new company to enter.

For example, in the US automotive industry a new entrant, Tesla, is running into regulatory roadblocks in several states that are preventing it from selling directly to consumers.[207] The regulations protect auto dealers and reduce consumer choice in those states. During the next round of automotive innovation, self-driving cars, there will be an accident. Someone will get hurt or killed, which may have the effect of casting doubt on the entire industry of self-driving cars. When that happens, governments should resist the impulse to enact highly restrictive regulations, similar to the UK's nineteenth-century "red flag" law,[208] that force the new technology to jump through much higher safety hoops than regular, people-operated cars (which crash too, with frightening regularity and results). If data empirically show that a new way of doing things is better than the old way, then the role of government isn't to prevent change but to allow the disruption to occur.

Big problems are information problems

As industries blow up and get re-formed, incumbents adapt or wilt, and new ventures grow, powered by visionary leaders and their ambitious

---

207. Steve Chapman, "Car Buyers Get Hijacked" (*Chicago Tribune*, June 20, 2013).

208. The law, enacted in the UK in 1865 as one of the Locomotive Acts, required that cars be preceded by a pedestrian waving a red flag to warn horses and riders that the contraption was coming. The same law set the speed limit of these "road locomotives" at two miles per hour in towns, and four in the country. It was repealed in 1896. See Alasdair Nairn, *Engines That Move Markets: Technology Investing from Railroads to the Internet and Beyond* (John Wiley & Sons, 2002), pages 182–83, and Brian Ladd, *Autophobia: Love and Hate in the Automotive Age* (University of Chicago Press, 2008), page 27.

smart colleagues, things will get better. We are technology optimists. We believe in the power of technology to make the world a better place. Where others see a dystopian future like *The Matrix*, we see Dr. Leonard McCoy curing the Saurian virus with a wave of his tricorder (and celebrating with a shot of Saurian brandy and a tranya chaser.)[209] We see most big problems as information problems, which means that with enough data and the ability to crunch it, virtually any challenge facing humanity today can be solved. We think computers will serve at the behest of people—all people—to make their lives better and easier. And we are quite sure that we, as a couple of Silicon Valley guys, will come under a lot of criticism for this Pollyannaish view of the future. But that doesn't matter. What matters is that there is a bright light at the end of the tunnel.

There are solid reasons underlying our optimism. The first is the explosion of data and a trend toward the free flow of information. From geological and meteorological sensors to computers that record every single economic transaction to wearable technology (such as Google's smart contact lenses)[210] that continuously tracks a person's vital signs, types of data are being collected that simply have never been available before, at a scale that was the stuff of science fiction only a few years ago. And there is now practically limitless computing power with which to analyze that data. Infinite data and infinite computing power create an amazing playground for the world's smart creatives to solve big problems.

This will result in greater collaboration among smart creatives—scientists, doctors, engineers, designers, artists—trying to solve the world's big problems, since it is so much easier to compare and combine different sets of data. As Carl Shapiro and Hal Varian note in

209. Both Saurian brandy and tranya were drinks in the original *Star Trek* TV series. We hope those of you who actually got these references relished them as much as we do. And that's our last *Star Trek* reference, we promise.

210. Smart contact lenses, under development by Google[x], are built to track their wearers' blood glucose levels by measuring glucose levels in tears. This would spare diabetics the necessity of regular, painful pinprick blood tests or of wearing a glucose sensor under their skin full-time.

Information Rules, information is costly to produce but cheap to repro-duce.[211] So if you create information that can help solve a problem and contribute that information to a platform where it can be shared (or help create the platform), you will enable many others to use that valu-able information at low or no cost. Google has a product called Fusion Tables, which is designed to "bust your data out of its silo" by allowing related data sets to be merged and analyzed as a single set, while still retaining the integrity of the original data set. Think of all the research scientists in the world working on similar problems, each with their own set of data in their own spreadsheets and databases. Or local gov-ernments trying to assess and solve environmental and infrastructure issues, tracking their progress in systems sitting on their desks or in the basement. Imagine the power of busting down these information silos to combine and analyze the data in new and different ways.

Speed is another hopeful factor. Thanks to technology, latency—the time between action and reaction—is getting much shorter. Again, this is a place where taking a historical view can be helpful in bring-ing the concept into focus. What economists call "general purpose technologies" (the steam engine or electricity are good examples) his-torically have taken a long time to go from invention to application to changing the fabric of how people live and markets operate. The Watt steam engine was developed in 1763 but it took the better part of two hundred years before the railroads transformed Kansas City from the trailhead of the cattle drive to a metropolis with a livestock exchange. By contrast, Netscape Navigator launched in 1994, and Jonathan proudly hooked up some of the world's first cable modems for Excite @Home in 1998. Less than a decade later these modern communica-tions technologies had transformed the way we communicate, hook up, shop, order food, and hail rides. The beauty of speed, however, is in the eye of the beholder: It seems like a bad thing when you are being

211. Carl Shapiro and Hal R. Varian, *Information Rules: A Strategic Guide to the Network Economy* (Harvard Business Review Press, 1998).

disrupted, since it is all upon you so quickly. But when you are building new ventures, the acceleration of everything works in your favor.

And the advent of networks is giving rise to greater collective wisdom and intelligence. When reigning world champ Garry Kasparov lost his chess match to IBM's Deep Blue computer in 1997, we all thought we were witnessing a seminal passing of the torch. But it turns out that the match heralded a new age of chess champions: not computers, but people who sharpen their skills by collaborating with computers. Today's grandmasters (and there are twice as many now as there were in 1997)[212] use computers as training partners, which makes the humans even better players. Thus a virtuous cycle of computer-aided intelligence emerges: Computers push humans to get even better, and humans then program even smarter computers. This is clearly happening in chess; why not in other pursuits?

The future's so bright…

It is hard for us to look at an industry or field and not see a bright future. In health care, for example, real-time personal sensors will enable sophisticated tracking and measurement of complex human systems. Combine all that data with a map of risk factors generated by in-depth genetic analysis, and we will have unprecedented abilities (*only* with an individual's consent) to identify and prevent or treat individual health issues much earlier. Aggregating that data can create platforms of information and knowledge that enable more effective research and inform smarter health-care policies.

Health-care consumers suffer from a dearth of information: They have virtually no data on procedural outcomes and doctor and hospital performance, and often have a hard time accessing their own health data, especially if it is held by different institutions. And pricing for medical services, medicine, and supplies is completely opaque and varies

---

212. Christopher Chabris and David Goodman, "Chess-Championship Results Show Powerful Role of Computers" (*Wall Street Journal*, November 22, 2013).

widely from patient to patient and facility to facility. Just bringing even a basic level of information transparency to health care could have a tremendous positive impact, lowering costs and improving outcomes.

Transportation will be another industry full of disruption and opportunity. What will happen when every car can drive itself? Ownership models will change, since personal car services will drop in price and become even more responsive. The only reason for *owning* a car will be for pleasure, not transportation. This will force planners to rethink transportation networks.

In financial services, more detailed information means more customized services. Today, for example, auto insurers are already starting to use information such as distance driven and location to assess the chances of a driver having an accident. How much smarter could they be if they agreed to lower your rates in exchange for getting access to *all* of your car's data: speed, location, operating hours, distances driven, traffic conditions, and maintenance records? Perhaps you wouldn't take the offer, but would you accept it for the teenage drivers in your family, hoping it would make them drive more safely?

In creative industries, there is more outstanding content and talent than ever before, and demand for it (at least when measured by media consumption) has never been higher. Despite the vast amounts of crummy, CGI[213]-driven action movies, technology has also created new ways for each of us to enjoy shows that rely on old-fashioned storytelling, like *House of Cards* or *Game of Thrones*, when we want to watch them, and on the devices of our choosing, be it a flat-screen, laptop, or wearable, glasses-like device. The Internet has decimated traditional media business models, but new ones have and will continue to emerge in their place. The result will be a much bigger, more fragmented and chaotic market for creators and endless choices for consumers.

Whether it's in fighting crime (analyzing crime patterns to enable "predictive policing"), agriculture (data-rich soil maps aiding poor

---

213. Computer Generated Imagery.

farmers), pharmaceuticals (sharing information to speed up drug development), defense, energy, aerospace, or education, every one of these pursuits will be transformed by the forces of technology in the first half of the twenty-first century, creating spectacular new products, birthing brand-new businesses, and replacing economic malaise with new jobs and development. And each one of these changes will be fomented by a small team of determined, empowered smart creatives.

This is what we believe.

The next smart creative

The two of us are not immune to these forces of change. For all of the things we have learned and then were forced to relearn, there are many more that we don't know. As much as we try to stay on top of technology and how it impacts our industry, we simply can't grasp it the way the next generation of smart creatives does. We grew up in an era when you used a landline telephone to ask someone out (and you called it a "date," not "just hanging out"), you *went* to movies, and broadband was when you got a bigger mailbox. We see the new breed, day in and day out, and marvel at their confidence and smarts. They tell us what's up and what's going to happen, and when it comes to deciding what to do next, they tell us as often as we tell them. Such is our fate, surrounded by up-and-coming smart creatives.

We are certain that for every one of these rock stars we meet in our daily work, there are dozens or even hundreds more who are doing their best to unseat us from our perch. Maybe all of them will fail, but probably not. Probably, somewhere in a garage, dorm room, lab, or conference room, a brave business leader has gathered a small, dedicated team of smart creatives. Maybe she has a copy of our book, and is using our ideas to help her create a company that will eventually render Google irrelevant. Preposterous, right? Except that, given that no business wins forever, it is inevitable.

Some would find this chilling. We find it inspiring.

Acknowledgments

We must start by thanking Larry Page and Sergey Brin for their wisdom and friendship and for the incredible company that the two of them started. Google's founders are really as good as we describe them. The privilege of working with the two of them every day, to learn about and understand the future, is a once-in-a-lifetime gift. Many of the brilliant things that made Google so great—the strategy, culture, and emphasis on hiring excellence—were set well before either of us joined the company. Imagine having, in your mid-twenties, the presence of mind and the vision to see what Google would be and could do. Over and over, Larry and Sergey pushed hard to challenge convention, question authority and incumbency, and go their own way in building a truly great company. Google not only changed our lives, but it changed and continues to change the lives of billions of people, every day, everywhere. There is no adequate way to thank them for what they have done for us except to say we are humbled by their support and by everything they do.

Much like Google itself, this book was made possible through the help of a lot of amazing, interesting, caring, fun, good people. We are grateful for that help, but even more so for having had the privilege to work with and know these smart creatives as both colleagues and friends. Thank you to...

Ann Hiatt, Brian Thompson, and Kim Cooper, who always found

time amidst crazy schedules for the authors to meet and who gave us plenty of good feedback. You manage the chaos with serenity.

Pam Shore, who began her journey with Eric at Novell and was very much a part of building Google and his staff.

Scott Rubin, Meghan Casserly, and Emily Wood, who are PR people who know how to have interesting conversations. We look forward to having many more of them.

Rachel Whetstone, who was the other person on the to: line when Eric sent the email to Jonathan suggesting we do this book. Rachel has been our communications partner for nearly a decade and a partner on this book since its inception. She is a tireless advocate not only for Google but for always doing the right thing by people. Our thank you to Rachel is for far more than just her assistance in this book.

Kent Walker and Marc Ellenbogen, a pair of brilliant lawyers who got off their horses, rolled up their sleeves, and helped us make the book so much better. Marc was particularly helpful, and his advice seemed to get even more sage during that week he worked with us while on his Caribbean vacation.

Dennis Woodside, who somehow found the time to read our book and give us his thoughts while leading Motorola.

Urs Hölzle, the founding father of many of Google's people-management and hiring practices.

Alison Cormack, who is simply the best reader ever and perhaps the most gracious Googler around.

Jared Cohen, Eric's partner on *The New Digital Age*, who learned all about publishing just in time to help us.

Laszlo Bock, who helped preserve Google's culture and standards as we grew, whose upcoming book on talent gets into the nitty-gritty details of how to make all this happen, and who always seems to be smiling, perhaps because he used to appear on *Baywatch*.

Nikesh Arora, whose invitation to address his team started this whole project.

Susan Wojcicki, Salar Kamangar, Marissa Mayer, and Sundar

Pichai, who taught Jonathan that sometimes a good manager just needs to get out of his people's way. If a manager's work product is the sum of his people's, then Jonathan stands on a mountain created by these four.

Lorraine Twohill, who helped show us the Googley, smart-creative approach to creating truly amazing, inspiring art disguised as marketing.

Clay Bavor, one of the smartest creatives we know and whose work speaks to the culture of Google. (Google his weekend projects "The Google Logo in 884 4×6 Photographs" and "Clay Bavor Lincoln Portrait in Pennies.")

Brian Rakowski, who had the good sense to include page numbers and searchable word strings in the multiple sets of comments he provided.

Margo Georgiadis, whose perspective on how C-level execs in big companies think was a constant source of insight.

Colin McMillen, whose Memegen invention is only one of the many cool things he's done.

Prem Ramaswami, who gave us the perspective of a Harvard Business School teaching fellow and made suggestions about how to make the work accessible to students.

Devin Ivester, our resident expert in all things books and movies; creative whizzes Gary Williams, Ken Frederick, and Lauren Mulkey, who contributed a lot of great ideas that we didn't use; and Jonathan Jarvis, whose design created a book that looks more elegant and handsome than its authors ever do. And that's saying something.[214]

Hal Varian, who makes economics entertaining. That's saying something too.[215]

Alan Eustace, who personifies Googley so much that he, with Jonathan's help, wrote the first Googler handbook.

Shona Brown and David Drummond, who for years were the

---

214. It isn't.
215. It is.

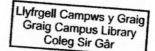

other two members of the management hiring review committee with Jonathan.

Cathay Bi and Chadé Severin, who calmly supported Jonathan in his role running products for Google and have been thoughtful critics from the outset of this project.

Jeff Huber, who worked with Jonathan at Excite@Home and showed up at Google to build a robust ad and revenue engine so that Jonathan could focus on managing smart creatives.

Patrick Pichette, whose operational rigor, Googley sensibilities, orange backpack, and I-ride-my-bike-to-work-even-when-it's-raining attitude continue to inspire us.

Gopi Kallayil, who is not only the best presenter we've ever known but a constant critic with insightful improvements.

Jill Hazelbaker, to whom Jonathan always turns, especially when he creates a PR problem (which is often).

Jared Smith, who helped us with details on China and is a great leader of smart creatives himself.

Bill Campbell, who is the most gifted of all management coaches, with an eye to people and how organizations work. We didn't know we needed a coach until we had one. Bill was a key person in the success of Apple and Google, now two of the most valuable corporations in America. Everyone smiles when Bill enters the room, and his ability to tell a great story is matched only by his humility in refusing the credit for the extraordinary role he has played in Silicon Valley and the success of generations of entrepreneurs.

John Doerr, Mike Moritz, Ram Shriram, John Hennessy, Art Levinson, Paul Otellini, Ann Mather, Diane Greene, and Shirley Tilgham, current and former Google board members who always take the long view of our impact on the world, and our customers, partners, and shareholders. As they should.

The many other current and former Googlers, who helped us get our stories straight while continuing to teach us some of the finer points of managing smart creatives: Krishna Bharat, Jeff Dean, Ben

Gomes, Georges Harik, William Farris, Vic Gundotra, George Salah, and Martha Josephson (not technically a Googler, but as true a partner as can be found).

Jonathan's family—wife Beryl, son Joshua, and daughter Hannah—who always remind him that he needs to walk that management talk about empowering others and staying out of their way at home as well as in the office. This helps keep Jonathan humble, and for that everyone who knows Jonathan should thank them.

Jonathan's mother, Rina Rosenberg, who was a strong advocate for women and headed the Commision on the Status of Women for Santa Clara County. It is in deference to her that we start out describing our smart creative as a she. Jonathan's father, Professor Nathan Rosenberg, who is formally and accurately footnoted in the text as a leading scholar on technological innovation. What greater acknowledgment can a son offer than to show his father that through all the years, he really was listening?

Karen, Gordon, and David Rosenberg, Jonathan's siblings, from whom he learned a great deal about decision-making. The four of them continually fail to reach consensus on who owns the family title of smartest creative. Frankly, kids, it's time for Mom and Dad to ring the bell.

Dr. Lorne Rosenfield, who regularly banters with Jonathan about great quotes and life wisdom. Several references in the book come from those conversations. Lorne's daughter, Lauren, who provided more than enough corrections to prove her point that she is a more learned literary critic than Jonathan. And her brother Michael, who burnished his smart-creative credentials by giving us plenty of examples that he assures us will resonate with the college set.

Dan Chung, who had the insight that the original manuscript was "written with entrepreneurs in mind" but could be expanded to be "useful to any businessperson."

Matt Pyken, who helped polish Jonathan's papers in college and lent us a "Hollywood eye" for dramatic flair and storytelling.

Glenn Yeffeth of BenBella Books, who was the only expert on publishing Jonathan could ask for help when he embarked on this project.

Adam Grosser, who rejected misguided jokes that were not funny and generally helped elevate the tone and encouraged us to be more rigorous in our definitions.

Professors Susan Feigenbaum and Gerald Eyrich, who were prescient in their insistence that Jonathan learn statistics and provided the necessary adult supervision to help him complete his BA.

Professor and Dean Jeff Huang, and his colleague Julia Easley, who read the manuscript "like a student thesis" and provided almost as many corrections, and mercifully omitted a grade.

Professor David Teece, who gave this a read from an academic economist's perspective and pointed us at much of the excellent additional literature.

Gary Leight, Betsy Leight, Dora Futterman, Libby Trudell, Cathy Gordon, James Isaacs, Dean Gilbert, and Richard Gingras, who are all former Jonathan bosses. Jonathan is eternally grateful for your wisdom and forbearance.

Professor Jeff Ullman, who took a scraggly Princeton teenager named Eric Schmidt and turned him into a computer scientist, almost before there was such a thing.

Bill Joy, Sue Graham, and Bob Fabry, who at Berkeley trusted Eric as a computer scientist enough that they built a team around him.

Mike Lesk and Al Aho, who while working on Unix at Bell Laboratories taught Eric the value of volume, open source, and scale.

Jim Morris, Butler Lampson, Bob Taylor, and Roy Levin of Xerox PARC, who invented the future.

Scott McNealy, Andy Bechtolsheim, Bill Joy, Vinod Khosla, Bernie Lacroute, and Wayne Rosing of Sun, who gave Eric his first hands-on experience in managing in a business. Only in tech would a person with no prior management experience be trained on the job so very well.

Raymond Nasr and John Young at Novell, where the journey was the reward.

Peter Wendell, who gave Eric the opportunity to teach at Stanford's Graduate School of Business, and the thousands of students for whom Eric initially formalized his thoughts on "lessons learned the hard way."

Nishant Choksi, whose beautiful and fun illustrations perfectly capture our points in ways that we couldn't have imagined.

Melissa Thomas, a fact-checking whiz, who we would never, ever want to face in a game of *Jeopardy!*

Marina Krakovsky, our research partner, who always goes about two steps farther than we expect. She is as insightful and thoughtful as she is diligent and thorough. All great things! She's the best.

David Javerbaum, a world-class humor writer who helped make us funny too, or at least funnier. One of our proudest moments came when David saw one of the jokes that we had written and deemed it "not too bad." Thank you, David, for your help, and especially for that high praise.

Jim Levine, our agent, who helped us understand the publishing world, and our editor John Brodie, who guided us wisely from rough manuscript to finished work, from Microsoft opening to Downton Abbey conclusion. And we guided John to see the awesomeness of working with Google Docs.

Sometime in the mid-'70s, a couple of kids met while pumping quarters into the world's first coin-operated video game, *Galaxy Game*, which resided in the Coffee House café at Stanford's Tresidder student union. Jonathan regularly vanquished Alan Eagle at *Galaxy*, but the two were more evenly matched in their classes at Gunn High. While they were battling for space supremacy and tackling chemistry and math, they could not have possibly predicted that thirty years later they would start working together at a company called Google. Or that nearly forty years later they would collaborate on a book about business and management. Yet that's exactly what happened. Imagine the unimaginable, indeed. Thank you to our coauthor, Alan Eagle.

Glossary

AdSense

The ads product that places ads on a large network of publisher sites.

AdWords

Google's flagship ads product, this engine generates most of the company's revenue.

ah'cha'rye

English rendering of the Hebrew for "Follow me," the rallying cry in the Israeli army.

Android

Google's open-source mobile operating system.

API

Application Programming Interface, which enables other applications to interact with it.

APM

Associate Product Manager; APMs usually do two twelve-month rotations before they become full-fledged product managers.

cloud computing

Technology that enables Internet users to access files and run applications that reside on computers in another location. These remote computers, which are sometimes called servers, are usually clustered in large data centers that feature thousands of individual computers.

Coase's law

The principle, expressed by Nobel Prize–winning economist Ronald Coase, explaining that large firms emerged because, when you take transaction costs into account, it's often more efficient to get things done within a firm rather than contracting out on the open market. Because the Internet has lowered transaction costs, Coase's law implies that these days it's often more efficient to outsource work rather than doing it internally.

Dory

A Google internal system for posting questions for executives and voting others' questions up or down.

Excite@Home

A former employer of Jonathan's that was formed when Excite, a pioneer in web portals, merged with @Home, which helped to popularize Internet access via cable modems.

Googlegeist

Google's annual employee feedback survey.

Google[x]

A team working on some of Google's most ambitious projects, including self-driving cars, Google Glass, Project Loon, and smart contact lenses.

HiPPO (or simply "hippo")

Highest-Paid Person's Opinion.

learning animals

People who have the smarts to handle massive change and the character to love it: They so enjoy learning that they aren't afraid of asking dumb questions or getting wrong answers.

market capitalization (or "market cap")

The total market value of the issued shares of a publicly traded company.

Memegen

A Google internal site that lets Googlers create memes in the form of pithy captions attached to images, this is a fun way for employees to comment on the state of the company.

Moma

Google's intranet, used for sharing all kinds of company information among Googlers.

Moore's Law

The prediction, made by Intel cofounder Gordon Moore, that the number of transistors on a chip—and hence computing power—would double every two years. Moore initially predicted, in 1965, that the doubling would occur annually, but he revised his prediction to every two years in 1975.

multisided market

A place where different user groups can connect and provide each other with beneficial services.

Noogler

New + Googler (new Google employee).

obligation to dissent

The expectation that if someone thinks there is something wrong with an idea, they must raise that concern.

OKR

Objectives and Key Results, a performance management system used effectively at Google and other companies.

open

Sharing intellectual property such as software code or research results, adhering to open standards rather than creating your own, and giving customers the freedom to easily exit your platform.

open-source operating system

An operating system, like Linux and Android, in which the code is available at no charge to the public for use and modification. The opposite is a closed operating system, whose code is tightly controlled by the company that owns it.

payback period

The length of time needed to recover the cost of an investment.

platform

A base of technologies or infrastructure on which additional technologies, processes, or services can be built.

ROI

Return on investment.

scale

To grow something very quickly and globally (verb) or quick, global growth (noun).

smart creative

A person who combines deep technical knowledge of his or her trade with intelligence, business savvy, and a host of creative qualities.

tenurocracies

Companies in which power derives from tenure, not merit.

TGIF

Google's company-wide meeting, initially held every Friday afternoon, now held on Thursdays so that Googlers in the Asia Pacific offices can participate.

user interface

The part of a product with which the user interacts.

Wave

Google Wave was a system that let groups of users communicate and collaborate in real time. Google stopped working on Wave in 2010, and open sourced the code.

Web 2.0

The set of technologies that make the web what it is today (an upgrade of Web 1.0 of the 1990s).

Index

A Note About the Authors

Eric Schmidt joined Google in 2001 and helped grow the company from a Silicon Valley start-up to a global leader in technology. As executive chairman, he is responsible for the external matters of Google: building partnerships and broader business relationships, government outreach and technology thought leadership, as well as advising the CEO and senior leadership on business and policy issues. From 2001 to 2011, Eric served as Google's chief executive officer.

Prior to joining Google, Eric held leadership roles at Novell and Sun Microsystems, Inc. He holds a bachelor's degree in electrical engineering from Princeton University as well as a master's degree and PhD in computer science from the University of California, Berkeley. He is a member of the President's Council of Advisors on Science and Technology and the Prime Minister's Advisory Council in the UK, and serves on the boards of the Economist Group, the Mayo Clinic, and Khan Academy. Eric's philanthropic efforts, through the Schmidt Family Foundation, focus on climate change, including support of ocean and marine life studies at sea, as well as education, specifically cutting-edge research and technology in the natural sciences and engineering.

Jonathan Rosenberg first met Larry Page and Sergey Brin in 2000 and finally accepted a job at their company the third time they offered it, more than two years later. He served as senior vice president at

Google and ran the Google product team until April 2011. In that role, he oversaw the design, development, and evolution of Google's products for consumers, advertisers, and partners. He helped develop the company's hiring processes and was influential in setting its communications and marketing practices. Today Jonathan is an advisor to Google CEO Larry Page.

Prior to joining Google, Jonathan ran products and services at Excite@Home, managed the eWorld product line for Apple Computer, and directed product marketing for Knight Ridder Information Services. Jonathan holds an MBA from the University of Chicago and a bachelor's degree with honors in economics from Claremont McKenna College, where he graduated Phi Beta Kappa.

Alan Eagle has been a director of executive communications at Google since joining the company in 2007. In that role, he led speechwriting and other communication activities for several Google executives, including Eric and Jonathan.

Alan has held sales and product management roles at several Silicon Valley start-ups, including Tellme Networks and Octel Communications. He holds a computer science degree from Dartmouth College and an MBA from the Wharton School.